HELLO, I'M
PAUL PAGE
"IT'S RACE DAY
IN INDIANAPOLIS"

Paul Page and J. R. Elrod

When I get together with Paul, we tell the stories that never ever end, the good times, the crazy times, and of course the unforgettable times.

—Bobby Unser,
Sportscaster and three-time Indy 500 champion

The wealth of knowledge that Paul has and his genuine demeanor towards racing was always exciting to listen to and be part of.

—Nigel Mansell,
IndyCar and F-1 champion

To this day, when I hear the voice of Paul Page, I feel like it is race day and our cars are about to take the green flag. For years, Paul has helped bring racing to life, taking his listeners and viewers inside the pit box and underneath the helmet with his passion for the sport and his insight into the personalities and the stories going on behind the scenes. He has narrated us through some of racing's greatest performances and most dramatic moments as the play-by-play voice of the Indianapolis Motor Speedway Radio Network and INDYCAR racing on network TV. But as skilled as he is describing the racing action, it is his unique way of creating a connection to the competitors while bringing the fans closer to our sport that has made him so special. I appreciate all that Paul has done to help take racing in new directions and I hope you enjoy looking back on his journey through motorsports.

—Roger Penske,
Winningest IndyCar team owner,
Owner of the Indianapolis Motor Speedway

Like me, he has such a great passion for racing and I think that helped make him the voice of our sport. He's always been such a great storyteller and I'm excited to read about some of his favorite moments and memories from his career in motorsports.

—Helio Castroneves,
Four-time Indy 500 champion

Paul and I have been friends for nearly fifty years. In the booth there were great and funny moments, especially when Bobby Unser was there too. . . . We worked together at NBC in the early CART days, and I think we brought new fans to IndyCar.

—Johnny Rutherford,
Sportscaster and three-time Indy 500 Champion

I met Paul for the first time as a rookie driver at the Indy 500 in 1983. He helped me significantly to understand the sport and culture of American Indy car racing. He was the best television announcer I ever worked with. He had a great set of pipes that helped generate excitement as he told the story. . . . It was obvious why he became the Voice of the 500.

—*Derek Daly,*
Author, sportscaster, and Indy car and Formula One driver

My profession has afforded me the ability to become close with many people whom I consider "legends," a potentially awkward balance between admiration and friendship. Paul is as big an icon as there is in motorsports, and I knew that very well in 2005. In 2021, he's that, but he's also just my buddy Paul.

—*Jack Beckman,*
Funny Car Champion

Paul is by far one of the most talented auto racing announcers in sports broadcasting. I swear he was born with a stopwatch in his brain—his innate ability to follow direction made this producer's job much easier. . . . He is, by far, the gold standard of sports broadcast announcers and one that I measure all others by.

—*Deb Luginbuhl,*
Emmy award-winning network producer

When I heard that Paul Page was going to be our play-by-play announcer for the ESPN drag racing series along side of me, I was thrilled to say the least. When he started he never took advantage of being the motorsports icon that I saw him as. He came in and worked to learn our sport, our production, and to do the best show possible every time which made me respect him even more. We had a lot of fun doing those shows and I can honestly say working with Paul is one of the highlights of my career. For me he will forever be that motorsports icon and the voice of the Indy 500.

—*Mike Dunn,*
Sportscaster, Top Fuel, and Funny Cars Champion

There are only a few non-drivers' names you hear that you immediately associate with the Indianapolis Motor Speedway, and the Indy 500 in particular. Paul Page is one of those iconic IMS figures. Through his voice, Paul painted pictures of and brought the excitement of the Indy 500 to fans from around the world.

—*Doug Boles*
President of the Indianapolis Motor Speedway

ISBN: 978-1-64234-164-5

LCCN: 2021934601

Cover Art by Yker Moreno
Design by Tom Heffron
Copyedited by Dani McCormick
Proofread by Faith Garcia
Interior Illustration by Heni Muslimah / Shutterstock
All photos courtesy of the author unless otherwise noted

Octane Press is based in Austin, Texas

Printed in the United States of America

CONTENTS

DEDICATION

For Sally, Brian, Marlo, Abby, Finn, and Coco.
—Paul Page

For LCB and HKE, the two lights of my life.
—J. R. Elrod

"You haven't won the Indy 500 until Paul Page says you did."
—*Al Unser Jr.*

FOREWORD

aul Page is no rat. He protects his friends. He was around drivers and crews for a bajillion years and never let the secrets out. He has a moral compass. He was so closely tethered in our inner sanctum, and we were always comfortable with him in his role of broadcasting our sport. He never as much as told a joke on the air at someone else's expense.

That's how he earned respect from his colleagues, from drivers, from race crews, and fans. Respect is a direct reflection of how you treat others. In racing, you have to stack quality years on top of quality years—and then you get the respect you deserve. Mission accomplished, Paul!

Paul Page always seemed happy. Over the moon, really. And why not? He's on a joyride. He's a big time broadcaster in his dream job in IndyCar racing, and he's an insider. He's laid-back, likes kibitzing, likes eating in dive diners as much as he does drinking fine wine at my winery in Napa Valley. And he never gets flustered . . . even when we refuse to forget that he can pronounce Lamborghini but not Countach.

So it seems that Paul Page now is in the mood to share his story—thus we have this book.

I hope he tells us what is really important from his broadcasting days, shares some of the pearls of wisdom he has picked up, tells us about the life lessons and friendships and what he misses, maybe the hiccups along his way and how he navigated those speed bumps. I'd like to read that.

It's important for racing to have great broadcasters, and it's important to have great people around. Paul Page is an example of both.

So without further ado, here is *The World According to Paul Page.*

—Mario Andretti

PREFACE

W hen you know guys like Mario and a long list of my friends are going to read this, it can be scary. What stories can you tell? I like good stories about good people. That's what you will find here. My life has taken so many twists and turns, it was hard to know where to start. I wasn't sure until my coauthor realized that the story of my life can't be told without telling the story of the Indianapolis 500.

Writing a memoir creates innumerable questions about what happened and when. The opportunity to reconnect with so many friends and piece together the good old days has been an unexpected reward of its own.

My coauthor brought a vision for this book that pushed beyond a collection of anecdotes and toward an earnest firsthand account of this magnificent race across six decades. So, there are really two voices here: history and a view inside the sport over sixty years. In this far more ambitious endeavor, I hope we have done justice to this enduring legacy.

INTRODUCTION

Mario Andretti once said, "The crashes people remember, but drivers remember the near misses." A joke at Indy is that the pit wall is getting higher and the straightaways shorter. Memories change and fade. Likewise, the stories in this book are how I recall them. Everyone knows my memory is terrible. If others remember things differently, I can only offer my honest recollection.

This book covers my first Indy 500 in 1960 through the one hundredth running in 2016, when I entered semiretirement. Too many people think of a particular time as the best era of racing. In truth, every era is the golden age. No matter the decade, every Indianapolis 500 is one of a kind.

The 1960s brought something completely new to the Speedway every year, with brilliant mechanics who relied on gut instinct and trial and error to find more speed. The rough-and-tumble drivers of the 1970s, flush with big sponsor money, lived life in the moment with no fear of consequences, in interviews and bar brawls alike.

The technological advances of the 1980s brought incremental improvements every year and also record entrants—scores of long-shot contenders living an Indy 500 dream on a hope and a prayer. Speed continued on its upward trajectory and peaked in the 1990s, even as the open-wheel racing split threatened to destroy the 500 itself.

In the 2000s, the cars and engines became nearly identical. Corporate speak trickled from most drivers in interviews. But parity put to rest those arguments in earlier eras—whether driver x would have won x many 500s with a better car. Winning came down to racing, strategy, and teamwork, not the mischance of a blown engine.

No decade has a monopoly on great racing—daring passes in Turn One and sprints on the final lap electrify the fans time and time again.

Anyone who comes to Indy is fiercely competitive, including drivers, owners, and media. Racing has its ugly side: ego-fueled rivalries, cut-throat business betrayals, accusations of cheating, and tough-luck cuts from the team or the broadcast. And yet, time seems to heal all wounds as the love of the Indy 500 overshadows even the nastiest feuds. In hindsight, everyone realizes being a part of the Indianapolis 500 was the best time of their lives. The only regret is they didn't stop to enjoy it more.

In the years when I struggled to make my way, I never lost focus on my passion for the Indianapolis 500, but I never felt certain I would succeed, nor for how long. Drivers in all eras live what I call a life of festival desperation. They know what they're doing can hurt them—it can kill them—and after five seasons, or twenty-five seasons, the end will come too soon. But they go out and do it, and therefore live the rest of their lives fairly open and fairly friendly. I think I've learned that lesson from them.

Most of all, I hope this book inspires others to find a passion and pursue it, much like a few words from a driver once did for me.

CHAPTER 1

On Top of the World

And these men have a rare combination of sacrifice, hope, triumph, and despair. The climax of their ambition is this pilgrimage to the object of their dreams—Indianapolis.
—*Sid Collins*

At an altitude of five hundred feet, our news chopper soared above the Indianapolis Motor Speedway, the greatest place on earth. It's a special vantage point from the sky. The entirety of the two-and-a-half-mile track cannot be seen from the ground, not even from the top row of the grandstands. Visible from space, its sheer size is breathtaking. From the dawning of the age of the automobile, the contours of this sacred racecourse have remained unchanged.

The lush green grass of the infield contrasted sharply with the gray asphalt of the oval. Bracing against the late-autumn cold in a goose-down jacket, I gazed at the barren track below. It filled me with awe.

Like an actor alone on a stage or an athlete crossing an empty field, I could feel and hear the past.

As I watched the iconic scoring pylon cast its thin shadow across the stands, a grin crept over my face: it had really happened. The prior May, I called the Indianapolis 500 as chief announcer for the radio broadcast. In my mind, "The Voice of the 500" would always be Sid Collins, my mentor, who spent the last quarter century calling the race. I found myself in his broadcast seat. How I got there would forever remain a bittersweet memory—in the midst of tragedy, a dream came true.

Ever since I was fifteen years old, I only dreamed of the Indianapolis 500. The rest of the year I spent waiting for May: the drivers, the cars, the speed.

It's not just a race for Hoosiers, it's a rite of passage: children playing in the infield beside a picnic blanket during practice, young debutantes blooming as the thirty-three 500 Festival Princesses, the rowdy youths carousing in the Snake Pit or the Coke Lot, runners stooping low to "kiss the bricks" halfway through the Mini Marathon, casual fans old and young playing hooky from work or school on a perfect May afternoon because "it's too nice a day to be anywhere but the Speedway." Tickets are handed down within families across generations.

The whole month of May is the Indy 500: a sprint to crown the pole-sitter followed by the battle over the remaining thirty-two spots. Then the heartbreak of Bump Day, where the bottom of the pack can only wait and see if their fastest was fast enough. The pressure builds during practice days leading up to Carburetor Day, the 500 Festival Parade, and finally Race Day.

Race Day, like the universe itself, starts in darkness until the silence is pierced by the big bang. That predawn aerial boom—a solitary firework—announces the gates are open. It unleashes the tide of spectators and the land-rush of staking claims in the infield. As the sun rises, the streets clog with cars and buses and police escorts, and the track swarms with high school marching bands and Boy Scout troops. The race is near when hundreds of thousands of fans sing in unison to "Back Home Again in Indiana" and the sky bursts into color with the balloon launch.

The 500 is an all-consuming vortex of sights, sounds, and emotions as race cars blaze through eight hundred left turns—two hundred laps—each one a tick closer to the checkered flag. Time seems to stop as the winner crosses the yard of bricks and coasts once more around the track to Victory Lane. For a brief moment, that stage becomes the center of the world: a mass of princesses, cameras, media, crew members, and four blaring Gordon Piper bagpipes. The wreath is worn; the trophy is hoisted; the quart of milk is emptied. As the fans drift away, their thoughts turn to those words of infinite hope, "next year." This is Race Day in Indianapolis, and it's spectacular.

Spring felt far away as the chopper followed its shadow beyond the cloistered confines of the track and meandered among the barren trees of the surrounding neighborhood. On that first day of December 1977, I had an office in the sky as a reporter and personality for WIBC radio in Indianapolis. I had a drawer full of broadcast journalism awards and at least a bit part in the history of the Indianapolis 500. Nothing could bring me down. I was on top of the world.

Until I wasn't.

The helicopter lurched and bucked. I looked left to my two companions. Worry washed over their faces. A crack and then a grinding sound brought abject fear. The tiny Hughes 269-B was in serious trouble. I looked past photographer Ed Moss to John Connolly, the pilot. John stared straight ahead as his hands fought the controls. The airspeed indicator spun well past our autorotation speed of eighty knots. I didn't need to look at the altimeter, I could feel the free fall. I learned in jump school it's preferable to have a parachute when you're falling from the sky. I didn't have one.

John jerked the cyclic stick like he was mixing dough. With his left hand he tried to pull the collective straight up. I looked to see where this ride would end. We were headed directly for Speedway High School.

I saw the main rotor frozen, unmoving. No main rotor meant no lift, and none of that famous autorotation that helps helicopters land in an emergency. We were stuck in a homesick brick aimed at a school full of kids.

The aircraft jerked and spun around. As if looking through a camera lens, the ground zoomed closer and closer. We barely cleared the school building as we flashed past the stadium lights for the football field. I ripped at my seatbelt, undoing the clasp. I'd seen enough fiery crashes to fear burns more than broken bones.

The last thing I saw was the empty green turf of the football field.

I can't say my life flashed before my eyes as the chopper descended that day. But if I could relive one moment, it would be my first Indy 500 in 1960. I was fifteen years old. My Uncle Harry took me in style behind a police escort. We rolled down 16th Street like kings, passing thousands of cars waiting in line to gain admission to the 44th International 500-Mile Sweepstakes.

An ocean of people bottlenecked in front of the main gate at 16th and Georgetown. We slowly ebbed toward the threshold. Each of the gate's red brick pillars was topped with a checkered triangular support adorned with a red "500." These columns held aloft a crossbeam emblazoned with "INDIANAPOLIS MOTOR SPEEDWAY." Above the beam rose the iconic "winged wheel" emblem—a graven image dating to the very first race—arrayed with the seven flags of the Speedway.*

The origins of the checkered flag remain a mystery. No doubt it dated to horse racing long before the invention of the automobile. Some suggest it started when women waved checkered tablecloths at the county fairgrounds to signal lunch was ready. While some of the Speedway's flags had different meanings prior to 1937, the checkered flag has always meant victory at Indianapolis.

I felt butterflies in my gut as we swarmed through the gate. Others plunged beneath the track through one of the six tunnels to emerge in the bright sun of the infield, that great jumbled mass of people and cars. The iconic old Pagoda was gone, replaced by the Master Control Tower and Speedway Offices. The first museum, just an open room beside the ticket office, featured a u-shaped shrine with the cars of past winners. The golf course hosted its first PGA tour that May. The pros grumbled about race cars roaring past during their backswings.

Massive modern grandstands walled off much of the track. The old weathered wood bleachers of Grandstand D still stood below the south chute. In the open patches along the infield, enterprising fans erected rickety makeshift scaffolds. I noticed the small creek, known as Dry Run or Dry Ditch Creek, that enters the track from the west, meanders down along Turn One, and disappears under the short chute. Nearby, a sign warned that throwing a bottle on the track could cause a bad wreck. It was a hint of the darker side of racing and the infield.

The green flag starts or restarts the race. The yellow flag denotes a caution—cars must slow down and maintain their positions. The white flag flies for the final lap. The blue flag (with an orange diagonal stripe) is a courtesy flag that indicates a driver is being followed by a faster competitor. If the blue flag is furled and pointed at the driver, it means they are required to give way immediately. The red flag means all cars must stop. The black flag sends a driver to the pits due to a penalty or an unsafe car. Two flags not found on the logo complete the set. The red-and-yellow striped flag indicates a slick track, usually due to oil. The black flag with a white cross stops a driver's laps from being scored. Since 1935, yellow and green lights along the track have also flickered in tandem with the flags.

We weaved through the enormous crowd to our seats in Grandstand B. To my left, I could see the pits, the Control Tower, and all the way up the main straightaway to Turn Four in the northwest. To my right, I could see Turn One into the south chute. Even today, out of the 257,000 fixed seats in the world's largest sports venue, I still think that's the place to be.

Directly across from our seats, the infield Tower Terrace grandstand stopped abruptly beside an empty patch of scrubby grass. I soon learned that plot was the most prized real estate in racing: Victory Lane. In 1971, the festivities moved to a platform in front of the Master Control Tower and became the "Victory Circle." To me, it's always Victory Lane at the end of the Indy 500.

On that bright, clear day everything shined, and the world sizzled. The great, deep voice of legendary track announcer Tom Carnegie echoed off the nearly mile-long grandstands lining the outside of the track. A light breeze carried the aroma of hot dogs and fried chicken and the occasional whiff of exotic fuels. I remember the Purdue University All American Marching Band, the huge drum, and the sequined baton twirlers: Golden Girl and the Silver Twins.

A mass of people surrounded the thirty-three "Champ Cars" on the straightaway. Referred to as Championship racing in those days, "Indy car" later became the more common terminology. Sparkling metallic colors flashed between the pit crews and friends gathered around the machines. More convertible than cockpit, the cars left the drivers exposed from the waist up. They needed arm room to manhandle the steering wheels and overcome the gyroscopic effect of the heavy front wheels.

A jitter went through the stands as a shiny white Oldsmobile 98 slowly rolled out of the pits: the pace car. Tom Carnegie's unforgettable baritone boomed: "It's time now for—."

I didn't know it then, but I was observing a ritual, a series of traditions with roots dating to the creation of the Speedway in 1909 and the first 500-mile race in 1911. Each of these rites, added on from generation to generation, led to this signature moment.

I could feel the anticipation build around me as Tom announced the name of Tony Hulman, owner of the Speedway. The crowd hushed as everyone strained to hear those magic words. Only the sounds of a scraping shoe or stifled cough broke the stillness.

Tony stood next to the pace car and faced the eleven rows of three race cars. He held in his left hand a three-by-five index card. It contained only four words, but these words must be spoken perfectly and with a singular inflection. Tony took a deep breath, and the massive public-address system blared the cutting words of:

"Gentlemen! Start. Your. Engines!"

The instant roar of the responding thirty-three cars was pure exhilaration. Nobody could describe that moment better than Tony: "After I say 'Gentlemen, start your engines,' I feel like I just pulled the pin on a hand grenade."

The smell of exhaust drifted over me. The cleanup crew, with vacuum cleaners in hand, cleared the dirt trampled on the track by well-wishers and fans. The safety patrol, in their blue wool uniforms and silver pith helmets, ushered people off the track. A decade later, they ditched the helmets and stood watch much more comfortably in their signature yellow shirts.

The excitement slowly grew as the Olds 98 pace car pulled ahead, followed by a white race car, the number 6. The man inside would become my hero. He was the pole-sitter, Eddie Sachs. Thirty-two race cars followed in formation, each row fifty feet apart: the Field of 33.

The wait for the pace lap to end was excruciating.

I heard the cheers move from Turn Two to Turn Three and grow louder near Turn Four. Finally, the pace car appeared in the north and turned down pit lane. With the swing of the green flag, thirty-three race cars thundered down the straightaway at full throttle. It took my breath away. The speed, noise, and vibration overwhelmed my senses. The rushing succession of blurs enveloped me.

This feeling blindsided me. I saw my first auto race as a child in Germany, race cars on a road course. On the train ride down to Indianapolis from Chicago I figured the Indy 500—cars going in circles—would be boring. It was the most exciting thing I could ever imagine.

In that instant of cars flashing by I thought, "This is it. This is what I want to do with my life." Somehow, I had to be a part of this. I was on top of the world.

In the infield overlooking the northeast corner, over a hundred fans paid five bucks each to watch from a scaffold stacked seven platforms high. As they leaned over to watch the first lap, the scaffolding tilted forward and fell like a tree onto spectators seated on the grass before it. Two were killed, and another eighty were injured. Blissfully unaware of the tragedy across the infield, the sleek circuiting cars simply mesmerized me.

In life, the first time is often the best time, but I am not alone in thinking 1960 was the best Indy 500 ever. Everyone had high hopes of seeing a sixty-second lap. Pole-sitter Eddie Sachs's qualifying lap at 146.59 miles per hour wasn't the fastest in the field—it was the fastest on the first day of qualifications, Pole Day. Jim "Herk" Hurtubise, a rookie, caught the fastest time at 149 mph. He was just a hair away from the long-awaited, yet so far unattained, 150-mph lap: around the track in sixty seconds.

At the Speedway, top speeds on the straightaway are only part of the picture. It's not drag racing. Drivers earn their pay daring to drive deeper and faster into the turns. Accordingly, the most heralded record at the Speedway is the fastest lap: the time it takes to make a single revolution around the track. Qualifying speeds are also measured in average lap speed. Because these records are averages, the cars achieve much faster top speeds before diving into the turns.

Race fanatics, called railbirds, sit with their own stopwatches timing the drivers. The old mechanical stopwatches came in sets with two independent timers, encased in rubber and counted down to 1/100 of a second. They used a template, usually glued to the back of the stopwatches, to convert the time to lap speed. Because of the perfect geometry of the racecourse, spectators can time laps, turns, and straightaways. Baseball fans' box scores are child's play compared to railbirds' charts at the Speedway.

No car broke the 150-mph barrier in 1960. Eddie led twenty-one laps, but his magneto failed and ended his day. It came down to the battle between Jim Rathmann and defending champion Rodger Ward—a rematch. The year before, Rodger edged out Jim for the win. The crowds around me jumped to their feet as the two traded the lead fourteen times. They both darted into the pits for their last stops with the whole race on the line. Back on the track, Rodger had the lead, but his worn tires slowed him down with three laps to go. Jim closed in fast and passed Rodger for the win. At the time, it was the second-closest finish in Indy 500 history.

As I took the bus back to Chicago, I felt like I had just passed through an initiation. As a teenager, most of us are searching for something to believe in, something that will come to define who we are. I think my mom Jeanne Page was afraid of what I might become. I could have run the gamut from a criminal to a priest.

I inherited my zest for life from my mom. She left Evansville, Indiana, to find adventure in the Navy's WAVES (Women Accepted for Voluntary Emergency Service) during World War II. The spirited and striking redhead became an air-to-air gunnery instructor. She also found the first two of her three husbands. The second husband was my father. She gave birth to me back home in Evansville on November 25, 1945. As I grew, I'm sure she saw her own spark and rebellious inclination in me.

I never knew my real father, a navy aviator and flight surgeon. They split early on, and my mom found her last husband, a lieutenant colonel—she had a thing for men in uniform. My stepfather treated me more like a soldier under his command than a son. As the years went by, my younger brothers and sister arrived, and I really felt like the odd one out. My mother's free spirit fell captive to the conformist culture of a military base in the 1950s. She soared only with the aid of her gallon jug of sherry.

As an Army brat, I didn't have a hometown. By the eighth grade, I held report cards from at least six different schools. In Stuttgart, Germany, I saw the still-raw devastation from the war in the ruins of bombed-out buildings. We lived in a house confiscated from an SS officer. My stepdad finally landed at Fort Sheridan, Illinois, on the banks of Lake Michigan. When he retired from the military and took a civilian job as an efficiency expert, we stayed close to the base in Highland Park about thirty miles north of Chicago.

Wherever we moved, I claimed one spot for my own: beneath the staircase in the basement. Woe be to my younger siblings if they invaded that space. We were always a bit isolated. My stepdad forbade guests in the house in case my mom wasn't presentable. Our friends could never come over to play.

All things considered, I had a good childhood. My worst moment was getting glasses at about twelve years of age. In the movies, the hero never wore glasses. They cast me as a bystander rather than the leading man I felt inside.

Growing up, I saw a unique cross section of America. In an officer's family, we were better off than a lot of my friends whose fathers were enlisted men. As a caddy at the Old Elm and Lakeshore golf courses, I met some of the wealthiest in Chicago, like Ben Florsheim of Florsheim Shoes and Leonard Wood of Sears, Roebuck & Co. Perhaps because I didn't feel like I belonged anywhere, I felt comfortable with everyone.

Maybe that's part of the attraction of the Indy 500. It's a place for everyone: the wealthiest sponsors, owners, and stars; the middle-class ticketholders; and the blue-collar fans in the infield. Unlike so many sports these days, a family of limited means can still afford to get in the gate and bring a cooler and a picnic basket from home.

By the time the checkered flag flew on that perfect day of May in 1960, I was hooked. It became my life's mission. Most people find a youthful passion, but it fades over time. My obsession never left me. It had staying power, like the Speedway itself.

The Speedway is a true original dating to the very beginning of the automobile era. Race officials in Indianapolis even coined the term "motorsports" in 1914. The Indianapolis Motor Speedway arose out of the unbridled ambition of Carl Fisher, a Hoosier and true rags-to-riches story.

The son of an attorney who abandoned his family, Carl quit school at age twelve to work at a grocery store. While still a teenager in the 1890s, he tapped into the national bicycle craze, became a competitive rider and mechanic, and opened a bicycle dealership.

Later, Carl helped promote a bicycle track where Indianapolis native Marshall "Major" Taylor set the track's unofficial mile record at age fifteen. Major faced down discrimination—Carl's old cycling club, the Zig Zags, refused to let him join—and became the greatest cyclist in the world. Major holds a special place in history as the first African American world champion in any sport.

After owning early electric and steam vehicles, Carl saw the future in the internal combustion engine. At the turn of the century, he sold his interests in bicycles and opened an Oldsmobile dealership. In 1901, he barnstormed county fairs throughout the Midwest, racing his car against any horse, and splitting the ticket sales with the fairground. By the next year, the excitement became cars racing cars, not horses. Indianapolis was right in the middle of it all. In 1903, Barney Oldfield set a world record averaging 60.4 mph around the one-mile track at the Indiana State Fairgrounds on 38th Street. The city soon became home to hundreds of automobile manufacturers.

As fate would have it, Carl met PC Avery, the inventor of an innovative carbide-based lamp. The kerosene lamps on carriages were fine at slow speeds, but the automobile needed something brighter. PC was near ruin because the established car manufacturers thought the volatile carbide was too dangerous. Carl and another investor put up $2,000 in capital for the Prest-O-Lite brand of lamps. After devising a way to safely fill the canisters, the business became an astounding success. Thirteen years later, the company sold for $9 million.

Some years later, the company erected a factory south of the Speedway. It featured a towering brick smokestack with Prest-O-Lite in vertical lettering. It blew a steady stream of black smoke, and, for decades, drivers blazing down the main straightaway used it to gauge wind direction.

Carl conceived the Indianapolis Motor Speedway as a racetrack and proving ground, and he erected it on 320 acres of level farmland outside the city limits. Geometrically, it is not an oval, but rather a rectangle with rounded corners. The architect started with a perfect one-mile circle, intersected and divided it into fourths (creating the 1/4 mile turns) and extended it by 5/8th of a mile north and south (creating the main straightaways) and 1/8th of a mile east and west (creating the short chutes).

In 1909, the Speedway opened to the world with its signature white buildings with green trim. The Speedway set three thousand hitching posts and marked ten thousand spaces for automobiles. The inaugural season saw races of cars, motorcycles, and hot air balloons. Unfortunately, the gravel track was unsafe—drivers and spectators were killed.

Carl would spare no expense in his pursuit of perfection. In a colossal undertaking completed in a few short months, 3.2 million ten-pound bricks were laid, most stamped with "W. C. Co. Culver Block, Pat. May 21, 1901." A solitary "gold" brick was laid in the center of the start/finish line, made of the exact alloy of brass and bronze used in the carburetors built at the local Wheeler-Schebler factory. The freshly-paved curves and straightaways soon garnered the track nickname: "the Brickyard."

After two seasons, Carl concluded the Speedway would be most successful with one grand race rather than multiple events. He scheduled one race for 1911—the race of all races—the International 500-Mile Sweepstakes Race. The length of the race was purely practical. At speeds in that era, a five-hundred-mile race took about six-and-a-half hours to finish: enough time for the crowds to arrive, enjoy a long race, and leave before nightfall.

Carl selected Memorial Day for Race Day to ensure a holiday crowd. The track opened for practice on May 1 to allow the mechanics plenty of time to perfect their cars. Springtime in Indianapolis would never be the same.

No matter how many years go by, the thrill of the race remains the same. The cars change, the names change, but the essence of the 500 endures. The tradition, the pageantry, the speed, the action, the crowds—it defies any description except one, "The Greatest Spectacle in Racing."

CHAPTER 2

A Letter to Eddie Sachs

I felt that all I was, or ever hoped to be, I owed
to the Indianapolis 500-mile race.
—*Wilbur Shaw*

Back home in Highland Park, I read anything I could find on the Indy 500. I checked out Wilbur Shaw's *Gentlemen, Start Your Engines* a dozen times from the school library. Every May, I temporarily subscribed to the *Indianapolis Star* and *Indianapolis News*. I loved learning about the drivers.

The sportswriters dubbed Eddie Sachs "The Clown Prince of Auto Racing" for his antics and sense of humor. He quickly became my favorite. Chris Economaki, an announcer and sportswriter who met more drivers than anyone, described Eddie as one of the most colorful and charismatic people he ever met, with an incredible charm that overshadowed his somewhat-homely face.

Eddie used to tell a story featuring the Conkle Funeral Home, which still sits a block away from the Speedway. In those days, race-tracks commonly employed funeral hearses for ambulances. The Conkle hearse was always on call at the Speedway. Eddie said, "If you're charging a turn at Indy, there are signs that count down to the wall. Three, two, one, *Conkle*. Don't drive as deep as Conkle." That led him to the story of a racer who awoke lying on a stretcher in the back of the Conkle "ambulance." The racer became very worried he wasn't headed to the hospital.

A few weeks after my first race, I wrote a fan letter to Eddie. I expressed how I wanted more than anything to be a part of the Indianapolis 500. I suggested, "Maybe I could write stories about you, Mr. Sachs." I mailed it to Eddie, care of the Speedway. I hoped with my whole heart for a letter in return.

It might seem surprising that I dreamed of a seat in the press box as much as a seat in the cockpit. But I learned from my Uncle Harry that you can play a big role in the world of sports even if you're not a player.

For almost twenty years, Harry Geisel worked as an American League umpire. When baseball was everything, he made the calls in the World Series (1930, 1934, and 1936) and a couple of All-Star games. He stood behind the plate in Shibe Park in Philadelphia on June 3, 1932, as the Philly Athletics faced the New York Yankees and Lou Gehrig hit four home runs. In Game 7 of the 1934 World Series in Detroit, fans in left field rioted over one of Harry's calls and threw garbage from the stands onto Navin Field.

In the off-season, Harry announced boxing matches and officiated at billiard tournaments. His career as an umpire ended when Yankees pitcher Spud Chandler collided with Uncle Harry at home plate. He spent seven weeks in the hospital. In gratitude, the American League paid Harry his regular salary until his death.

In retirement, Uncle Harry went on the dinner speaker circuit. When asked about Game 7 of the 1934 World Series, he told a story about a bat boy named Seymour Wax. Harry and pitching legend Dizzy Dean both noticed Seymour's shoes were falling apart. Without a second thought, they went out and bought him a new pair. Harry had a soft spot for children.

I spent many summers in Indianapolis with Uncle Harry and Aunt Norna in the 5800 block of North Delaware Street, a perfect neighborhood for a bike ride on a summer day. We cooled off with a dip in the pool at the Riviera Club.

Uncle Harry encouraged my interest in broadcasting. He helped me stage television shows in his basement. We converted floor lamps into flood lights by removing the shades and wrapping aluminum foil around the bulbs. A chrome bud vase became the mic. I asked the Pfeiffer sisters next door to be a singing act. Uncle Harry even built a big TV studio camera out of plywood with "SNBS TV" painted on the camera: "Skipper's National Broadcasting System." The Skipper nickname came from my father being a naval aviator. No one calls me Skipper anymore. No one.

Uncle Harry knew Fort Sheridan had a large "radio shack" for hobbyists, and he pushed me to earn my amateur radio license. I spent a lot of my free time in the shack listening to the world over shortwave, fascinated by the bright glow of the vacuum tubes inside the huge military BC610 transmitter and the RAS-5 battleship receiver. I joined MARS (Military Affiliate Radio System) and mastered Morse code sufficiently enough to earn my license.

As a Freemason and Shriner (and 1953 Potentate of the Murat Shrine in Indianapolis), Uncle Harry enthusiastically supported the Shriners Children's Hospitals. On occasion, he brought me along when he had meetings at the Murat Temple: a massive yellow brick building in downtown Indianapolis with a Middle Eastern design and a towering minaret. Its large theater is still a major concert venue. Uncle Harry would take me up, sit in the fourth row, and make me tell stories from the stage. I didn't realize it then, but he was training me in the art of public speaking.

When we went to an Indianapolis Indians baseball game at the old stadium on 16th Street, Harry took me up to the press box to meet play-by-play announcer Jim McIntire and watch him work. Even as a teenager, I noticed how smoothly he segued into a commercial.

Uncle Harry made me believe anything was possible. If I wanted to be in broadcasting, I could do it. And he would help me any way he could.

Only a week had passed when I ran to the mailbox at our house on Hyacinth Place and found an envelope with the logo of the "Champion 100 MPH Club." Sponsored by the Champion spark plug company, membership included those drivers who completed the Indianapolis 500 without a relief driver and achieved a 100-miles-per-hour average for the entire race.

Postmarked from Allentown, Pennsylvania, and signed by Eddie Sachs, the handwritten letter offered a few words of advice:

> Many people will say they will do these things. But many forget and go on to other stuff. You must stick with something if you want it.

I've carried those words with me ever since.

I think they left an impression because Eddie didn't patronize me or treat me like a child. He wrote something he meant—something he really wanted me to take to heart.

Most drivers take their interactions with kids seriously. Perhaps more than any other type of athlete, racers seem to connect with young people. In a lot of ways, racers and children are the same age emotionally: they relate. Like Jack Arute, the longtime pit reporter for ABC Sports, used to say of Tony Stewart, "He's a like a fifteen-year-old with a credit card."

One might say I was a bit of a Tony Stewart in high school. I did well in the courses I liked: straight A's in public speaking, debate, and drama. Math, chemistry, and sociology, not so much. I skipped 90 percent of my homework. Fortunately, I usually nailed the tests and scraped by with Ds on my report card.

The one thing I really took seriously was my work on the Suburban League student programming at WKRS in Waukegan, Illinois. Every Saturday, I spent a twelve-hour day writing news segments and working the "board," the large control panel. I learned the ropes, and even the announcers and engineers handed off their work to me.

Never far from my sight was a plaque on the wall that read: "Proud Member of the Indianapolis Motor Speedway Radio Network."

In May of 1961, Melvin "Tony" Bettenhausen nearly broke the 150-mph barrier on a practice lap. Later he test-drove a car for Paul Russo. As Tony applied the brakes, a bolt fell out of the arm that controlled the steering to the wheels. He hit the outside wall, flipped over, and slid upside down along the wall and catch fence. Tony didn't survive.

Eddie Sachs caught the pole for the second year in a row. His white Ewing roadster sported a big blue number 12. Anthony Joseph "A. J." Foyt Jr. put his Trevis-built roadster, a Watson copy, in Row 3. A. J. Watson designed some of the most beautiful Indy cars ever made. They dominated for years; the front row was all Watson roadsters in 1958. With George Bignotti as his owner and mechanic, A. J. Foyt would be tough to beat.

Less noticed was a tiny car in British racing green with white stripes and a number 17 in a solid white circle—the Formula One style. Two-time F1 World Champion John "Sir Jack" Brabham, an Aussie, drove the rear-engine Cooper Climax. The Indy gang considered any green car to be bad luck. They didn't know Brabham's marked the beginning of the end of the roadster.

On Race Day, Eddie and A. J. fought it out tooth and nail. In the closing laps, A. J. made his last stop for fuel, but something went wrong. A problem with the fuel tank valve forced another pit for fuel, giving Eddie the lead, and likely the race. But with three laps to go, Eddie saw a white line spinning down his right rear tire. An exposed white cord usually meant the tire was dangerously worn.

Eddie played it safe and headed to the pits. The crew used hammers to loosen and tighten the giant wing-nut lug on each tire. As Eddie roared out of the pit, A. J. flashed by on the straightaway, taking the lead. A mechanic threw his hammer after Eddie's car in a fit of frustration. He knew something Eddie didn't. The white line on the tire was the warning strip, not the tire cord. That unnecessary pit stop handed A. J. his first checkered flag at Indy.

Because it was a dangerous sport and nothing can top winning the 500, a lot of drivers said they would retire in Victory Lane. Only two drivers actually did: Ray Harroun and Sam Hanks. Eddie often teased the other drivers saying the only way to get rid of him would be to let him win the 500. Legend has it that Eddie, unwilling to retire, decided to throw the race and let A. J. win.

I never believed it for a minute.

Later that summer, I learned to drive in a battleship gray 1952 Plymouth Cambridge—six cylinders and three on the tree (a manual shift on the steering column). A dream car it was not. Rusted out and with a piece of plywood for the floorboard, it always stalled on me in hilly Highland Park. But it had bench seats, allowing your date to scoot closer to you. Where she sat was a good gauge of how well the date was going.

On Pole Day 1962, Rufus Parnell "Parnelli" Jones broke the 150-mph barrier, taking his Watson roadster, *Calhoun*, around the track in less than sixty seconds. Henry "Smokey" Yunick, a legendary mechanic, became the first to mount a wing on an Indy car to increase down-force. Mostly known for his dominance in NASCAR, Smokey spent many Mays in Indy in his white shirt and pants and an old beat-up cowboy hat, trying out new ideas.

Strides in technology and innovation date to the very first 500. In an era before dashboard gauges, most drivers needed a riding mechanic to pay attention to the engine. Ray "the Little Professor" Harroun designed his car's engine and raced solo. He won the 1910 National Championship racing series in his single-seat Marmon called the Wasp and retired. To his competitors' disappointment, Ray came back for the inaugural 500.

On the eve of the race, Ray learned some of his opponents were grumbling to the officials that the Wasp was unsafe without a riding mechanic. Who would warn him about vehicles passing from behind? They hoped to get Ray and the Wasp disqualified. In response, Ray fastened a mirror on his car in a manner he had once seen on a horse-drawn carriage. It was the world's first rearview mirror on a car.

Some of the drivers thought Ray had an unfair weight advantage without a passenger because the tires would last longer. In reality, Ray determined he could get substantially more miles on a tire by driving at an average lap speed of 78 mph rather than 80 mph. In a real-life version of "The Tortoise and the Hare," Ray drove slower, pitted less often, and won the first Indianapolis 500.

Single-seat race cars were banned the next year and came in and out of favor in the decades that followed. Similarly, no one took much notice when George Bailey put the first rear-engine car in the second row in 1939 or when Jack Brabham's Cooper finished ninth in 1961. When rookie Dan Gurney put team owner Mickey Thompson's rear-engine car in Row 3 in 1962, teams took notice of its potential.

For Race Day 1962, Bill and his brother Tom rode with me on the train from Chicago. I acted like a big shot and showed them around the Speedway. After getting to our seats, I left them in the stands so I could watch and listen from all angles: in the tunnel feeling the cars above, beside the straightaway, up high, down close.

The place meant more to me than they could understand.

Eddie Sachs started twenty-seventh, and my hero put on quite a show, finishing in third place. Parnelli Jones lost his brakes and yet still completed the race by angling into the pits, bouncing off tires set up as bumpers, and scraping Calhoun to a halt against the pit wall. Rodger Ward owned the second half of the race on his way to his second win.

Over the years, layers of asphalt began to hide the bricks of the Brickyard, first in the turns and then on the straightaways. Over the summer of 1961, the last portions of the track were covered in asphalt. When Rodger caught the checkered flag, only a three-foot-wide row of bricks remained at the start/finish line: the yard of bricks.

I graduated in the bottom 10 percent of my class. Later in life when I achieved some level of success, Highland Park High School overlooked my academic deficiencies and invited me annually to its Festival of the Arts banquet. Then Gary Sinise came along; he and my brother Tracy were classmates. After Gary's Oscar-nominated role as Lt. Dan in *Forrest Gump*, my invitations to the banquet stopped coming.

For graduation, Uncle Harry gave me a very nice Hammond watch, which was more than I could expect from my stepfather. I couldn't get out of Highland Park and back to Indianapolis fast enough. I longed for it year-round; Indy was my home, and the Speedway was my shrine.

In May of 1963, the brand new ninety-six-unit Speedway Motel rose outside the southeast corner. When the Beatles sold out the

Coliseum at the Indiana State Fairgrounds, they secretly stayed at the Speedway Motel as a sanctuary from the fans. The Fab Four took a spin around the track in a Cadillac. On Pole Day, Parnelli Jones seized the pole again, still driving Calhoun. Scotsman Jimmy Clark and Dan Gurney qualified the last cars with carburetors instead of fuel injectors. Rookie Johnny Rutherford qualified near the back of the field.

The new British Lotus-Ford rear-engine cars proved real contenders. To fans, the "funny cars" seemed contrary to the laws of nature: engines belonged in the front. Sam Posey sat in the stands that year and quipped that the Lotuses were about as popular as the Japanese had been at Pearl Harbor. In the garages, they joked that rear-engines were for men who liked to be pushed around.

If fans hated the Lotus, they loved the Novi. As Chris Economaki put it best, "no racing machine at Indianapolis came close to the powerful sound and fury of the Novi." The beastly power of the Novi engine made those cars the most challenging ever driven at the Speedway.

The big Novi engine needed a big chassis, and the Kurtis race cars looked different from everything else in the field. Pronounced with a long *i*, they were produced in the Detroit suburb of Novi, Michigan, named after gate "No. VI" of an early toll road. Two stone race cars are set in front of the Speedway Museum and Hall of Fame: a Foyt Coyote and a Kurtis Novi. The Novi's 1963 return to the field made Herk Hurtubise and rookie Bobby Unser instant fan favorites, no matter where they finished.

On Race Day, Parnelli led the pack in the closing laps when Calhoun began leaking oil from a crack in the left external oil tank. Chasing him were Eddie Sachs in a Watson roadster and rookie Jimmy Clark in a Lotus-Ford. Their owners stormed over to the starting line to confront Chief Steward Harlan Fengler. They demanded a black flag for Parnelli as a track hazard. Parnelli's owner, J. C. Agajanian, in his signature white cowboy hat, hollered back that the oil level had dropped below the crack and no longer leaked. Harlan, in his red fedora, shouted back his decision to let them race.

Eddie tried to pass Jimmy and spun out, hitting the wall and causing damage that eventually resulted in Eddie losing a wheel. Parnelli got the win, followed by Jimmy. In true Eddie fashion, he found his lost wheel and rolled it along the track on his way back to the pits, waving to the raucous amusement of the fans.

The loudest cheers don't always go to the winner. In 1912, Ralph de Palma led 196 laps before his engine locked on the second-to-last lap. Ralph and his mechanic got out and pushed, igniting the roaring encouragement of the crowd. Joe Dawson finally caught up to the lead lap and passed them to take the checkered flag. Exhausted, Ralph paused for a moment, but the cheers erupted louder and louder. They heaved the car on to the finish line.

Never shy of controversy, Eddie loudly proclaimed that Jimmy should have won and blamed his own spin on Parnelli's oil. The next day, he continued to run his mouth at the Speedway Motel. Parnelli warned Eddie not to call him a liar. Eddie didn't heed the advice, and the very muscular Parnelli landed a heavy blow before both men went to the floor wrestling.

I enrolled in the broadcasting program at Tulsa University and headed to Oklahoma in the fall of 1963. I worked as much as I possibly could on the campus station. In the evenings, I hitchhiked out to Sand Springs for my first paid radio job DJing country music on KTOW. In that tiny, cramped station I had to be careful not to lean too far back in my chair—it would hit the power button on the transmitter and shut it all down.

I pledged a fraternity, but that wasn't for me. I stayed at the YMCA instead. My study habits from high school continued. At the end of the school year, I was named campus station manager for the upcoming semester. Unfortunately, my grades were so bad that I flunked out of college. I spent my last fifty-four dollars on a plane ticket to Indianapolis. I showed up at Uncle Harry's door unannounced. That old familiar block of Delaware Street was cool and green and welcomed me home. I'm fairly sure Uncle Harry called my mom to let her know where I was.

In May of 1964, I spent almost every day at the Speedway. I waited for the John Zink Racing team as they rolled a car back to Gasoline Alley, and I started waving and shouting. I had visited their shop in Tulsa a few times, just to see it. They remembered me, and John Zink gave me a bronze badge (garage pass). That golden ticket put me behind the scenes for the first time. I've never been shy, and a willingness to put myself out there, to be "that guy," has opened lots of doors over the years.

More lightweight rear-engine cars arrived that May. They ran on gasoline rather than methanol to leverage its better fuel efficiency for fewer pit stops. They might run the entire race without a pit stop. It had happened before—in 1931 Dave Evans finished without ever refueling his Cummins diesel. Gasoline isn't as efficient as diesel, so the teams increased fuel capacity by extending the fuel tank around the cockpit. A. J. Foyt decided to stay with his roadster, warning the rear-engine cars were "like sitting in a bathtub of gasoline."

Team owner Mickey Thompson brought his low, aerodynamic, rear-engine "flying saucers." Their fenders wrapped around the wheels—meaning they weren't open-wheel. The original design required small, twelve-inch tires. A late rule change mandated larger wheels, and Mickey's crew worked around the clock cutting up the fenders and compensating for the change in height.

On Race Day 1964, I sat next to my Uncle Harry in Grandstand E. Jimmy Clark led from the pole, while rookie Dave MacDonald sat in one of Mickey's cars in Row 5. Eddie Sachs sat in Row 6. As the cars dove into Turn One on lap two, I saw Eddie chasing Dave. As I watched Jimmy come back around and pass the start/finish line, I heard a boom and turned to see a giant ball of flames and black smoke rising out of Turn Four. An indescribable inferno erupted along the track. Billowing black smoke blocked out the entire sky to the north. Flames consumed an enormous sycamore beside the track. That same ominous tree was featured in *The Big Wheel* with Mickey Rooney.

I looked for Eddie, but he wasn't there. No more race cars came by, only firetrucks and ambulances. For the first time in Indy 500 history, the red flag stopped the race for an accident. The fire burned and burned. The public address system went silent. I listened to the radio broadcast on my portable transistor radio, but we knew nothing.

Eventually, an ambulance rushed down the straightaway, turned into Victory Lane, and exited a gate that led to the track hospital two hundred yards away. The patient was visible from the windows. Someone behind me said, "That was Dave MacDonald in there." An hour passed before I heard the announcement over the track speakers:

> Driver Eddie Sachs was fatally injured in the accident on the main straightaway.

Later in the race, the radio broadcast announced Dave's death as well.

On that fateful second lap, Dave lost it coming out of Turn Four. He hit the inside wall and slid out to the center of the track. Eddie reacted with the accepted pro move: aim where the out-of-control car is now, and its momentum will keep it moving out of the way. While true for the big front-engine cars, Dave's lightweight, rear-engine machine stayed put. Eddie hit it square, and he likely died on impact.

As other drivers hit the brakes and risked stopping in the inferno, Bobby Unser shouted, "Goddammit, stand on it you sombitches."

He plowed his heavy, four-wheel drive Ferguson Novi through the black smoke, knocking rookie Ronnie Duman's car clear of the fire. Crumpled against the outside wall, Bobby watched the fire crews cover Eddie's car with a tarp.

Five years earlier in the same spot coming out of Turn Four, Bobby's brother Jerry wrecked on a practice lap. Still conscious and wearing only a T-shirt, he called to the crew putting out the fire: "My legs are on fire. Call my wife." He died at Methodist Hospital two weeks later. Jerry's death became the impetus for mandatory fire-resistant suits for all drivers.

After Bobby sent Ronnie free of the conflagration, he went rolling over the inside wall, still engulfed in flames. He suffered severe burns, but he recovered and returned to racing. Years later Ronnie died in a grisly wreck at the Milwaukee Mile.

When Johnny Rutherford came to a stop, he noticed debris from the wreck around his legs in his cockpit. He found a lemon hanging from a shoestring. Eddie always wore a lemon on a string around his neck during a race—something juicy to nibble on to keep from drying out. While being treated for burns at the track hospital, J. R. sat right beside Dave as the doctors worked on him. He noticed a pink liquid drip down Dave's cheek; he learned it resulted from inhaling fumes.

After the race restarted, Mickey Thompson's other car pitted several times for mechanical problems and fell way behind the leaders. When Mickey learned of Dave's death, he packed it in.

In the stands that day, I couldn't believe it. Eddie Sachs, this larger-than-life personality who led bands down the front stretch, who laughed off a loss but cried during "Back Home Again in Indiana," was dead. As an invincible teenager, my heroes were supposed to be invincible too.

Clutching my little radio, I listened to Sid Collins deliver words of comfort. In the months that followed, the IMS Radio Network received over thirty thousand requests for a copy of what became known as the "Death Has a Thousand Doors" eulogy:

You heard that announcement from the public address system. There's not a sound. Men are taking off their hats. People are weeping. There are over three hundred thousand fans here not moving, disbelieving.

Some men try to conquer life in a number of ways. These days of our outer space attempts, some men try to conquer the universe. Race drivers are courageous men who try to conquer life and death and they calculate their risks. And with talking with them over the years I think we know their inner thoughts in regards to racing. They take it as part of living.

A race driver who leaves this earth mentally when he straps himself into the cockpit to try what for him is the biggest conquest he can make [is] aware of the odds, and Eddie Sachs played the odds. He was serious and frivolous. He was fun. He was a wonderful gentleman. He took much needling and he gave much needling. Just as the astronauts do perhaps.

These boys on the racetrack ask no quarter and they give none. If they succeed, they're a hero, and if they fail, they tried. And it was Eddie's desire and will to try with everything he had, which he always did. So the only healthy way perhaps we can approach the tragedy of the loss of a friend like Eddie Sachs is to know that he would have wanted us to face it as he did. As it has happened, not as we wish it would have happened. It is God's will, I'm sure, and we must accept that.

We are all speeding toward death at the rate of sixty minutes every hour, the only difference is, we don't know how to speed faster, and Eddie Sachs did. So since death has a thousand or more doors, Eddie Sachs exits this earth in a race car. Knowing Eddie, I assume that's the way he would have wanted it.

At this point, Sid paused and asked Freddie Agabashian in the booth to offer his comments. Sid then continued:

Byron said, 'Who the gods love die young.'

Eddie was thirty-seven. To his widow Nancy, we extend our extreme sympathy and regret. And to his two children. This boy won the pole here in 1961 and 1962. He was a proud race driver. Well, as we do at Indianapolis and in racing, as the World Champion Jimmy Clark I'm sure would agree as he's raced all over the world, the race continues. Unfortunately today without Eddie Sachs. And we'll be restarting it in just a few moments.

As I learned the trade of broadcasting, I marveled that Sid could ad-lib such an impressive speech. The truth was, he didn't. Sid knew the result for an hour before the PA announced it. There was plenty of time to think it out. So it wasn't ad-lib, but that didn't matter. It was a great piece of oration. After Sid's death, I found among his files an envelope labeled "fatalities." It contained several poems on death and the meaning of life, along with draft remarks with blanks for the driver's name. Sid felt he had not handled the deaths of Bill Vukovich and Pat O'Connor in earlier races as well as he should have. He was ready when death came for Eddie. I didn't adopt Sid's use of draft remarks, but I certainly framed the appropriate responses in my mind so I would be ready.

Anyone who raced in this era knew the dangers. Of the thirty-three drivers in the 1958 Indy 500, a dozen would go on to die from racing injuries. Even top drivers raced whatever and whenever they could: sprints, midgets, stocks—nearly all on dirt tracks. Even half of the Indy car races were on dirt tracks like the Indiana State Fairgrounds. Dr. Steven Olvey, the long-time medical director for the Indy car series, estimated that 7 percent of drivers died every year in those days.

The big show went on without my hero. A. J. Foyt led 146 laps on his way to claim his second checkered flag. He won ten of the thirteen races in the series and claimed the title.

What I felt in the stands was heartbreak. The prior fall, I drove from Tulsa to Dealey Plaza in Dallas with a journalist's curiosity. Unlike many in my generation, JFK's assassination was not the quintessential loss of innocence for me. Eddie Sachs's death was.

Eddie's words lived on in me. I bit down harder. I resolved to follow my passion wherever it led.

CHAPTER 3

On And Off the Airwaves

I would rather win that race than anything in the world.
I would rather be Ralph de Palma than president.
—Ernie Pyle

Uncle Harry outfitted me with a '53 Buick for my job hunt. I landed at WAIV, a jazz and classical music station owned by some bigwigs at Eli Lilly, the landmark Indianapolis pharmaceutical company. From the top floor of the Dearborn Hotel, the studio overlooked the sprawling RCA television factory.

Both genres were new to me, but one of my courses at Tulsa required me to learn how to pronounce composers' names. It came in handy. I pumped out light classical in the afternoon, with Vivaldi's "Four Seasons" as the opening. In the evening, the sound of an airplane taking off led into "Jazz Flight 805," and my background looped the brass horns of the *James Bond* theme music. WAIV later became WTLC, and Jazz Flight continued for decades.

I moved on to WATI, DJing and reading the news in a basement studio in downtown Indianapolis. The programming included a religious show sponsored by a local funeral home. To my shock, I heard the pastor deliver a grossly anti-Semitic sermon. As a young hire, I realized I shouldn't make waves, but I didn't hesitate to tell the station manager. I've always believed doing the right thing is more important than the consequences. The station cut the program.

Soon after, WATI went automated. Timing is everything in this business. Losing that job led to a spot in the news department at WIBC, the home of the Indianapolis Motor Speedway Radio Network. I felt like I won the lottery.

Assigned to the crime beat, I spent a lot of time hanging around the police station, courts, and even the morgue. I asked lots of questions. I learned how the coroner's office handled the aftermath of the 1963 propane explosion at the State Fairgrounds' Coliseum during the Holiday on Ice Show. With scores of spectators killed, they needed to keep the bodies cold during the identification process. I saw pictures of the bodies laid out on the ice of the hockey rink.

About four months in, I was assigned to cover an important Indianapolis racing tradition: the annual Soap Box Derby, where children race engineless homemade carts. The hillside track located just west of downtown is named for three-time Indy 500 champion and Hoosier Wilbur Shaw. The race endures to this day.

I interviewed the kid who won and delivered my tape to the booth. Sid Collins happened to be in the hallway when it went live over the speakers. I noticed Sid listening attentively. I held my breath, hoping it might leave a good impression. Sid was the man—literally "The Voice of the Indianapolis 500." Not only the chief announcer, he also chose the other broadcasters and engineering staff for the race. Sid was the one person I needed to impress.

When my segment ended, Sid looked at me and said, "That's the worst interview I've ever heard."

It hit me like a baseball bat.

If Sid thought I couldn't interview a twelve-year-old kid, I had no hope of working on Race Day.

Perhaps sensing my distress, Sid walked me to his office and spent the next three hours teaching me how to properly conduct an interview. He must have seen some potential, otherwise he wouldn't have wasted his time on me.

I picked up a lot of great advice at WIBC, much of it from veteran reporter Bob Hoover. He'd been around forever. As a young photographer, he captured an iconic picture of John Dillinger. He loved to tell the story of the day the Ku Klux Klan chased him off, having taken some exception to his questions. Before an interview Bob would remind me, "Don't let them know what you know. Keep your mouth shut. Don't interrupt. And don't be afraid of silence."

In May of 1965, I experienced life as a teenager with press credentials. I spent almost every day of May at the track. I drank it all in: the sights, sounds, cars, and faces. Eleven rookies made the field, including future greats Gordon Johncock, Al Unser Sr., and Mario Andretti. Just months after breaking his back in a wreck in January, A. J. Foyt smashed the 160-miles-per-hour barrier and seized the pole. All but six of the cars in the field were rear-engine.

I spent every dime I had at the Allied Radio Company in Chicago buying a reel-to-reel tape recorder with a wireless microphone. I set it on top of a fifty-gallon drum in Gasoline Alley and walked up and down the garages interviewing anyone who would talk to me. Jimmy Clark was intrigued by the cordless mic, and I explained some of the technology behind it. The World Champion stood about five-seven with dark wavy hair and a handsome smile. He was chatting with *me* like I belonged at the Speedway.

I stood only a few feet away when Mario removed the three rookie stripes from the back of his car, signifying he passed his rookie test. The stripes were a warning to watch out for the new guy. In the '80s, the Speedway started a rookie orientation program where new drivers found their bearings before the Speedway opened for practice in May.

Passing the rookie test was no sure thing. Even greats like my hero Eddie Sachs didn't make the cut their first time around. In this era, the test started with ten laps at an exact 120 mph average lap speed. Rookies could fail if they varied more than a half mph. The speed increased to sets at 125 and 130 mph. On the fourth run, veteran drivers spread out around the track to observe. They reported back to the Chief Steward, who made the final decision. Either the stripes came off, or the rookie heard those devastating words, "You need a little more time."

On Race Day, A. J.'s gearbox broke shortly after the halfway mark. Jimmy Clark, in his British racing green Lotus-Ford, led 190 laps and reached the finish line nearly two laps ahead of second place Parnelli Jones. Mario came in third on his way to winning the series as a rookie.

For me, the drivers, owners, and crew members became people I knew, not just people I read about.

When May ended, it was a huge letdown. The crime beat kept me hustling as I waited for spring. When I heard the call on the police scanner for Car 83, the homicide detective, I packed up the mobile news equipment and followed. I parked on New York Street in a tight-knit neighborhood on the East Side. The hardened officers leaving the house were visibly shaken, something I had not seen before. I soon learned the unfathomable: a sixteen-year-old girl named Sylvia Likens had been starved, tortured, and murdered by a woman with the help of her school-age daughters and several neighborhood children.

Gertrude Baniszewski, a mother of seven, agreed to provide room and board to Sylvia and her younger sister while their parents traveled with a carnival for the summer. When payments from their parents slowed, Gertrude took it out on Sylvia through beatings, starvation, cigarette burns, and sexual assaults. Gertrude encouraged her teenage daughters and neighborhood children to watch and join in the abuse. Some neighbors looked the other way while others dismissed the stories as wild rumors too horrible for belief.

In those days, when reporters worked with facts rather than opinions and political narratives, we had near-unlimited access to crime scenes and police facilities. Bob Hoover brought me along to see the postmortem, but there wasn't room for a cub reporter. Sylvia's lifeless body revealed more than a hundred wounds and burns, and the words "I'm a whore and I'm proud of it" carved on her stomach

It became the city's most sensational story. I covered it from day one. It would also be my last crime story for a long time.

I made the mistake of admiring a beautiful car: a light blue '65 Mustang convertible with a V-8. Jim Hilliard, my station manager, wanted to unload it. I had to have it. I gave him a down payment, and he handed me the keys. Unfortunately, I soon learned I couldn't get a loan at my age. I stalled and made another payment, but I had to come clean. Jim took back the car, kept my payments, and told news director Fred Heckman to fire me.

It felt like the end of the world. I racked my brain every day for any possible way to get back in the good graces of WIBC—my only route to the IMS Radio Network.

Depressed and back in Highland Park for the weekend, my stepfather chose that moment to lay into me about the military. He told me I had better volunteer before my draft number came up. The ground war in Vietnam had already begun, and I was an unemployed, unmarried college dropout in perfectly good health.

I knew he was right. I faced a choice. I enlisted in the Indiana National Guard. When a nation is at war, some young men choose paths that will likely lead to the front line. These men must be forever remembered as heroes and warriors. I will never forget my debt to those men who braved the perils of combat.

On an icy day in February, my mom called with bad news. Uncle Harry had died. I went to the house, but Aunt Norna was inconsolable. Before I left, a couple of my mom's sisters accused me of taking Uncle Harry's jewelry: his baseball ring and two Masonic rings. I attended the funeral at Crown Hill Cemetery like an uninvited stranger. The rings turned up in a shirt pocket at the house three years later.

I knew he had heart troubles, but I wasn't prepared to lose my Uncle Harry. He had been the one constant in my life, my only real support. His house on Delaware Street was the only place I always felt welcome, and that came to a sudden end. Between alcoholism and raising my younger siblings, my mom had her own struggles. I felt like I was on my own without a safety net.

Winter gave way to spring, and I found work at WIFE in Indianapolis with its "window on the world" in the 1400 block of North Meridian Street.

During May of 1966, Mario Andretti claimed the pole, sporting the number 1—a privilege earned by winning the National Championship the prior year. Chuck Rodee fatally crashed on a warm-up lap.

I drove my director's pace car, a Mercury Comet Cyclone GT, to the track to do a promotion for the station. I left the top down after I parked, and someone stole the parking pass. He called me onto the carpet for it. I couldn't believe it: I almost got fired over a boss's car again.

On Race Day, the fiftieth running of the 500, I sat in the grandstand. On the first lap, a fourteen-car wreck piled up right in front of me. A. J. Foyt climbed the fence to avoid the incoming cars, injuring his hand. The crash knocked eleven cars out of the race, and a wheel hit a spectator. Mario dropped out early with engine problems. Jimmy Clark made an exceptional save on a spinout that kept him in the race. Only seven cars remained on the track when the white flag waved. Englishman Graham Hill, sporting his rakish pencil-thin moustache, took the victory in his rear-engine Lola-Ford. The World Champion found the checkered flag as a rookie to Indy.

Jimmy also drove to Victory Lane believing he won it. He challenged whether Graham Hill was on the lead lap. Even Graham admitted he was surprised to find himself in the lead at the end of the race. The IMS Radio Network scorers likewise put Jimmy in front. Ultimately, Jimmy's team declined to file a formal appeal.

Sometime mid-May, Graham asked Tony Hulman to make a few renovations to the garages. Men who have been to the Speedway are familiar with the long, wide-open "troughs" in the restrooms. Gasoline Alley was still men-only, and the restrooms lacked privacy. Among his uproariously funny remarks at the Victory Dinner, Graham thanked Tony for putting doors on the "loo."

Fans owe an incalculable debt of gratitude to Tony Hulman, the third owner of the Speedway. Other great racetracks were built around the same time in England and France, but the Brickyard is the only one from that era that remains. The Speedway's longevity is largely due to the luck of a series of exceptional owners.

Carl Fisher's commitment to fairness among competing manufacturers established a sustainable enterprise. He founded the City of Speedway as a modern town: the first in the United States to ban horses. Its elementary schools, Fisher, Allison, Wheeler, and Newby, are named for the four original investors in the track.

When racing paused during the Great War, Carl offered the Speedway to the war effort, and it became an aviation repair depot. He reopened the track after the war, but he wanted to sell it as he moved on to other ventures. After years with no success, Carl nearly sold the property to real estate developers.

In the nick of time, Captain Edward V. "Rick" Rickenbacker purchased the Speedway in 1927. Rick competed in the inaugural 500 as a relief driver and raced his own car the next year. During World War I, General John "Black Jack" Pershing chose Rick as his personal driver. It probably says something about a general when he chooses a race car driver for his chauffeur. Later founding the "Hat in the Ring" squadron, Rick became the most celebrated American fighter pilot of the war, the first Ace, and a recipient of the Medal of Honor. Back home, he founded Eastern Airlines.

The Speedway weathered the Great Depression under Rick's steady management. When the garages went up in flames the morning of Race Day 1941 and World War II arrived before year-end, the future of the Speedway became uncertain. The modern planes needed longer runways than the Brickyard's straightaways could offer. It sat fallow for four long years.

During the war, Wilbur Shaw returned to the Speedway to test tires for Firestone. He was appalled at what he saw. Grass grew knee-high between the bricks, and the groove had to be weeded before he could drive a lap. He thought the grandstands and garages looked like abandoned farm buildings. Wilbur learned Rick was disinclined to expend the capital necessary to reopen after the war. He planned to sell to developers for a housing subdivision. Wilbur arose as the Speedway's champion, as he wrote in his autobiography,

Gentlemen, Start Your Engines: "The track was the world's last great speed shrine, which must be preserved at any cost. I felt that all I was, or ever hoped to be, I owed to the Indianapolis 500-mile race. I accepted the situation as a personal challenge and started a one-man crusade to get the job done."

Wilbur soon realized most potential buyers wanted to use the Speedway to sell their products. He needed to find an outsider who would uphold Carl Fisher's principles of fairness. Wilbur found him in a businessman from Terre Haute, Indiana, who had no connection to racing: Anton "Tony" Hulman Jr.

The scion of a wealthy family of wholesalers in Terre Haute, Tony was born in 1901. Most people think of Tony as a grandfatherly figure, but he excelled as an athlete in his youth. At Yale, he lettered in seven sports. His standout football career included an undefeated season. Tony had brains as well as brawn and earned a degree in administrative engineering. Upon his return to Indiana, Tony expanded the family business into newspapers, banks, breweries, chemical companies, and even the Coca-Cola bottling plant in Indianapolis.

Though Tony's parents often hosted a large picnic in the infield at the Indianapolis 500, he had never actually bought a ticket for a seat in the stands. A business broker in Indianapolis first thought of Tony as a buyer and brought the idea to him and his top aide, Joe Cloutier. Joe was less than enthusiastic, calling the broker's proposition "ridiculous." Eugene Pulliam, a national publishing magnate who owned the *Indianapolis News*, told Tony he was crazy to even consider it.

After reviewing the books and touring the Speedway, even Joe came around. Tony's wife Mary was doubtful, calling it "a pig in a poke," and Tony started to waver before the closing. Joe finally said, "Tony, if you're not going to buy it, I will." That dispensed any doubts.

Above anything else, Tony wanted to preserve the Speedway for the people of Indiana. He considered the Indianapolis 500 to be a quintessential part of Indiana's identity, much like the Kentucky

Derby across the Ohio River. Like his contributions to the Rose-Hulman Institute of Technology, a top engineering college in Terre Haute, this legacy would benefit generations of Hoosiers.

Tony agreed to buy the Speedway if Wilbur Shaw would commit to serve as its first president and superintend its rehabilitation. The deal closed in a smoke-filled room at the Indianapolis Athletic Club on November 14, 1945. The 500 returned in May of 1946. For more than three decades, the Speedway thrived under the wisdom and dedication of Tony Hulman.

Already on thin ice over the stupid parking pass, my boss started giving me grief over my National Guard training commitments on weekends and over the summer. When it came time to ship out for basic training, I knew my job at the station wouldn't be waiting for me. On a brisk day in October, I reported to Fort Knox.

I'm sure I must have hated every moment of boot camp, but thinking back fills me with fondness. Senior Drill Instructor Walea saw combat in Korea where his unit was decimated. Having known war at its worst, he was earnest, fair, and demanding. Raised in Hawaii, he spoke with an almost British accent.

Walea had hundreds of Jody calls, the sing-song cadences drill sergeants call out and troops shout back during marches or exercises. His favorite exercise was the side-straddle hop. I can still see him standing on the PT platform as he shouted, "How many repetitions?" "One hundred," we hoped. He gleefully shouted louder, "*Three* hundred repetitions!" At about seventy reps, he started his Jody calls: "I want to be an Airborne Ranger; I want to live a life of danger." After dozens of his Jody calls, he started counting again at seventy-one, and we all moaned.

Exhausted, laying on my bunk in the barracks, I listened to the tank cannons boom during night maneuvers. The constant thundering somehow lulled me into a peaceful sleep.

I didn't mind the physical training. My parents vetoed playing football, but I wrestled varsity at the 169-pound weight class. At five foot, eight inches and wearing glasses, my athletic ability was often underestimated. Stocky and strong, I could always hold my own. Something about the hands-on method of army training clicked with me. As a kid, Uncle Harry bought me a .22 rifle, and I knew I was a decent shot. I should be, considering my mom's job in the WAVES. I qualified with the M14, the M16, and the M1 Garand.

After a few other courses following basic training, I headed to Defense Information School (Dinfos) at Fort Benjamin Harrison in Indianapolis. The courses on broadcasting and journalism were the best I ever had. As an honor graduate, I taught at Dinfos for the remainder of my commitment. For decades afterwards, I continued to teach as a guest lecturer.

The riots and protests in the late '60s and early '70s caused the National Guard units to spend much of their time training for civil unrest. Near the end of my commitment, I helped develop the ideas that became the *Indiana Military Domestic Emergency Plan*, a handbook and protocol for countering and de-escalating riots. Part of my research came from reviewing the After-Action Report on the Kent State shootings, which involved a detachment from the 38th Division. Kent State was entirely preventable: those soldiers should never have been sent out with live rounds. The firepower of a few strategically placed snipers would have provided sufficient protection for the soldiers. Their leadership set them up to fail.

My presentations on best practices were not always well received. One colonel dismissively retorted, "If one of those hippies tries to shove a flower down the barrel of a rifle, my boys will know what to do." As a sergeant E5, I probably should have kept my thoughts about the colonel to myself. I reported him up the chain—it was the right thing to do. The top brass had no more patience than I did for someone who had learned nothing from Kent State.

Back in those days, under a completely different system, too many of the officers in the National Guard were political appointees with questionable merit. Luckily, I had a chat with the Adjutant General of the Indiana National Guard, and he transferred me into his three-person state-level staff. Across the hall was an affable young officer in the 120th PIO named Dan Quayle. If that name sounds familiar, it's because he went on to become a US senator and vice president of the United States.

The Guard and 38th Division held summer camp at Camp Grayling in Michigan. With no role for a broadcast specialist in the war games, I played an "aggressor," one of the bad guys. We attacked our unit to test their preparedness. To tell us apart, our helmets had a ridge down the top. I enjoyed learning the strategy of combat.

I loved the camaraderie as well. My squad sergeant was a real live wire and typically carried a .30 caliber machine gun on a pistol belt around his neck. After we were captured in a nighttime exercise, they took our rifles and marched us off to battalion headquarters, hands in the air. In the dark, they didn't notice our Sarge's machine gun still hanging from his neck. As we stepped into the tent, he shouldered it and sprayed the brass with fake lead. None of us could keep a straight face as we all got hell for it.

At Grayling, I met Donald Davidson, who had enlisted in the Aviation Battalion. Sid Collins thrust the native Briton into the spotlight during Donald's first visit to the States. His encyclopedic memory of Indy 500 statistics created quite a stir. It landed him a job as the historian for the USAC and the Speedway, a role he would hold for over fifty years. I envied Donald because he had already made it on the IMS Radio Network. If Donald could follow his passion across the Atlantic, I figured I could make it too.

CHAPTER 4

Stringing in Indianapolis

Indy is one of America's oldest traditions and the ultimate
expression of the American fascination with the automobile.
—*Sam Posey*

T he 500 has uniquely deep roots. The Indianapolis Motor Speedway is one of the oldest sports venues in America. It predates Wrigley Field, Fenway Park, and the Rose Bowl. Most top sporting events—the World Series, the Super Bowl, the Olympic Games—are traveling festivals. The 500 happens "Back Home Again in Indiana" every year.

In terms of attendance, it's the world's largest single-day sporting event. It's held that title year after year, decade after decade. This event is literally etched on the face of the earth, and to prove it, I have on my wall a photograph taken by my friend astronaut Ed Lu while aboard the International Space Station (ISS 6).

Indy car racing in the early 1960s stood as the undisputed king of American motorsports, with midgets and sprint cars as the training leagues—all sanctioned by the United States Auto Club (USAC). All summer long, fans could find great racing at storied tracks around the Speedway's orbit: Winchester, Fort Wayne, Dayton, Salem, Terre Haute, and the Indiana State Fairgrounds.

Formula One, which organized in the 1950s, featured exotic road races for wealthy European owners. NASCAR reigned only in the South. Born partly out of moonshining hot rodders, teams employed equal lawlessness in cheating on the stock car rules.

Even putting aside the history, tradition, and enormous attendance, Indianapolis is the crown jewel of racing and the Motorsports Capitol of the World because of the racing. From Mario Andretti to Arie Luyendyk to Danica Patrick, the drivers use the same language to describe Indy: respect the track, or it will *bite* you. No street course has corners like Indianapolis. A driver must shoot deep into the turn to catch the ragged edge—the threshold dividing a fast lap from a spin into the wall.

With a track width of fifty feet on the straightaways and sixty feet on the turns, and a low bank of nine degrees, twelve minutes, drivers must have precision and absolute fearlessness. The wider superspeedways have higher banks that keep the cars from sliding. Some of the 2.5-mile tracks are measured from the outside wall. The Speedway is measured from two-and-a-half feet above the inside white line—a much larger track. With these dimensions, a heart-stopping pass on a turn in Indianapolis is like no other.

I had to be a part of it, and broadcasting seemed to be my only avenue.

After I finished my active-duty training, I pounded the pavement. I could only find stringer work here and there. I needed a steady job and worked security at an art cinema, the Esquire. A school-teacher moonlighted as the theater manager. Soon after I started, Nobel Pearcy, the prosecutor in Indianapolis, went after the theater for showing films he considered obscene, like *I, A Woman* and *Elvira Madigan*. The manager feared he might lose his day job and quit. I gladly took over for him. I wanted to back the owner and stand up for freedom of speech against that sanctimonious politician.

The Esquire was an old-school theater with carbon arc projectors and a ticket booth facing the street. Later I managed the Lyric, an old vaudeville theater turned cinema. Back in the day, all the greats, including Frank Sinatra and Elvis Presley, debuted in Indianapolis at the Lyric. I've always loved music. Back in Highland Park, I played rhythm guitar in a band called The Chaparrals with my best buddy Bill's brother Tom. We even booked the enlisted men's club at Fort Sheridan, our only paid gig.

My all-time favorite act—Wayne Cochran and the C.C. Riders—toured locally at the Holyoke Bar in Indy and Club 67 near Muncie, Indiana. Known as the "King of Blue-Eyed Soul," Wayne played bass for Otis Redding and became pals with James Brown and Elvis Presley. In a tiny venue, belting out from beneath a giant blonde pompadour in front of blasting horns and wailing backup singers, Wayne was a sight to behold. Jake and Elwood Blues in the movie *The Blues Brothers* somewhat imitated his style. An album from The Blues Brothers Band included a Wayne cover.

At Club 67, I met a Ball State University journalism student who went to all of Wayne's concerts. He came across as intense and funny, though so deadpan that his humor kind of snuck up on you. In the early '70s, I followed his career as we both moved around the local Indy media scene. He landed a gig as a weatherman on Channel 13. He soon became known for his on-air antics like congratulating a tropical storm for becoming a hurricane. Most memorably, he set a scale model of the TV studio on fire while live on the air. His name was David Letterman.

In 1975, David drove a red pickup truck to California to try to make it big. A few years later, I caught his act at a comedy club on the Sunset Strip. He joked about being so poor when he got to LA that he chipped dried toothpaste off the sink for a mint. Years later, I did voice-over work at the NBC studios in Burbank when David had his own show, and I noticed David's old red truck parked in a space reserved for Johnny Carson.

David always loved racing. He worked as a pit reporter on ABC's telecast of the 1971 Indy 500. When he sponsored his own racing team, our paths crossed more frequently. I gave him a copy of a boot-legged recording of Wayne I made at one of those '60s era concerts. David accepted it with enthusiasm.

On Pole Day 1967, Mario Andretti captured the top spot for the second year in a row. Team owner Andy Granatelli brought the tur-bine: a race car powered by a Pratt & Whitney J-4 turbine engine normally used in helicopters. I recorded the team starting up the "Whooshmobiles." The muted roar was unlike anything heard at the track before—almost like a vacuum cleaner. In Silent Sam, Parnelli Jones would be tough to beat.

Andy was a fun and gregarious man who loved to talk. Because I kept my promises on things told off the record, he let me in on all kinds of tactics and strategies. He once installed a hydraulic airbrake that popped up whenever the car braked. At his reserved table at his favorite restaurant in downtown Indy, Andy captivated his guests as only a great storyteller can.

Mickey Thompson brought a race car with all-wheel steering, a concept that would not be used in the domestic auto industry until the '90s. When the driver turned the front wheels to the left, the rear wheels would turn to the right, creating a more efficient turn and better rear tire grip. Mickey let me sit in it—my first time in a real Indy car.

Even among the vivid personalities at the Speedway, Mickey stood out. Brilliant and wealthy, he wore white work pants and work shirts and sported a flattop, true to his blue-collar mechanic bona fides. The self-taught engineering genius claimed the land speed record at over 400 miles per hour by linking four engines together in his Challenger I. Smokey Yunich said he had "the balls of a dinosaur and the persistence of a hungry tiger."

Until 1967, the weather had generally smiled on the 500. On Race Day, rain arrived on lap seventeen and halted the race on lap nineteen. For the first time after a green flag, officials postponed the race to the next day. On the restart, Parnelli stayed in control, leading 171 laps. Nearly a lap ahead with only four laps to go, a transmission bearing that cost about six dollars failed. Parnelli pushed his car to the pits while A. J. Foyt weaved through a late accident for the checkered flag. Three wins out of seven Indy 500s—that's how a legend is born, and a nickname like "Super Tex" is earned.

A. J.'s car rolled into Victory Lane with Goodyear tires. Every winning car for over forty years straight had Firestone tires. Goodyear had returned as a supplier a couple of years earlier, and the rivalry let loose big sponsorship dollars for the teams and drivers. The Unser brothers, Bobby and Al Sr., put proud parents Jerry and Mary "Mom" Unser in a difficult position by securing competing tire sponsors. They cut a couple of the sponsors' jackets in half and resewed them. In 1967, Jerry rooted for Goodstone and Mom for Fireyear.

As a stringer for WCFL in Chicago, "The Voice of Labor," I covered Robert Kennedy's campaign stop in Indianapolis. At the Marott Hotel, I waited in the lobby for Kennedy's staffers to come down the elevator. As the doors opened, I asked for a reaction to President Lyndon Johnson's decision to end his reelection campaign. Unaware of the news, the staffers were stunned speechless. The doors closed and the car went back up.

With the Indiana primary approaching, the Kennedy campaign scheduled a rally for April 4, 1968, at a park in a largely African American neighborhood. Shortly before the rally, the radio station called to warn me of a report that Dr. Martin Luther King Jr. had been shot. I arrived early. As people from the neighborhood filled the park, I could tell they hadn't yet heard of the shooting.

The police warned the organizers they couldn't guarantee the candidate's safety and suggested canceling the event. From my training in the Guard, I knew the police were right. None of the elements necessary to control a crisis were in place. The campaign's advance staff couldn't make the decision, so we all just waited for the candidate to arrive.

Whatever anyone might think of Bobby Kennedy, he was no coward. I stood only a few feet away when he hopped atop the back of a flatbed truck. He faced the crowd, took a slow breath, and announced the great civil rights leader had been slain. The whole crowd gasped. I hadn't yet heard the shooting was fatal. We all froze in anticipation of the reaction.

Bobby didn't.

He delivered an emotional speech he jotted down on the plane ride over. To the surprise of his staff, he mentioned the sting of losing his brother, something he had never publicly done before. He offered the words of the Greek poet Aeschylus:

> Even in our sleep, pain which cannot forget
> Falls drop by drop upon the heart
> Until, in our own despair, against our will,
> Comes wisdom through the awful grace of God.

The five-minute speech called for unity and prayer in the face of hatred.

It never occurred to me that I was witnessing a historical moment. I only feared what might happen next. While riots spread across so many cities that night, the heartbroken people around me retired to their homes. I rushed back to the theater and transmitted my report across the telephone to WCFL. I had one of the only recordings of that speech.

That patch of grass is now known as Kennedy-King Park. In its center, a bronze edifice features the likenesses of these two men, murdered just months apart. It memorializes that special moment when a speech inspired our better angels, when hate and violence would not be answered in kind, when a city grieved together.

May arrived in 1968 without one of my favorites. Jimmy Clark died in an accident at the Hockenheimring in Germany in April. Mike Spence, a British driver, took his slot for Indy. After getting the turbine up to speed, Mike hit the wall. A wheel ricocheted back, striking him in the head, knocking off his helmet, and killing him. As qualifications continued, only one roadster made the field, a Mallard driven by Herk Hurtubise. Joe Leonard and Graham Hill took the top two spots in the turbine-powered STP "door-stops," named for their wedge-shaped design.

Hollywood invaded the track to film the movie *Winning*, starring Paul Newman. He drove an Eagle painted to match Bobby Unser's car. The scene on Victory Lane, with my pal Lou Palmer playing himself, required multiple takes. On the first try, Paul braked too hard, bunching up the black and white checkered carpet and lifting the car into the air. A silly fight ensued over the tires. Goodyear paid the studio a fee to have views of its tires in the movie. To the chagrin of the Goodyear reps, the stagehands dirtied up the tires for realism, obscuring the logo. As the stagehands left, the Goodyear guys ran in and cleaned the tires, and so it went.

The movie director wanted to film Tony Hulman's command at the starting line in the film. As Wilbur Shaw once said, "there are no sweeter words in the English language than the traditional command at the Indianapolis Motor Speedway." Tony was nervous and wanted to get it right.

Though educated out East, Tony still had a rural Indiana drawl. In his first couple of years, the line came across as "Gentlemen, starch 'ur engines." Tony asked Ralph "Luke" Walton, broadcaster and adman for the IMS Radio Network, to tutor him as a voice coach. Every race, Luke wrote out the command phonetically on a cue card. Tony nailed it for *Winning*, the best he ever gave it.

Work at the theater kept me away on Race Day, and it burned me to no end. In retrospect, listening on the radio gave me new insight into the craft. I gained a deeper understanding of what Sid Collins did to make listeners feel as if they were at the Speedway.

On Race Day, Bobby Unser took the lead early. Joe Leonard finally caught up and passed him on lap 175. Still in front with only eight laps to go, Joe's fuel pump went out. As the next car in line, Bobby took the checkered flag. He fought gearbox problems most of the race, and only his raw talent kept him from stalling on his way out of the pits.

Bobby turned down a huge offer from Andy Granatelli to drive a turbine that year. He stayed loyal to his sponsors and his team, the Leader Card Racers, winning his first 500 and going on to win the championship.

As the roadster became obsolete, so did a breed of race car drivers: the muscular men who could physically will the cars to do more. Some, like A. J. Foyt, would evolve. Others, like Jim Hurtubise, would rage against the dying of the roadster. Nicknamed Hercules (rhymes with Hurtubise), and long ago shortened to "Herk," he always fired up the crowd. When I interviewed him over the public address system at the Hoosier Hundred race at the State Fairgrounds that summer, it seemed like ten minutes before the cheers of "Herk! Herk! Herk!" faded enough to ask him a question.

Severely burned in a racing accident not long after Eddie Sachs's death, the doctors permanently molded a bend in his hands so Herk could still hold a steering wheel. I knew the story, but it was something else to see those gnarled knuckles in person.

Herk was one of the old guard—a purist who wanted the grace, beauty, and handling of the old front-engine roadsters. Back then, a great driver could get a lot more out of a mediocre car. That changed too fast for Herk.

After 1968, Herk doggedly tried to qualify a roadster each year and failed. In 1972, he gave in and qualified a rear-engine Coyote. But, to everyone's surprise, Herk towed his Mallard roadster to the line shortly before the six o'clock cutoff on Bump Day. He would have to withdraw the Coyote to try to qualify the roadster. If he failed, he would miss the show.

As the clock ticked down, Herk jumped out and removed the engine cowling. Where the engine should have been was a tub filled with ice and beer. The starter pistol ended Bump Day, and Herk handed out cold ones to the pit crews and race officials. Since Miller High Life sponsored Herk, it seemed like a lighthearted prank. He kept the roadster full of beer in his garage the rest of May and for years after.

Fast forward to Bump Day 1978, again close to the cutoff. I looked down from the booth in the Control Tower to see Herk towing the Mallard to the line for qualifications. Unamused, Chief Steward Tom Binford ordered Herk to get the obsolete roadster out of the line. Herk hadn't proved it could make it to competitive track speeds. The veteran, who first competed in 1960, thought he had earned the right to give it a try. What's the harm if he was too slow?

Tom wouldn't budge, and Herk snapped. In protest, he ran over and sat in Bob Harkey's car. It got tense. Other drivers still needed to make runs to qualify that day. Eventually Herk got out and ran down the track, with officials and yellow shirts in pursuit. Driver John Martin caught up and walked Herk back to his garage. Tom banned him for the rest of May, but all was forgiven in the years that followed.

After the Lyric and Esquire theaters closed, I ran the Tibbs Drive-In and the General Cinemas at the Glendale and Lafayette Square Malls. I learned a lot of business and managerial skills, but I remained frustratingly far away from my dream of broadcasting the Indianapolis 500. I felt no closer than I was the day I flew in from Tulsa five years earlier.

On Pole Day 1969, Leon "Jigger" Sirois clocked a mediocre first qualifying lap. His team waved him off to try again later. It started raining and washed out the rest of the day. Jigger would have won the pole if he had finished his run. Later that May, he crashed and missed the show entirely. As the years passed, Jigger never made the field at Indy.

In honor of that monumental mistake, the American Auto Racing Writers and Broadcasters Association created the Jigger Award to honor the driver with the worst luck each year. In Jigger's defense, qualifying strategy is extremely complicated.

The Indy 500 has determined starting order based on qualifying speeds since 1915. The guarantee of the first slot to the fastest first-day qualifier started the next year. The origin of the word "pole" for the fastest driver dates back to horse racing when a wooden post often marked the starting line. The first horse beside it was "on the pole."

Pole position is critical. At this writing, nineteen drivers have won from the pole at Indy, but the pole means much more. Back when there were four qualifying days and the pole was determined on the first, there was greater value. The pole-sitter was in the media spotlight for two weeks as opposed to the winner who held the media for a week. Some people, including my producer at ABC, Bob Goodrich, have incorrectly presumed the pole is the vertical scoreboard, or scoring pylon, that lists the order of qualified cars (and the positions of the cars during the race). The pole is figurative, not an actual structure. It refers to the left or inside spot in Row 1.

The four-lap average has long been the standard for qualifications. Cars are qualified, not drivers. Each car is put through two inspections, including a road test of ten laps at "racing speed."

The order of qualifying used to be first come, first serve. Eddie Sachs always wanted to be first for good luck. He lined up every year at the crack of dawn. Since 1965, the order has been determined by drawing a numbered ball, or "pea" from a box. The cooler temps in the late of the day tend to result in the fastest runs. Around five o'clock, when the shadows of the stands cover the main straightaway, it's known as "Happy Hour."

Many of the rules for qualifications have changed over the years, but I'll summarize the basics in this era. All drivers get a Day One attempt (a try for the pole), even if it takes two days to get through them all. The first cars line up at eleven o'clock. A late or no-show driver loses the guaranteed attempt and goes to the back of the line. Each car is limited to three qualifying attempts total.

The drivers qualifying on Day One fill the rows by order of speed, with the fastest on the pole. Later day qualifiers fill the remaining spots in order of speed for that day. This continues until thirty-three cars qualify. Then the slowest car in the field (referred to as "on the bubble"), in whatever position, gets bumped if a later car qualifies faster. Because the order depends on the day of qualification, some of the fastest cars might start in the back rows.

A driver cannot qualify two cars in the field at the same time (the qualified car must be withdrawn before attempting to qualify another). Once bumped, the car becomes ineligible and cannot be qualified again. A bumped driver can only get back in by qualifying a new car (a different chassis and engine).

The stakes are high, the chances are few. The decisions all fall on the crew chief, the master of the team, and the actual "entrant" of the car (who, back then, also claimed the prize money). Is it suitable for the style of that particular driver? How fast will be fast enough to make the field? It also means tweaking the car to go as fast as possible over the course of four laps, not two hundred. Horsepower is dialed up and fuel is "popped" with additives. Engines, and drivers, are pushed to their breaking point. Scott Dixon calls it the toughest day in racing.

Once the car is ready and the track conditions are right, the driver takes a couple of warm-up laps. The team clocks the driver to confirm the time is fast enough to qualify. Back then the driver waved to the chief steward with a Day-Glo orange band around his forearm to signal the first qualifying lap. Even after the driver starts qualifying, the team can "wave-off," or quit and try again later.

A driver may rue waving off, as Jigger did. Even the brilliant Roger Penske won the Jigger Award in 1991 for waving off Emerson Fittipaldi's qualifying run. After the rains arrived, Emmo dropped from a likely second slot down to fifteenth.

On Race Day 1969, A. J. Foyt rolled out front in the pole position. Directly behind him in Row 2 started rookie Mark Donohue and Team Penske's debut at Indy. I watched from Grandstand B, and a drunk behind me yelled, "Come on, Mario, let's go," every single lap. It evidently worked because Mario Andretti led 116 laps and found the checkered flag. Owner Andy Granatelli planted a big kiss on Mario's cheek in Victory Lane. It remains the only win by the Andretti family.

As the summer of 1969 ended, I landed steady work doing weekend news at WXLW. I kept pushing my good friends at WIBC Chuck Riley and Lou Palmer to convince Fred Heckman to hire me again. Five years after I lost my job over the Mustang fiasco, Lou finally wore him down. Fred put me on an "Ask a Question" community feature and the evening news. Finally, I caught the break that could get me out of the stands on Race Day and on the air.

CHAPTER 5

Journalist, Paramedic, Race Car Driver

But when things are right, you can feel the tires in your nerve ends.
And when you take a car down into the corner as deep as it'll go and
you know it's on the ragged edge, it's just like a shot in the arm.
—Johnnie Parsons

Wilbur Shaw described the Indianapolis 500 as "a world series, a heavy-weight championship fight, a National Open, a Rose Bowl game, and a Kentucky Derby all rolled into one tremendous spectacle—with a touch of the pomp and ceremony of a coronation." He spoke for race fans everywhere, but not everyone can be in the stands on Race Day.

The 500 became a Memorial Day tradition across America through the imagination and talent of Sid Collins, then a young radio personality. He conceived a plan to bring the race to every home in the country and even around the world.

While first relayed on the radio in 1922, the broadcast of the 500 was sporadic in the years that followed. When racing resumed in 1946, the Mutual network offered limited coverage: a fifteen-minute introduction, half-hour blocks at the beginning and end of the race, and five-minute updates on the hour.

Sid joined the Mutual broadcast team to cover Turns One and Two for the 1948 and 1949 races. In 1950, the previous chief announcer left for baseball, and Bill Slater, his planned successor, faced a long recovery from an illness.

Speedway president Wilbur Shaw called Sid to his office. He looked across his desk at the twenty-six-year-old and asked, "Kid, do you think you can handle the chief announcer's job on the Mutual race broadcast?" Sid responded, "Yessir." Wilbur proposed Sid to Tony Hulman, who replied, "Let's give the kid a chance." Bill recovered his health and co-hosted the race. Sid went solo the following year.

Unfortunately, Mutual struggled to find sponsors. WIBC took on a bigger role in the broadcast, but the business model was failing. Sid pitched a plan to Wilbur and Tony for broadcasting the entire race. The Speedway would create its own network of radio stations that would pay subscriptions for the race, and WIBC would be the flagship. It required running AT&T Long Lines to each station, at significant expense to the Speedway. Wilbur reacted with skepticism:

> Gosh guys, racing has been my entire life, but I think a broadcast of automobiles driving around in a circle will be boring as hell.

Tony owned a radio station in Terre Haute and felt comfortable with the challenge. To bring the whole race—flag to flag—to all of America, it was worth a try. Disappointingly, most station owners shared Wilbur's sentiments. Out of five thousand solicitations, only twenty-six stations signed up for the first broadcast.

Covering the race had its own logistical problems. It required a large cast of broadcast professionals in the booth, turns, and pits. Where would he find the talent? Sid's solution was to bring in WIBC's competitors. Other local stations could carry the race for free in return for furnishing engineering crews and announcing staff. Such a collaboration among competing stations was unprecedented.

While Sid might find greater talent elsewhere, he wanted locals who spent the entire month of May in Indy getting to know the drivers, owners, and teams. In a typical pep talk for his staff recounted in *Stay Tuned for the Greatest Spectacle in Racing*, Sid had a vision of how he could bring the race to life:

> This is color radio. The car is never red, it's candy apple red. It's never green, it's lime green. . . . Let's smell it! Let's see it! Let's taste it! Let's have the listener see it as though he were right there in person.

He succeeded. The network increased to 110 stations the next year and steadily grew for the next two decades. By 1965, over eight hundred stations carried the race, including the Armed Forces Radio Network and Radio New York Worldwide. Translated into Spanish, Portuguese, French, and Italian, millions of listeners tuned in around the world. None of this could have happened without the ingenuity of Sid. Tony Hulman saved the Speedway. Sid Collins brought the Indy 500 to the world.

I would not hesitate to say that Sid brought the City of Indianapolis to the world. Wherever I've traveled internationally, people know my hometown because of this race.

As the roadster disappeared, many of the great mechanics and drivers still had difficulties mastering the rear-engine cars. Only one driver would win the Indy 500 in both front- and rear-engine cars: A. J. Foyt. Newcomers who learned to race in rear-engine sports cars in the Sports Car Club of America (SCCA) had an advantage. One of them was Bill Simpson.

Bill started in drag racing and popularized the use of parachutes, the same kind used for military planes, to slow down the dragsters. He moved on to racing sports cars. He also sold safety equipment, including Nomex fire suits, after he learned about the material from astronaut Pete Conrad. The other big fire suit supplier was Lew Hinchman in Indianapolis.

Bill first showed up at the Speedway in 1967 to promote his fire suits with a demonstration. About ten of us stood around as he suited up and set himself on fire. The fire suit worked fine, but once extinguished, he forgot his helmet might still be very hot. When he reached up with a bare hand to take it off, he got a nasty surprise. We all busted into laughter at the imperfect safety lesson. Bill was only singed.

After seeing the Speedway, Bill felt he had to race there. He eventually formed his own team and arrived in Indy a few years later. Hailing from California, Bill and his crew wore their hair long—a big contrast from the buzz-cut drivers and mechanics of the old guard. One night, A. J. Foyt, Lloyd Ruby, and the Unser brothers showed up at Bill's garage with barber's clippers and announced Bill's team couldn't practice until they all got a haircut. Bill wasn't about to permit such hazing. Using stronger words than I'll repeat, Bill told them they better not try or there'd be a serious fist fight.

The veterans were cut from a different cloth. As Johnny Rutherford wrote in his autobiography *Lone Star J. R.*:

> There are very few of us who made it through that time. I came from the dirt track—dirt-under-the-fingernails, T-shirted, beer-drinkin', flat out racin', after-the-race-fight fraternity of race car drivers. It may have been an unsophisticated time, but for me, it was an unforgettable and profound education.

In Sam Posey's words, sportscar drivers like himself were maligned as "effete snobs who had no right to share the track with these sprint car veterans." USAC drivers referred to the "wine and cheese" circuit as "squat and pee" (roughly rhyming with the "SCC" of Sports Car Club).

In the garage that night, the veterans could tell Bill wasn't bluffing. He earned a bit of respect, and the older drivers backed down.

In May of 1970, Al Unser Sr. narrowly edged out Johnny Rutherford by just three thousandths of a second to take the pole. His blue Johnny Lightning-sponsored PJ Colt became an iconic car.

On Race Day, after a short rain delay and a wreck on the pace lap, the green flag unleashed Lloyd Ruby. The wily veteran and crowd favorite shot from twenty-fifth to fifteenth on lap one and broke the top ten by lap three. Soon "Hard Luck Lloyd" climbed to the lead, but his namesake proved true once again. Black smoke from his grinding gears brought out the black flag, and Lloyd ended his day on lap fifty-four.

Al Sr. owned the race, leading 190 laps, and hoisted the milk for the first time.

At WIBC, I wanted to be a hard news reporter, but news director Fred Heckman thought I might be better in a feature role. To prove myself, I chased every story I could, listening to the police scanner and getting to the scene first. My hard work paid off. Fred gave me a company car and free reign on news assignments.

I did a series on Dr. Henry Bock and two other doctors who started ALS Medicine, Indiana's first modern ambulance service, at Marion County General Hospital (now Sydney & Lois Eskenazi Hospital). Henry was also my roommate and the head of the track hospital at the Speedway. The casualties of the Vietnam War led to medical advancements in emergency care. These doctors knew they could save lives here at home by bringing the hospital to the patient.

On ride alongs in the ALS Medic-1 ambulance, I followed Steve Barr, Dennis Brockman, and Gary Gilliam, the first certified paramedics in Indiana. My "Medic One" series received Associated Press and Indianapolis Press Club awards. Watching these guys save a life, pulling someone from the brink, truly inspired me. I enrolled in the DePauw University paramedics course at Methodist Hospital. Less than a year later, I received my license. I worked shifts on ambulances, in the ER, and even at the track hospital. I also helped with the formation of the first ambulatory helicopter service.

Sometimes my careers intersected. In the WIBC news chopper covering a bad accident with multiple victims, I saw the Life-Line helicopter touch down. They didn't have a paramedic on board, and they radioed us to see if I could hop in and attend to the patient. I ducked under the rotors, carrying my broadcast equipment with me.

On the news chopper, I had a running joke about "stepping out on the patio to take a closer look" when DJ Chuck Riley asked about the traffic. As I watched over my patient in the much larger lifeline chopper, I heard my lead-in and said, "If the chopper sounds different, it's because I'm out on the patio." The show must go on.

All paramedics have great war stories, and I saw my share. One night, we responded to a bar in a rough area of town for a gunshot victim. We followed the police inside through the packed narrow bar. No one seemed concerned about the shooting. We had to push our way through the crowd to the last booth. On one side a man sat with a gun, and on the other a woman sat next to the victim. It was the eternal love triangle: one woman, two boyfriends.

The officer disarmed the shooter as we went to work on the victim. We had the same trouble getting the patient through the crowd on the way out. The girlfriend didn't appear any more concerned than the rest of the patrons. As one boyfriend exited on a stretcher and the other in handcuffs, she bellied up to the bar and asked if somebody would buy her a drink.

In May of 1971, Peter Revson took the pole, but Al Unser Sr. looked hard to beat, tearing around the track in his number 1 Johnny Lightning. George Bignotti built Al Sr. a new car nearly identical to the one he used to conquer the 500 and the series the year before.

Race Day began with a wreck away from the race cars. Eldon Palmer, owner of the Palmer Dodge car dealership, drove the Dodge Challenger pace car to start the race. He had Tony Hulman, ABC's Chris Schenkel, and astronaut John Glenn on board. After the pace lap, Palmer veered into the pits as the race cars roared down the straightaway.

Watching from Grandstand B, I heard squealing tires. I turned to see the orange pace car hit a yellow shirt, flipping him into the air. Still screeching, the pace car crashed into the photographer's stand—a set of bleachers set atop a flatbed truck parked at the exit of pit road (it would be driven away after the start). The collision sent the yellow shirt and twenty others to the track hospital. Inside the car, Tony Hulman sprained his ankle. Chris Schenkel lost his nerve and couldn't do the broadcast. John Glenn joked it was the only time he ever crashed on reentry.

The use of a pace car and a "flying start" dates to the original Indy 500 in 1911, which was also the first major race to institute the pace car. Carl Fisher realized it would be safer if the cars were running en masse at a minimum speed before letting them really go, allowing time for stalled cars to get moving or get out of the way. Carl himself drove the pace car.

While it's unusual for the pace car to wreck, the parade and pace laps are surprisingly treacherous for race cars. The cars' high gears make it difficult for drivers to maintain consistent slow speeds (the roadsters only had two gears, high and low). Heading into the green, drivers have one foot on the throttle and one on the brake, preparing for the start. In later years, riding the throttle and brake could trigger the pop-off valve, and more recently, the stuck-throttle shut-off. Drivers heat their brakes with short accelerations and hard stops. With cars intentionally and unintentionally darting ahead and braking hard, accidents are surprisingly common on a pace lap. The drivers also warm up their tires for better traction by weaving back and forth. With the race cars three deep on a fifty-foot-wide track, it's easy to accidentally touch tires.

Lap one is by far the most dangerous lap of the race. The entire field is bunched up and jockeying for position. With thirty-three cars entering so closely, Turn One becomes an unimaginable sea of air turbulence. Often described as mini-tornadoes, the winds created by the vacuum randomly push and pull the cars. While every driver knows you can't win the 500 on the first lap, races aren't won by just letting cars go by. With so much passing and blocking in the same space, lots of accidents happen. The teams, safety officials, and broadcasters all breathe a sigh of relief when the cars make it around to the yard of bricks.

Only ten laps in, Steve Krisiloff lost a bunch of oil coming into Turn Three. Mel Kenyon caught the oil patch and slammed into the wall. Crumpled and awaiting the safety crew, Mel saw Gordon Johncock losing it as well and coming at him. Mel sank as low as he could in the cockpit as Gordy went right over him. With only a cut on his leg, Mel headed to the track hospital. Sitting on a cot, he noticed Gordy's tire marks on the top of his helmet.

Al Unser Sr. took control during the second half and claimed a back-to-back victory on his thirty-second birthday.

With federal law banning televised advertisements of tobacco, racing found big sponsorships in big tobacco. The 1971 Champ series became the USAC Marlboro Championship Trail. Dirt tracks became a separate division, a sign of the sport outgrowing its roots. USAC also decided its midget and sprint car divisions would forever remain front-engine, creating a mismatch of racing minor leagues. The pipeline prepped young talent for front-engine stock cars, not rear-engine open-wheel racing.

In those days I drove a green Fiat 124 Spider convertible. I entered it in a few gymkhanas at Indianapolis Raceway Park. These were timed events where one car at a time raced around cones and obstacles. Perfect for novices, you could even race with a passenger on board. I won a few cups and decided I should find out if I really had the chops for racing.

I fitted my Fiat with a rollover bar and enrolled in driving school. The very first day my engine started knocking due to a spun bearing. A friend let me borrow his ride: a Lotus 51 Formula Ford with the British left-handed gearshift. Soon it was mine. I competed in SCCA events in Indiana, Ohio, Illinois, Wisconsin, and Minnesota. I started to understand racing from a driver's point of view.

I also learned the limitations of the Lotus 51. The gear sets in its Renault gearbox couldn't be changed. Changeable gearboxes let you set the gear ratios to suit the track, especially the turn that leads to the longest straightaway. The goal is to find as much speed as possible off that curve and keep it into the straight.

I needed a better ride to move up. Jack Baldwin had just won the US Formula Ford Championship in an Elden Mark-10C Falconer, and I picked the same. I sold my Lotus 51 for $2,000 and, with a little help from a sponsor, bought a shiny red Elden for $3,500. When an orange car arrived, I complained about the mistake. I was told there was no error; that's what the Brits called "pirate red." I painted it white.

To haul my race car to SCCA races, I bought a camper with a ramp originally designed for snowmobiles. It had a small kitchenette and a couple of bunks unfolded over the car. With the help of Johnny Miles, his son Ricky, and Gail Sherman who was my best friend for years, I would load the trailer, drive overnight, and hope to qualify during the early morning emergency practice session. Racing attracts wonderful people, and I have very fond memories of hanging around the paddock with drivers and their families.

I qualified for an SCCA national license, an FIA B, and a USAC stock car license. Over the years I had a few good races. I competed against several rising stars, like an eighteen-year-old Chip Ganassi who left me in the dust.

I became a race chairman and a regional executive for the SCCA. I gained a lot of insight into the promotional and organizational side of racing. To improve communications at the corner stations at Indianapolis Raceway Park, I talked the local Marine Corps Reserve into running their radios at our races as an exercise.

I helped form the Indy Racing Organization to promote the use of doctors, nurses, and medical workers in staffing race events. We trained firefighters and paramedics on how to get a cervical collar underneath a driver's helmet. We came up with a narrower stabilizing board that could safely ease a driver out of a race car. The organization became an important part of the USAC series.

When I first bought my Lotus 51, I invited a few of the guys at Patrick Racing to try it out. They returned the favor by tweaking my car in their garage at 38th and Industrial, not far from my apartment. Before long, I worked for the team as an unpaid gofer in exchange for the use of their garage. By the time I got the Elden, the team let me keep it there. I learned a lot about how race cars should be set up. With their direction, I fashioned an undertray for my engine and modified the nose to reduce turbulence. Going to the garage for a couple of hours was the coolest shop class ever.

Marathon sponsored my race car with gas vouchers. The company happened to book Sid Collins to speak at a corporate dinner in Toledo, and they asked me to come along as the warm-up act. Sid negotiated the arrangements, and we flew on a private plane—a first for me.

Sid was a master at demanding the best for his speaking engagements. If someone asked him to speak for free, he would ask if the caterers were also working for free. If they were too far apart, he would ask about their budget. When the Rolling Stones played the Coliseum at the State Fairgrounds, I used my press pass to get into the green room. The top roadie showed me the band's contract with their absurdly long demands, down to the number of bowls of M&Ms. By demanding lots of small things, the roadie thought it ensured everything got done, both the important and the trivial.

On the flight back from Toledo, Sid admitted he was impressed with my comments and delivery at the dinner. Perhaps seeing a glimmer of hope cross my face, he quickly added, "But there is no place for you on the IMS Radio Network. We're full."

Even if Sid wasn't yet sold on my abilities as a broadcaster, my peers noticed. Between 1972 and 1974, I received every state and local broadcast journalism award I could get at least twice and the Excellence for an Individual Reporter award three years straight.

In the fall of 1971, my Aunt Norna called. My mom was in the hospital, and it looked bad. Her alcoholism had caught up with her. I drove to Great Lakes Naval Hospital to see her. Somewhat lucid, she chatted with me until the nurses shooed me off around eleven in the evening. She died the next morning. She was only fifty-two.

On Pole Day 1972, Bobby Unser blazed to the front with a new track record of 195.9 miles per hour, a monster jump of 17 mph from the prior year's pole. The boost came from new rules allowing bolt-on wings. Bobby's advantage came from Dan Gurney's invention of the "Gurney flap," or "wicker bill," a spoiler added to the trailing edge of the rear wing.

High speeds pushed drivers to their limits. With laps reaching the mid-190s, veteran Jim Malloy hoped to break the 200-mph barrier in his Eagle, but he veered right and hit the wall in Turn Three. He died four days later. Art Pollard broke his leg in another wreck. In those days, a loud horn sounded in the press room when a caution came out during practice and time trials. A small bus loaded up the press and traveled to the site of the accident. I always dreaded riding that bus.

Speed on an oval requires keeping traction in the turns. The increases in speed during the late '60s had reflected advances in weight distribution in the rear-engine cars. With independent suspensions, stagger became the industry standard: better traction from using different sized tires, typically a larger circumference for the right rear tire.

By 1972, advances in aerodynamics changed everything by using wings to create downforce to keep the cars on the track. Building race car wings is the reverse of airplanes. The front and rear wings force the cars down onto the track instead of up into the air, leading to more traction. This also explains why an Indy car takes flight if it spins 180 degrees at high speed: the wings lift the car off the ground like a glider.

Engines were changing as well. The standard very rough-running four-cylinder Offenhauser, relatively unchanged for decades, evolved to the smoother eight cylinder. The Ford engines also competed until the dominance of the Cosworth by the end of the '70s. When I covered a race for CBS in 1978, the Offy was such a dying breed that some teams wore black armbands in protest of the rules they felt favored the Cosworth.

Construction of the chassis moved from tubular to unibody. The tubular models of the '60s were a series of welded pipes creating the frame. Unibody or monocoque construction had a unitary body-chassis frame: a "tub" bolted to the engine. This design made the car more rigid and durable.

Also in 1972, the Electro Pacer system debuted: a series of electronic panels for enforcing cautions. Instead of the honor system for drivers maintaining their distances as they existed before the caution, a number for each driver would appear on the panels based on an 80-mph speed limit. The system became a constant source of complaints and accusations of cheating for years.

On Race Day, singer Phil Harris showed up with a wide smile and unsteady legs. Track organizers worried he might not make it through "Back Home Again in Indiana." Jim Nabors happened to be a VIP guest with Bill Harrah, owner of the Vegas casino. Tony Hulman saw Jim's show in Tahoe, and he asked Jim if he would sing for the opening ceremonies. Jim agreed and walked over to the director of the Purdue Band to find out which key they would use. The director said there's only one key. Jim had expected to sing the National Anthem, which has two keys. When they told him what song he'd be singing, Jim said, "I'm from Alabama—I don't really know it." Fortunately, he did know the melody. With no rehearsal and the words written on his hand, the Alabaman became a forty-year Hoosier tradition.

After the green flag, it looked like Gary Bettenhausen had the race in the bag, leading 138 laps. But an ignition problem ended his run on lap 182. Mark Donohue took the lead with thirteen laps to go and found the checkered flag, handing team owner Roger Penske and the McLaren chassis their first wins.

Race car drivers come from all walks of life. Mark, nicknamed "Captain Nice," was an Ivy Leaguer with an engineering degree from Brown. He could hold his own against the best and won the first IROC (International Race of Champions) against Bobby Unser and

A. J. Foyt. Mark's promising career ended much too soon in Austria before the 1975 F1 race, when he wrecked his Penske PC-1 and suffered fatal injuries.

Later that summer, Art Pollard asked me to help out Robin Miller, a local sportswriter who had just bought a new Formula Ford. Robin needed a trailer, and Art thought of mine. We took Robin's car to the 5/8-mile track at Indianapolis Raceway Park. After firing it up, the engine started smoking. Art pulled the cowling off, and we saw a sign taped to the engine that read "NO OIL." With no permanent damage done, Robin sorted out the gears and broke her in.

Robin is another lifelong lover of racing and the Speedway. His hero was Herk Hurtubise. As a kid in Terre Haute, Robin shoplifted beer and brought it to Herk at the track, just to have an excuse to talk to him. At eighteen, still not old enough to be in the pits, Herk snuck Robin into the garage as an unpaid gofer and stooge for the team. But Robin got fired when he scratched the race car and taped Herk's goggles to his hair instead of his helmet. Later Robin worked for Bill Finley's team. When Robin started racing, he bought a midget car from Gary Bettenhausen. He entered it at Kokomo back when a lot of Indy car drivers still raced midgets. He competed with thirteen drivers who were also in the field for the Indy 500.

A bit of a rivalry existed between us. On Mondays, Robin would get together with a few mechanic and driver pals for lunch. They would often tell Robin I did very well in a race over the weekend. Finally, Robin broke down and paid fifty-four dollars to have several years of race results faxed to him, just to see if it was true. It wasn't. They were ribbing him.

In print, Robin could be tough on me at times. When Robin started at NBC, he saw things from a different perspective, and he apologized to me for some of his harshness. Today, he is still the best writer in motorsports, and I am lucky to call him a close friend.

Hanging around his garage, I got to know team owner U. E. "Pat" Patrick—another bigger-than-life character. An accountant turned Michigan wildcatter, he made his fortune in oil on his eighteenth dig. He sometimes entered a number 18 car in hopes of another lucky strike. When he started building his own race cars, he named them Wildcats.

Coming into the 1973 season, Pat lured the best master mechanic to his team, George Bignotti. He also recruited big name drivers Gordon Johncock and David "Swede" Savage. Gordy was your typical tough-guy driver. Young and athletic, Swede was a blond-haired California surfer-type with an easy smile.

During May, Pat mentioned to me he wanted a better set of two-way radios to communicate with the drivers during a race. The days of chalkboards held up by a trackside team member would soon be a thing of the past. I figured a setup similar to what we used on the ambulance would be perfect. I was thrilled when Pat tasked me with ordering them—it seemed a big step up from gofer and parts washer.

All I ever wanted was to be a part of the Indy 500. In the pits, the track hospital, or the broadcast booth, I'd take what I could get.

CHAPTER 6

Live From Pit Road

This was the "big show," and I was part of it.
—*Wilbur Shaw*

E veryone describes the 1973 Indy 500 as jinxed. That word isn't strong enough. A darkness hovered over the Speedway even worse than in 1964. On Pole Day, during a practice lap, Art Pollard crashed into the wall in Turn One, spinning, flipping, and bursting into flames. Close behind, Johnny Rutherford dodged the debris. I was on the air at WIBC when Lou Palmer called it in. Shaken by the news, Lou asked me to do the report for him on the newscast. It was the first death of a friend on the track. It wouldn't be the last. They all stung, each worse than the one before.

I couldn't get out of a shift at the station on Race Day, a Monday morning. For once, I was happy a long rain delay postponed the start. I zipped through the light traffic behind a three-wheeled motorcycle police escort. The new main entrance with its gaping four-lane tunnel welcomed fans for the first time. A buddy on Mike Hiss's crew gave me the silver badge backing for crew members. I wandered my way through the pits to my favorite location: a spot at the south end beside Dry Ditch and near the old Victory Lane. When the cars raced, you could see all the drama on the track from the main straightaway to the pits and into Turn One. During downtime, you could see all the drama in the rowdy area of the infield known as the Snake Pit.

When the track finally dried, the Field of 33 rolled toward the start. As the pace car turned aside, Pat Vidan, in his signature white tux jacket, stood beside the low inside wall and unfurled the green flag, igniting the rolling roar. Seven seconds later, David "Salt" Walther touched wheels with Jerry Grant's car, launching him into the air and against the catch fence dividing the track and the spectators. The car looked like a floating Fourth of July pinwheel—spewing fuel that immediately caught fire—as it ripped away the fence.

What should have been a beautiful flying start became a freeway pileup. Race cars desperately bobbed and weaved. A hundred yards from where I stood, Salt landed upside down in a burning hulk of a car, its nose and much of its rear gone. The engine slid down the track by itself. Salt's legs stuck out from the front of the flaming overturned tub.

The stands filled with screams for someone to help Salt. I found myself yelling too. Wally Dallenbach came to a stop in the grass as fire rained down on him and melted his face mask. He ran over to Salt. Clad in fireproof gloves, he grabbed ahold and heaved, but it was too heavy. Help arrived, and they overturned the car. Wally averted his eyes. He didn't want to see Salt like that. An ambulance raced him to Methodist Hospital

Crews tended to the ten race cars involved. A dozen fans who sat in folding chairs beside the wall sought treatment for chemical burns at the track hospital. The rain returned. Officials postponed the race to the next day.

Salt suffered severe burns to 40 percent of his body and a smashed knee cap. The burns to his hands were so bad his fingertips were amputated. After many agonizing months of surgery, Salt eventually recovered and raced again.

The rain continued the next morning, a Tuesday. It finally tapered off. A restart looked promising as emergency trucks and vehicles drove laps to hasten the drying of the track. The cars started the parade lap, but rain returned and never stopped.

On Wednesday, buckets of rain brought another delay. The unruly denizens of the Snake Pit escaped that mud-filled swamp by tearing down the fence on the inside of Turn One. They reveled and slid down the embankment while awaiting the start of the race. To my surprise, when Tom Carnegie announced the race would resume, they dutifully cleaned up and returned behind the fence.

Finally, the magic of the race returned with the green flag. I stood beside driver Mike Hiss's scoring stand just north of the pylon and less than fifty feet away from the main straightaway. From my perch, the track was frightening, breathtaking, and exciting all in the same instant as the deafening blurs flashed by. With no speed limits in the pits, the cars screamed down at 160 mph and braked at the last second. After pitting, the slow push from the crew ignited the unbelievable acceleration out of the pits. I fell into that blissful haze of absorbing the race until awakened by a boom.

On lap fifty-eight, a gigantic explosion filled the entire width of the track just north of the pit entrance. It sounded like a bomb went off. The crowd began to scream and point. A car had come high out of Turn Four and brushed the outside wall. It shot across the track and into the inside wall with unimaginable impact. The tub slid back to the center, surrounded by a lake of fire.

Crew members bolted toward the wreck. From my left, a Speed-way pickup truck loaded with fire equipment rushed up pit lane, against race traffic. I saw George Bignotti and Armando Teran, a boardman for Graham McRae's team, running ahead. Then I saw only Armando's shoes on the track where he last stepped in front of the truck, blindsided. Armando landed in front of Wally

Dallenbach, a hundred yards away. He died instantly. It wasn't the first time something like this had happened. In the 1961 race, while responding to a wreck, a firetruck backed over safety worker John Masariu, killing him.

The driver stranded in the flames was Swede Savage. Having refueled just before the wreck, the seventy-five gallons of methanol blazed against the firefighters' efforts. Finally extinguished, we could only pray as the ambulance rushed him to Methodist.

Just before the wreck, Swede passed his old teammate Bobby Unser. In their days on Dan Gurney's All-American Racers, Bobby didn't think the motorcycle and sports car champ was his equal. When a magazine rated Swede a top-ten driver, Bobby said he didn't think Swede belonged in the top hundred. Some wonder if Swede tried to prove something passing Bobby on his way into Turn Four. Bobby watched it all happen. He told me Swede just got too high up in the marbles—the accumulated bits of tire and other debris. The path most cars take around a track is called the "groove." The passing cars keep that route clear, but the marbles build up on the outside of it, and they can cause an instant loss of traction.

After crews finished clearing the track, the cars resumed until lap 133. A final rain shower mercifully extinguished the race. Only eleven cars remained as the checkered flag dropped with Gordon Johncock in the lead. Patrick Racing, my team, found the checkered flag. The 500 that everyone would just as soon forget, the "72 Hours of Indianapolis," was over.

The Victory Dinner had already been canceled. Pat Patrick and Gordy picked up fast-food burgers on their way to the hospital to visit their teammate Swede. His lungs were in bad shape. He received tainted plasma and refused an amputation. Swede died a month later, at only twenty-six.

On that tragic day, Swede's wife was pregnant with their daughter Angela. She would know him only through stories. At age forty, she built up the courage to see the Speedway and the site of the crash. The organization treated her like the racing royalty she is. Many of us who knew Swede accompanied her on the tour. We all cried.

When Angela had occasion to visit my home, I showed her my memorabilia collection. I noticed an old mechanical set of timing watches given to me by George Bignotti with his name scrawled on the back. I realized these had been used to time her father. I offered them to Angela, and she accepted.

The radios I ordered for Patrick Racing arrived just in time for the race at Phoenix. I opted for helicopter helmet microphones for the drivers. The team hired Wally Dallenbach to replace Swede. Pat asked me if I would run the headset for Wally. I said, "Yessir." No longer just a garage gofer, I was on the crew.

I learned the sport from the inside out as I traveled with the team. The best teacher was George Bignotti, master mechanic and engineering genius. Like many of the greats, he demanded a garage floor clean enough to eat off. When he saw the tangled mass of wires from the base station of my radio unit, he insisted I properly bundle them. Whether discussing Indy cars or my Formula Ford, George explained the dynamics in a way that made sense. As the years went by, I helped assemble the Wildcats at the garage. I knew my way around enough to put a car on the scales and "string and bump steer," a process for adjusting the suspension.

George was married to Kay, the daughter of three-time Indy 500 champion Louis Meyer. Kay also held a USAC mechanic's license and worked on the crew. The strong-willed couple never held back. I remember a race where the two argued over whether the driver should pit. Neither backing down, they both grabbed for the microphone, and it fell to the ground in the struggle. Kay got to it first, and the driver pitted.

On my first trip to California, I drove the team Winnebago overnight with the Meyer family to the Long Beach Grand Prix Formula
5000. We stopped in Las Vegas around three in the morning, and
Kay taught me how to play blackjack at Caesar's Palace. A few hours
later, on the final stretch of road, June "Mom" Meyer chatted with
me to keep me awake. Seeing my heavy eyes, she ordered me to pull
over and get out of the driver's seat. I protested to no avail. At around
seventy years old, she plunked down, hiked her skirt a bit, and hit the
gas hard. She looked over and reminded me she had done this before.

Back in the '30s, June and Louis Meyer were a team. When a
race ended, June hopped in the sedan and towed the trailer across
the country while Louis slept back in the race car as they bumped
along—it was the only place he could stretch out. She crisscrossed
the country back when the roads were few and poorly paved.

Los Angeles was all I hoped it would be. We stayed on the Queen
Mary, the famous old passenger ship then moored in the harbor as a
hotel. The crew crammed into a room, and I slept on the floor. In those
years, with Long Beach's start/finish line at the top of the hill, it was
breathtaking watching the cars tear down Ocean Boulevard at the start.

As I learned the mechanics of racing from George, I learned the
history from Louis Meyer. With six wins between the two over a
thirteen-year span, the rivalry between Louis and Wilbur Shaw was
legendary. In 1927, Louis took the wheel as a relief driver for Wilbur,
a rookie that year. The next year, Louis got his own car, and his first
win, at only twenty-three years of age. The tradition of drinking milk
in Victory Lane started with Louis. He liked to drink buttermilk as a
sort of energy drink during races. Thirsty after the checkered flag, he
tilted back his quart bottle of buttermilk in 1936. The sports pages
carried a photo of that moment, and someone from the milk lobby
realized it was the perfect promotion. Louis also had the distinction
of being the first face added to the Borg Warner Trophy.

After a scary crash, Louis retired but stayed in the racing business. He and Dale Drake bought the Miller-Offenhauser brand in

the '40s. They manufactured the "Offy" engines that dominated from the post-war era through the '70s.

Louis had a great sense of humor. On a hospital visit, Louis regaled me with his stories: "Back in my day, if we wanted to know if a part worked, we put it in and drove. If we didn't crash, we knew it worked."

He reeled us in when he asked, "Did you know we invented the seat belt back in our racing days at the Speedway?" I told him I hadn't heard that. With a wink he said, "Well, it wasn't for the drivers. We lashed in our riding mechanics so they wouldn't run away during pit stops."

Touring with the team helped me understand how different drivers' skill sets can be. A fast and bold driver, Gordon Johncock knew nothing about cars. In a road race at Mid-Ohio, we had spotters around the track to listen for when Gordy shifted gears so adjustments could be made. A surprising number of great drivers, including my hero Eddie Sachs, were just as mechanically disinclined.

At the other end of the spectrum, Wally Dallenbach owned a construction business with his cousin. He ran a beautiful dude ranch in the Frying Pan Valley near Basalt, Colorado. In his early days, he set up his own cars. Bright and laid back, Wally knew how to drive but always seemed to have bad luck on Race Day.

After the fatalities of 1973, the Speedway overhauled the track for safety. Major renovations raised the outer wall from thirty-six inches to fifty-four inches, moved the pit access to Turn Four instead of the straightaway, and lengthened each pit to forty feet.

New rules reduced the size of fuel tanks to forty gallons, shortened the rear-wings, and required pop-off valves to reduce the horsepower in turbocharged engines. For the first time, these rules were designed to slow down the cars for safety. The rules at Indianapolis had always encouraged innovation and, inevitably, faster speeds. The tension between innovation, speed, and safety has shaped racing ever since.

In a break from tradition, officials announced the 1974 race would be held on a Sunday. Due to traditional religious considerations, the race had never been held on a Sunday before. With federal law fixing Memorial Days on Mondays, Sunday has been Race Day ever since.

In February of 1974, Julie Eisenhower-Nixon, the president's daughter, was hospitalized in Indianapolis during her pregnancy. She worked for Beurt and Corena SerVaas, an influential Indianapolis couple who owned several businesses and publications including *The Saturday Evening Post*. When Julie recovered enough to travel, President Nixon arrived in Indianapolis on Air Force One to fly her home. Coinciding with the height of Watergate, I covered the departure of Air Force One. Sid later told me it was this reporting that confirmed in his mind I was ready for the IMS Radio Network.

Sid asked me to listen to the prior year's race tapes and propose possible changes to the broadcast. I suggested the expanded pits would require another pit reporter. Sid replied, "Well, I think you should take the fourth position then." I about fell out of my chair. Then I froze, fearing it was all a joke. When no punchline arrived, I calmly thanked him, doing backflips on the inside. He told me, "Now show me some style on Race Day—not just the way you talk, but the way you look and act."

On Race Day 1974, I took Sid's advice literally and wore a brand-new suit. In the opening segment, Sid introduced me to a hundred million listeners with a backhanded compliment on my white suit. Perhaps it wasn't the best fashion decision, particularly for a pit reporter.

The green flag waved from the new elevated starter's stand, and a dream came true. I was part of the Indy 500. I nearly forgot I had a job to do as I watched A. J. Foyt lead the field from the pole position.

I covered the north pits, where the worst drivers were assigned. They tended to be out early, which meant I always had someone to interview. The pit reporter has a dangerous job. Gary Gerould was on the job when a fuel tank exploded in Herm Johnson's pit at the Michigan 500. People had to scale the cyclone fence to get to safety, and it looked like one pit would go up right after the other. It's not much safer in the turns. Gary literally patted out Bobby Unser's smoldering fire suit as he interviewed him following a wreck in Phoenix. At Pocono, Bill Canell had a front row seat to Michael Andretti spinning into the wall. After his report I asked Bill if Michael was alright. Instead of describing the scene, Bill yelled down, "Hey, are you okay?" I could hear Michael shout back, "I'm okay." That's being close to it all.

At a lull in the action, Sid sent me to find and interview Evel Knievel. Sid encouraged celebrities to drop by the broadcast booth for interviews. Dinah Shore was a regular. While Sid loved giving airtime to celebrities, I didn't. I thought the race was more important. So I lied and told Sid I couldn't find the daredevil. Watching me from the Master Control Tower, Sid asked, "Aren't you standing right next to him?" Busted. I was wrong—you must do what your anchor asks. I started to worry this might be my only stint on the IMS Radio Network.

Wally Dallenbach set a competition record of 191 mph on lap two—quite an accomplishment with all the changes to push down speeds. On lap three, Wally blew a piston. George Bignotti had worried that might happen. He used a huge blower for qualifications, but to his surprise, officials wouldn't let him trade it out for smaller, safer one for the race. Johnny Rutherford blazed from twenty-fifth to third in just thirteen laps. The race shaped up as a fierce battle between "Lone Star" J. R. and "Super Tex" A. J. Foyt. When officials black-flagged A. J. for leaking oil on lap 140, J. R. never looked back.

After the checkered flag, fans rushed the track in Turn Three while drivers kept racing. This led to the rule that the race ends with the checkered flag, and positions at that moment determine the final order. Previously, the officials let the drivers continue to race for "a while"—usually five or ten minutes. Lloyd Ruby ran out of fuel late for a ninth-place finish, while wearing the last open-faced helmet.

During J. R.'s early rush to the front, he cut off rookie Pancho Carter, sending him spinning. In a testament to J. R.'s character, he apologized to Pancho while in Victory Lane.

Sid had become my mentor. We weren't exactly cut from the same cloth. He was debonair, perfectly dressed, always an overachiever. I wasn't.

Born Sid Cahn, his parents ran a general store on the northwest side of Indianapolis. He attended Shortridge High School, a prominent public school. Sid was co-editor of the student newspaper with Kurt Vonnegut, the famous novelist. He attended Indiana University, joined ROTC, and became an officer stationed in England during World War II. Back home, he easily found broadcasting work and soon landed at WIBC.

His entire career as the Voice, Sid stood with an Electro Voice 635 microphone hanging around his neck on a bent-to-shape coat hanger. When he started, most sportscasters spoke into a large mic like an RCA 44DX on a desk stand as they looked down on the playing field. Sid's playing field required him to crane his neck almost ninety degrees in each direction to catch the cars flying past.

For the second year of the IMS Radio Network broadcast, Sid wanted a better lead-in for commercial breaks. Alice Greene, a young staffer, suggested "Stay tuned for the greatest spectacle in racing." It remained the cue until Speedway President John Cooper changed it to "the greatest spectacle in sports" for 1982. He dismissed my arguments in favor of the grand understatement of the legendary cue. After John left the Speedway, I changed it back.

Under Sid's system, each announcer had an engineer. When something noteworthy happened, the engineer called the control booth. The producer answered and wrote down the message, something like "big wreck in turn two," on a three-by-five card and handed it to Sid. He arranged the cue cards in front of him and sent the lead out to the action. It was classic radio at its best. Sid painted the picture with action, insight, and detail.

The Indianapolis media market, to this day, is blocked from the live national television broadcast of the Indy 500. The only exceptions were the 100th Indy 500 in 2016 and the fan-less race in 2020. At Race Day parties throughout central Indiana, a radio blares over the sizzle of the grill, and lawn chairs are clustered close to the speakers. Listening to the 500 remains the tradition. In the evening, fans gather around the television to watch the delayed broadcast, experiencing the race for a second time.

The radio broadcast is riveting. The action is sent from the booth to the announcers in the turns and pits, one taking over right after the next in seamless coverage. Under a green flag, each announcer covers about ten seconds of each forty-five second lap, chasing the action streaking around the track at 230 mph. You hear the speed and the noise and the action, and your mind fills in the rest. It's the furthest you can get from the television sports of today, where many of the commentators talk about anything but the action on the field, and worse, about themselves. I was trained to tell stories, interesting and inside bits that inform and fascinate the viewer.

In 1983, *Sports Illustrated* ran an article comparing the tape-delayed, hindsight-based ABC coverage of the Indy 500 to the live work by the IMS Radio Network:

On the surface, you wouldn't have bet on the radio guys to win the checkered flag. Last year ABC got four Emmys for its Indy coverage. As far as is known, Page didn't even get a free meal at St. Elmo's Steakhouse in downtown Indianapolis. The IMS Radio

Network can only guess how many people its 700 affiliates reach. Suffice it to say that the network, now 32 years old, reaches the likes of Chicago, Lewistown, MT. and 10,000 service-station lube bays coast to coast. For all of ABC's artistry—Posey has become a superb analyst, and director Larry Kamm's cameras caught all of the action—Page and his 13 cohorts stationed around the track accomplished what their TV rivals didn't. The radio voices were genuine, not staged. There's no substitute for authenticity. As they relayed the call around the track among themselves, a listener could see in his mind's eye the sun glinting off Al Unser's brilliant yellow No. 7 and hear the engines 20 yards away. It was vintage live radio. As Page said before the race, "If you want to feel the emotion of the event, then you come live it with us."

In this era, the drivers, owners, and crews were very accessible to the public. Most stayed at the Speedway Motel or the Holiday Inn Northwest on Crawfordsville Road. Groupies had no trouble finding drivers. In that free-love era, some drivers compared their numbers of trips to the motel room. It only counted if the driver met the young lady for the first time that day. I read in Jackie Stewart's autobiography that he abstained before a big race. When we shared the broadcast booth, I had to ask the World Champion if it was true. He answered, "That was all rubbish."

The cafeteria under the Tower Terrace had a small roped-off section just for drivers. To get further away, a driver could head over to the "Oldtimers' Room," a private lounge. Oldtimers were people who had been involved at the track "for a long time." It included drivers, safety officials, even volunteers. After at least ten years, you could submit an application, but you still had to wait for the big ugly red trucker's hat. Three decades as an Oldtimer earns a yellow hat, four decades a white one.

Drivers and other VIPs, like Chuck Yeager, were always welcome in the lounge. The actor James Garner regularly tended bar in the Oldtimers' Room, chatting with everyone. A respected amateur driver, he often drove the pace car to start the race. He freely gave autographs, even on his way back to his room at the Speedway Motel carrying a sack of McDonald's.

At the track, wives, girlfriends, and moms of the drivers shared an area of seats above the pits known as the Rattlesnake Stands. Women weren't allowed in the pits and garages until the '70s, but lots of wives and girlfriends have told tales of getting smuggled inside that last bastion of testosterone. Everyone looked forward to Mom Unser's annual chili lunch. Alice Hanks, wife of Sam Hanks, was a tour de force. Even in her eighties, she was beautiful and glamorous and a whirlwind of energy. Her other great love was the air races in Reno.

The Snake Pit, located inside Turn One, attracted the revelers. Every day of May, it had the feel of a KISS concert. The dynamic included a Bourbon Street culture of exhibitionism, without the beads, and a shouted four-word request. So engrained were those words that, at the Women's Auxiliary's fashion show, one of the models unzipped a jacket to reveal a cardboard sign hanging from her neck that read, "Show us the pits."

The month of May had many receptions and events. Sid Collins started the Pole Position Mechanic banquet to honor the mechanics; the drivers sat in the back and cheered their crews. The Last Row Party roasts the drivers starting in Row 11. Checks were awarded in the amounts of $0.33, $0.32, and $0.31.

Off the grounds, the most popular hangout was Mate's White Front Café, always just called White Front. The standalone block building still sits on the south side of 16th Street, east of the rail overpass. Other favorites, like the Mug'n'Bun and Working Man's Friend, are still around and nearly unchanged.

Back then, drivers didn't care about reporters or the media and sometimes gave them a really hard time. Al Unser Sr. would ask me for money before he would do an interview. I always refused, and he always did the interview. To this day, I don't know if he was joking or not, or if other reporters ponied up.

Though I know Jack Arute ponied up. He and Al Sr., both unlucky in marriage, wagered a thousand dollars on bachelorhood—whoever remarried first would owe the other. Jack lost, but Al Sr. would only accept payment by a single twenty-dollar bill each time he saw him. During a live interview on ABC, Al Sr. demanded another installment. Jack pulled out his wallet and handed over an Andy Jackson. In the next segment, our producer forced Jack to explain to the viewers the reason for the transaction.

One of the most intimidating interviews for any reporter was A. J. Foyt. He had rules about when you could ask him a question: only after he got back to the garage and never during the walk back. If A. J. got hot enough, he was known to slug reporters for shouting questions at him. Even for veteran reporters, A. J. was difficult. He especially tortured Robin Miller.

For an interview on Channel 13, A. J. told me to pretend to come up to him "spontaneously" on his walk back later that day. Live and right on time, I saw a mischievous smile cross his face as I got closer. He barked at me for harassing him when he was trying to work and not knowing his rules, before ducking into his garage. When the spot finished, he came out and had a laugh. I gave him hell right back. He did the interview for real the next day.

That rough exterior hid a soft heart. When Johnny Rutherford hit the wall at Phoenix after an oil slick, followed by Roger McCluskey and Mario Andretti, Roger sat on the stretcher due to a concussion. A. J., already out of the race, ran over from the pits to help. He saw J. R. remove his glove, exposing a horribly burned hand. J. R.'s shoes were on fire too. After helping to get the flames out, A. J. hoisted Roger right off the stretcher and set him to the side, saying "Johnny needs it more."

I once stayed at A. J.'s ranch, and a mare died after giving birth. A. J. and I met the vet who proceeded to cut off the mare's hoof as part of his examination. A. J. turned white and quickly made an excuse to leave. That's A. J.: tough as nails on the outside, but a big heart of gold on the inside.

CHAPTER 7

A Heartbreaking
Succession

I still believe no one remembers who finished second,
and that luck is where opportunity meets preparation.
—*Johnny Rutherford*

O n a fantastic Pole Day 1975, second-year driver Tom Sneva caught a set of fast laps early in the morning. Bobby Unser and then Gordon Johncock ran even faster sets. As the day cooled around Happy Hour, A. J. Foyt blazed his way to a back-to-back seat on the pole, tying Rex Mays's record of four poles.

The pits looked a little different. Air hammers became standard issue for changing tires. It dropped pit stop times from around twenty-three seconds down to fourteen seconds. Powerful radios put the teams in constant contact with their drivers. They also interfered with each other's signals and the radio broadcast. Goodyear won the tire war; for the first time in nearly a half century, no Firestone tire could be found in the pits.

Sid asked me to join him in the booth during qualifications. The small room five floors up in the old Master Control Tower stood level with the surrounding grandstands. Outside the window, ropes kept the fans from blocking our view. We did one-hour reports at five o'clock recapping each day. I hoped this was a sign of better things to come. At the end of one shift, Sid said, "You have the reportorial skills, what I need to see is your passion for racing."

On Race Day, Tom Sneva touched tires with Eldon Rasmussen on lap 125, launching Tom airborne into the catch fence. Debris pelted fans in the luxury suites. The flaming cockpit rocketed down the track, violently flipping and spinning along. We all feared the worst, but Tom was unhurt until he tried to get out of his car. Unaware of the invisible methanol flames, he lifted his visor and put his hand down in the pool of flaming fuel, burning his hand and face. When I visited Tom at the hospital after the race, he also had odd square-shaped second-degree burn marks on his chest and arms. The sponsorship patches sewn onto his fire suit compressed the Nomex material, reducing its protection from heat.

Caught up in Tom's wreck, Dick Simon waited for repairs in the pit, and I interviewed him. Sid remarked it was the first time a driver had been interviewed while still in competition.

Wally Dallenbach held the lead for ninety-six laps. His hopes ended when his crankshaft broke on lap 162. A sudden downpour drenched the track and everyone in it. Several cars wildly hydro-planed out of Turn Four. The checkered and red flags dropped on lap 174 with Bobby Unser in the lead. His tires splashed through the standing water on his way to Victory Lane for the second time.

Sid Collins had a few quirks in his personality. I invited Sid to dinner at his favorite restaurant, Macri's Italian Village on North Meridian Street, so he could meet my brother Chuck. When we arrived, Sid stood out front and apologized for his cold hands as he greeted us. He stretched out his left hand to show a raw steak wrapped in paper. He explained he didn't think the restaurant served good meat so he brought his own.

Sid was, of course, being cheap. But because he broadcast interviews nightly from the restaurant and made it very popular, the proprietors indulged him. Folks watched for celebrities during Sid's radio show at the Village before heading south on Meridian to the Embers nightclub.

If frugal in some ways, Sid was generous with his advice, and I benefitted immensely. Over dinners and late nights at the station, he held nothing back when he discussed the trade of broadcasting. He would say, "Be descriptive: use your descriptors, colors, the name of the mechanic, what's happening in the stands, what the listeners are hearing. It's painting pictures with words. Always be motivating the audio—that's what makes the audience feel like they're there. Don't give away the end. Even if it's clear with twenty laps to go who will win, keep the mystery. But also foreshadow possibilities, records to be broken, pitfalls ahead." He often quizzed me about how I might handle particular situations, just to make sure I had given it some thought.

Like all broadcasting greats, Sid could find that "space" or "zone" or "rhythm" where he was aware of everything happening around him, instantly filtering and arranging them in descending order of importance, so the story could be told without distraction or tangents, and in the proper order. I preferred the phrase: "theater of the mind." I found my space and rhythm. I could predict things. It became instinctual: when drivers will pit, who needs tires, when someone will make a move.

As the years went by, Sid suggested a few times I would replace him as the Voice when he retired. I shrugged it off because I doubted

Sid would ever hang up his microphone. And besides, that decision would be up to Tony Hulman.

As May of 1976 arrived in Indianapolis, the quartz-infused concrete forming the white walls of the new IMS Museum and Hall of Fame blindingly gleamed in the sun. All the excitement surrounded Janet Guthrie, the first woman to try to qualify for the Indy 500. Lore has it that women raced each other during World War I when the track was an Army airbase, but this was something new.

Until five years earlier, the Speedway expressly banned women from the pits and garages. The rules only changed when Mari McCloskey, assistant editor of *Woman's World Magazine*, sued to gain admission as a journalist in 1971. Speedway officials soon issued press passes to reporters Bettie Cadou, Mary Anne Butters, and Myrta Pulliam.

In April of 1976 at Phoenix, Arlene Hiss, wife of my friend and driver Mike Hiss, became the first woman to qualify and race an Indy car. She finished fourteenth, but not without controversy. She was black-flagged for driving too slowly. Some drivers threatened to boycott if she entered the next race at Trenton. Arlene moved on to stock cars and never drove at Indianapolis.

The prejudice against women was part sexism and part superstition. Drivers are ridiculously superstitious. The color green has been considered unlucky since at least the 1920s. A. J. Foyt once refused to have his car towed by a green truck at Pocono. Back when Tom Binford owned a team, his driver Cal Niday threw a new pair of driving shoes back at Tom because he saw tiny green triangles on the tongues.

The old Gasoline Alley had eighty-eight garages numbered 1 through 89, so no one would get number 13. Wilbur Shaw didn't like what he called "upside down" numbers: 88 or 99. It's considered bad luck to eat peanuts in the pits; a relic of the era of wooden tracks when the seats hung over the track and spectators occasionally dropped peanut shells below. When someone noticed peanut shells inside a car after a fatal wreck, the superstition stuck. You never wish a driver good luck; like an actor before a show, it's considered a jinx, and by some drivers, fighting words.

Stories of tempting fate and losing are never forgotten. Floyd Roberts kept a big mean black cat in his garage in 1938. Floyd got the win. The cat came back in 1939, and Floyd's luck ran out. He became the first champ to die in a later Indy 500 race.

Ted Horn, who never won but placed fourth or better in nine consecutive 500s, had the series all wrapped up before the last race of the 1948 season. He asked his wife to wear a green dress in the stands. She did, and Ted was killed in a wreck.

When Janet showed up in 1976, she took a lot of heat, often through chauvinism. A lot of sponsors considered her a liability: what if she wrecked? How would the public react to a woman rather than a man dying in a crash? Many drivers supported Janet through their actions, if not their words. Bobby Unser loaned Janet one of his fire suits after the airline lost her luggage. Watching her on the track, A. J. Foyt knew it was the car and not the driving that kept Janet out of the show. Likely at Tony Hulman's suggestion, A. J. let Janet climb into his backup car and sent her out for a few laps. Janet's time would have made the field, proving to all the doubters she was the real thing.

Even without making the show, NASCAR noticed, and Janet found a seat in a stock car for the Charlotte World 600. She finished fifteenth. She took the rookie honors at the next Daytona 500, placing twelfth when her engine blew with ten laps to go.

The advent of women in racing reflected changes in technology as well as culture. Few women would have had the muscles of a Herk Hurtubise necessary to steer a Novi a decade earlier. Drivers needed leather hands and strong cardio for sprint cars on a dirt track, and most had demanding strength-training routines. With rack-and-pinion steering and other advances, A. J. Foyt's physical strength was no longer the asset it once was.

Also chasing a spot that May was my old friend from Formula Ford days, Eddie Miller. I happened to be in the chopper above the Speedway when I noticed his car coming down the straightaway. He lost it going into Turn One and lifted off the embankment, clearing a couple of fences, doing endos, and landing in the spectator area beside the trees and next to the tunnel. Eddie broke his neck and gave up any ambitions for Indy.

On Race Day 1976, the Texas Shootout of 1974 reignited between A. J. Foyt and Johnny Rutherford. J. R. finally passed A. J. on lap eighty. He held on until the rain red-flagged the race on lap 103. Under the rules, a rain-out after the completion of lap 100 (the halfway mark) can end the race.

The rain stopped, the track dried out, and the cars lined back up on pit lane. But before the pace car arrived, rain fell once more. Officials called the race, and J. R. walked to Victory Lane while his car was towed from the pits. I followed and interviewed him along the way—the first interview of a winner before reaching Victory Lane. It was the start of a lifelong friendship with J. R.

Sid Collins signed off in his typical heartfelt manner:

So now, the 60th running of the 500 here is now history. Since 1911, the hypnotic effect of speed upon driver and spectator alike is never dim. The run from the green flag to the checkered and on to Victory Lane here is a pursuit only one man in the world can accomplish once a year. . . .

The massive crowd of more than 350,000 has threaded its way towards the exit gates as their eyes have taken a final sweep over the track before departing. For some, this has been a once-in-a-lifetime experience, others will come back, but in every case, it's always difficult to relinquish one's grasp on the pulsating emotion that is the 500. And at this microphone we share that reaction of having to say goodbye to you across the many miles that separate us. But, another icy Indiana winter will come and go, and before we know it, springtime returns, it will be May, and the roar of engines will once again breathe life into the lazy Hoosier sky and bring us back together. God willing, I'll be here to greet you for this annual reunion through our mutual love of auto racing and the Indianapolis 500. . . .

So until next May, this is Sid Collins, the Voice of the 500, wishing you good morning, good afternoon, or good evening, depending upon where in the world you are right now. We're here at the Indianapolis Motor Speedway, at the Crossroads of America. Goodbye.

Over the years, I made connections at the FBI as a newsman. I knew the value of relationships as a reciprocal source of tips and leads. As a young reporter, I often visited the FBI office looking for a lead. On one of those visits, I chatted with Special Agent Bob Stouffer, and a call came in for a bank robbery. I asked if I could ride along, and he told me to hop in. It was a rush to watch an FBI manhunt up close.

When they learned I could be trusted, I became friends with Bob and Special Agent Weyland "Arch" Archer. They once asked for my help consoling a rookie the night after he saw his first real action. At the Knights of Columbus a glass of beer cost a quarter. At the end of the evening, we had an eighty-five-dollar bar tab, and the rookie felt no worries. None of us did.

On a snowy day in February 1977, I had lunch plans with Bob and Arch when a hostage situation came across the police scanner. Bob hopped in my car while Arch ran back to his. We arrived at the office building just in time to see a man with a gun marching another man down the street. The shotgun held to the back of the hostage's head was wired around the hostage's neck, down to his wrists, and back to the trigger; any false move and it was all over. As we tried to catch up, he hijacked a car.

Tony Kiritsis thought his mortgage broker swindled him out of some real estate. After the hijacking, he barricaded himself and the broker in an apartment. As the police evacuated the complex, we knocked on a unit with a good view and asked if we could use it. The lady enthusiastically agreed—even offering us the food in the fridge and the booze under the sink. The police and FBI congregated in a couple of units nearby. The FBI invoked the Hobbs Act and took over. I climbed up on the roof to hang out with the snipers so I could hear the chatter on the FBI radio.

An FBI hostage negotiator arrived from Washington, DC. His profile was dead-on. He predicted it would take three nights and Kiritsis would become increasingly volatile toward the end. Kiritsis wanted to talk to the media, and the FBI wanted to find a neutral party to help with negotiations. The agent in charge asked me to do it. I said, "Hell no."

To me, there was no question a reporter should never become involved in a story. Our only job is to report on how a story unfolds. We should never influence a story. I told them to call my boss, Fred Heckman, certain he would feel the same way.

To my surprise, Fred thought we should get involved. In the newsroom at WIBC, a group of us engaged in a long debate over the ethics of it: Fred, Tom Cochran, Lou Palmer, and Virgil Napier—an old coot of a reporter from Harlan County, Kentucky, who thought himself a wise old sage of yesteryear. Of course Fred was the boss, so it didn't matter what we thought. Fred convinced himself he needed to do this to save a life. Breaking a cardinal rule of journalism, Fred agreed to assist the FBI and became part of the story.

Around midnight I went home to get some shut-eye. I left the radio on. Around five in the morning, I awoke to the sound of obscenities shouted live over the air—at least five of George Carlin's "Seven Words." Fred had not only talked to Kiritsis, he agreed to let him air his grievances on live radio. I got dressed and sped back over to the scene.

Finally, Kiritsis agreed to let the mortgage broker go free in exchange for several legal documents, including some relating to the mortgage and others granting him immunity from prosecution. But he wanted a press conference first.

I waited for him in a room full of police, FBI, reporters, and TV crews. Everyone was tense. In came Kiritsis, still shouting, and the gun still wired around the hostage. An idiot photographer standing on a chair fell to the ground causing a loud slam. But by the grace of God, Kiritsis didn't flinch, and he finished his final rant.

I learned the FBI planned to take him to another room where Kiritsis would set the hostage free. I ran outside hoping to watch the action through the window. As I walked along the building, Kiritsis stepped out of a door just ahead of me, shotgun in hand. He fired. Just as quickly, he turned back inside. I paused to check for bullet holes—and to see if I needed to change my underwear.

It turned out Kiritsis negotiated the right to squeeze the trigger and fire a round into the air to prove he hadn't been bluffing all this time. I'm not sure he ever even saw me, but it sure scared the hell out of me.

Somehow, Kiritsis was found not guilty by reason of insanity. The events over those days became a case study at journalism schools.

We all came to know Sid was in ill health. He had neck surgery and a foot problem, but something else was wrong. At only fifty-four years of age, he began to lose his balance and walk with a distinct limp. We had to help him up and down the stairs of the Master Control Tower.

A group of friends presented him with a golf cart to help him get around the Speedway easier. Afterwards, he said, "Put that away and don't ever bring it out again." When he emceed the USAC awards dinner, I drove him to the hall early, arriving before anyone else. He took his seat on the dais and remained there until everyone left. He wanted to hide his use of a cane.

Sid was a proud man. In his famous "Death Has a Thousand Doors" remarks, Sid gave the wrong years for when Eddie took the pole. Sid caught the mistake after the fact. The LP of the 1964 Indy 500, recorded by Fleetwood Records, has a gap: it stops before the quote from Byron, omitting Sid's error. He swept it under the rug.

Sid's neurologist, an old friend who knew how he would react to his diagnosis, hid his condition from him. In late April of 1977, Sid had enough and flew to the Mayo Clinic for a second opinion. He came back with a diagnosis of ALS, also known as Lou Gehrig's Disease. Sid was openly suicidal. He had spent the last year mortified people would mock him as a drunk due to his stumbling. The thought of spending the rest of his days as a worsening invalid was unbearable.

I pleaded with Sid: "You can make it to thirty years as the Voice. You promised me we would announce that 500 together, just like your first year with Bill Slater. I need you. I'm not ready to do this by myself yet. You promised me." He was unmoved.

Henry Bradshaw, Sid's close friend and lawyer, took him to the psychiatric ward. Sid checked himself out the next day. I spoke with his doctor at the hospital, but he said if Sid really wanted to kill himself, no one could stop him.

Sid had no family. He wasn't in a relationship with anyone. He regretted causing the love of his life to wait too long, and she married someone else. He held out for something better. Early in his career, Sid auditioned for roles in New York City. His bosses at WIBC convinced him to stick around and move into selling advertising. It assured him financial success in addition to his fame as the Voice. Sid stayed home in Indy. He regretted it. Late in his career, he still pleaded with Dinah Shore to hire him for her show.

On Sunday, the first day of May, Henry and I went over to Sid's apartment to check on him. Sid had a hard look in his eyes. He freely discussed killing himself. He meant it. I brought up the annual network breakfast two days away, and he seemed buoyed by it. Henry suggested moving out of his two-story apartment and into a nursing facility. To our surprise, he agreed and asked us to come back the next day so we could tour a couple of options.

It was a relief.

It was also a lie.

On the morning of May 2, 1977, Sid called Russ Arnold, director of the IMS Radio Network, and demanded confirmation that I would be Sid's successor. Hearing the desperation in Sid's voice, Russ worried this unresolved issue might be the only thing stopping him from doing something rash. Russ stalled and kept Sid on the phone until he heard that Ray Trotta, a close friend, had arrived. Ray brought an early lunch, his favorite spaghetti from Macri's Italian Village.

Around noon, I pulled up to Sid's apartment in his pace car, an Oldsmobile, all filled up and ready for our outing. Henry pulled in right behind me. We knocked, but we heard only silence. The door was unlocked. We pushed it open and called out. No response. Our hearts sank as we walked up the staircase of that familiar apartment, expecting the worst. His cane rested against the baluster.

In the bedroom, we found Sid hanging in a closet from a necktie wrapped around the clothes rod. Henry got him down, and I called for an ambulance. I knew it was too late. I'll never forget the sight of my mentor lying dead in his pajamas on the floor of his bedroom.

The closet wasn't very tall. Sid went the hard way. He must have kneeled, pulling his legs up. He could have stopped at any time if he had second thoughts. Sid proved his willpower to the last. I recognized the tie around his neck as the same one he wore on the cover of *Hot Rod Magazine* commemorating his twenty-fifth year as the Voice of the 500.

We went through his things and found a tape recording—his version of a suicide note. It mostly recounted his diagnosis. He wanted it played on the air during the 500. That request would not be honored. His requested replacement as the Voice was a different question.

With the race only a few weeks away, a decision on the broadcast needed to be made immediately. On the evening of Sid's death, I met Russ and Tony Hulman at the restaurant in the Speedway Motel. As he did with Sid almost thirty years earlier, Tony decided to "let this kid have a chance."

Russ handed Tony a copy of the proposed press release. He made one edit. To the sentence naming me the chief announcer for the Indianapolis 500, he added, "for 1977."

CHAPTER 8

The New Voice and
a Hard Landing

Cars and bones may be mended. To a driver, the only
thing that matters is getting back to speed again.
—Janet Guthrie

T
he morning after Sid's death, I walked into the restaurant
at Stouffer's Hotel on North Meridian Street for the
IMS Radio Network's annual breakfast. Almost without
exception, Sid kept secret who would be on the broadcast. Everyone
had to wait for an invitation to the breakfast, and there he announced
assignments. Russ Arnold introduced me as the chief announcer, and
the room fell silent for a moment. Lou Palmer stood and began to clap,
as did the rest of the room. I choked up. It was a lot to take at once.

I helped Henry Bradshaw and Ray Trotta make funeral arrangements for Sid. At some point, Sid had become a Unitarian. He had
a deep spiritual side influenced by his Jewish roots. A huge crowd

gathered for the wake at the funeral home. Initially closed, I asked for the casket to be opened. Seeing his face again shook me hard. Some of us gathered at a friend's home afterwards, and I drank and drank my grief away. The next morning, I was too sick to make it to the burial.

I helped clear out Sid's apartment. Most of his awards never got hung on the wall. He had scores of unopened boxes of racing mementos; the kind of swag he liked to hand out when he spoke to groups. It all seemed such a waste. Everything about Sid's death made me angry, but I didn't have time to deal with my emotions.

On Pole Day 1977, the radio booth overlooking the Indianapolis Motor Speedway was mine for the first time. History stops for no one. Mario Andretti had unofficially broken the 200-miles-per-hour barrier on a practice lap. Tom Sneva officially broke the barrier and took the pole.

On Bump Day, Jim McElreath settled an old score. Already qualified himself, Jim watched as his son James made one last try shortly before the six o'clock gun. Jim could tell on the practice lap James wouldn't have the speed. He kept his son out anyway because Salt Walther was next in line.

Salt drove for his father's team, and he acted like it. When Salt finished dead last for the third time (his sole record of distinction), he got back in the race by relieving another driver on his dad's team. Another year when Salt failed to make the field, his dad bought a qualified car from a different team. They fired the driver, whose efforts earned its place in the show, so Salt could race. Jim was of the opinion that Salt's dad still owed him money from when he drove for his team several years earlier. With James taking up time on the track, the gun went off, and Salt lost his chance to qualify. Jim considered it payment in kind.

For all of Sid's talents, he had become complacent with an "if it ain't broke, don't fix it," attitude. Our team seized the opportunity to improve the broadcast. We upgraded to a system that allowed us to talk to each other through our headsets off the air. We retired Sid's three-by-five cards. We would report things as they happened in real time. When the topic came up, I voted against being called the Voice of the 500. I was overruled.

I wrote my opening material the night before the race. I settled down with Bloemker's history of the Speedway, *500 Miles to Go*, until I finally drifted off to sleep. Up before five in the morning, I had breakfast with the crew, an annual tradition. As we chatted, I kept looking at my watch and the "Order of the Day" for the Speedway:

5:00 a.m.	Salute Bombs—All Gates Open
8:00 a.m.	The Big Band-O-Rama marching bands
8:30 a.m.	Race Cars on Apron in Front of Respective Pits
	Spectacle of Bands
9:45 a.m.	Crews push race cars to starting position
	"On the Banks of the Wabash" by the Purdue Band
10:00 a.m.	Celebrity Caravan
10:34 a.m.	Final inspection of racecourse by chief steward
10:41 a.m.	Combined Armed Forces Color Guard
10:42 a.m.	"Star Spangled Banner" by the Purdue Band
10:45 a.m.	Invocation
10:46 a.m.	"Taps" by the Combined Armed Forces Color Guard
10:48 a.m.	"Back Home Again in Indiana" by Jim Nabors
	Balloon Spectacle
10:51 a.m.	"Gentlemen, Start Your Engines" by Tony Hulman
10:52 a.m.	The Parade Lap—pace car driven by James Garner
10:55 a.m.	The Pace Lap, Bomb Crescendo, Galaxy of Flags
11:00 a.m.	Start of Race

The aerial bombs might seem out of place, but the tradition dates to the first races at the Speedway. Like the use of flags, the firework booms were cues for the drivers: when to line up, when to start the engines. They could be heard above the roar of the crowds and the race car engines.

We arrived late to the track. Some quarrel between the Speedway and the Sheriff's office resulted in us losing our escort. After pleading with the Indianapolis Police Department, they came through for us.

The stage fright really hit me on the way down 16th Street—I felt like that fifteen-year-old kid with my Uncle Harry on my way to my first 500. Once in my office underneath the Tower Terrace grandstand to the north of the Master Control Tower, I closed my door and tried to calm myself with last minute matters. All the guys stopped by to wish me well, each sending my panic a little higher.

Like Sid used to do, I went for a walk through the pits and garages to take in the feel of the track. I stopped by Pat Patrick's garage and chatted with Gordon Johncock. On my way back up to the booth, a yellow shirt stopped me. I explained who I was, but he insisted I needed a letter to go up to the fifth floor. I marched back to my office and took out my aggression on an old typewriter, banging out a letter on IMS Radio Network letterhead from myself to myself granting myself access to the booth.

As I headed back, my ire changed to amusement at the whole situation. Any stage fright melted away. The yellow shirt looked blankly at the letter and let me pass.

Inside, we tested the lines and an amplifier blew. They told me they could fix it with a bigger fuse. I had my doubts, but it seemed to work.

I put my headset on and looked over to my producer Jack Morrow. His final words of wisdom were just what I needed: "There are over 110 million listeners out there, so don't screw this up."

I chuckled and soaked it all in for a moment. Here I was, in a place I revered, doing what I never thought I would be able to do.

At 10:17 a.m., Jim Shelton opened the broadcast and held a moment of silence for Sid. I nearly choked up as he introduced me:

Now here is Sid's good friend, race driver, broadcaster—a well-qualified man and our new Voice of the 500—Paul Page.

In an instant, something I barely had the courage to dream came true. It threw me for a split second. I swallowed hard and launched into my prepared remarks:

Thank you, Jim Shelton, and greetings from Indianapolis. . . . We hope you will join us in dedicating this sixty-first running of the 500 mile race to Sid Collins.

It is May 27, 1977. This is race day at Indianapolis. The place, the world's greatest racecourse, the Indianapolis Motor Speedway. The spirit is running high here, this day has already dawned as the spectacular finale to a magnificent month. At this moment, the skies are hazy gray. The temperature is seventy-nine degrees and the humidity sixty-seven percent.

I am speaking to you from the Master Control Tower situated above the starting line and commanding a view of the main straightaway and the pit area. . . . This year, once again, you and your radio set at home are tuned in to the world's largest radio network. Our signal covers every inch of the continental United States and Alaska and Hawaii. We are being beamed by shortwave radio to the Armed Forces radio and television service throughout the world. I am Paul Page, proud to serve you as the Voice of the 500.

The prerace festivities continued. Time stood still at 10:51 a.m. as Tony Hulman made his way to the microphone for the command. The anticipation grew palpable. For the first time, no one was quite sure what he would say.

In a green and white *Bryant Heating & Cooling Special,* Janet Guthrie qualified as the first woman in the field for the Indy 500. In the process, she set a closed-course speed record and became the fastest woman in racing. She also shook off a wreck in Turn Four earlier in the month, showing her toughness.

Leading up to the race, the press asked Tony if he would change the command since it wasn't only gentlemen this time. He responded that the mechanics actually start the engines, not the drivers, so it might still be accurate. Indy cars aren't equipped with starters; the crews use portable starters to fire the engines. While I think Tony was being facetious and had every intention of being inclusive, this created a bit of controversy. Kay Bignotti announced she would be the mechanic to start Janet's car, removing any pretext for delivering the usual line.

As the moment arrived, Tony gripped the microphone and announced:

> In company with the first lady to ever qualify at Indianapolis, gentlemen, start your engines.

The crowd erupted in cheers.

At the same instant, the amplifier fuse blew again in the booth. Our headphones went silent. We could only hope for a quick fix as the parade laps went by. Our mics were fine, but I had no idea what the announcers in the Turns were saying. They could hear me, but I couldn't hear them. After the green flag, the engineers pointed in the directions of the turns and cued when I should jump into the narration. By lap four, I had a transistor radio in the booth so I could hear the others. It took until lap twenty-one for everything to function properly.

The race came down to Gordon Johncock, who led 129 laps, and A. J. Foyt, who challenged close behind. Gordy really suffered from the heat. The crew dumped ice water on him during his last two pits.

Heat exhaustion is a real danger for drivers. Carl Scarborough died from heat exhaustion at the 1953 race. In 1913, Frenchman Jules

Goux coped with the heat of the ninety-degree day by downing an entire bottle of champagne at each of his four pit stops. On Victory Lane he announced to the reporters, in his native tongue, "Without the good wine, I would not have won." While historians are skeptical as to how much he drank, officials expressly banned alcohol for the next season.

With only sixteen laps to go, Gordy's crankshaft broke. The Wildcat let out a plume of smoke, and the car came to a stop. Gordy ran straight over to the infield and jumped into Dry Ditch Creek to cool off. A. J. took the lead and a record fourth checkered flag at Indy.

On the victory lap in the pace car, A. J. asked Tony Hulman to ride beside him in the back of the convertible—Tony had always sat in the front passenger seat. Fans never cheered as loud as they did for these beloved men of the Speedway.

I will always think of A. J. in Victory Lane, arms raised, tossing his signature red gloves. He seemed to be looking right at me. In retrospect, it occurs to me he might have been looking at the 500 Princesses in the row just below the booth. He held up four fingers, one for each victory. A. J. offered words of advice that reminded me of what Eddie Sachs once wrote: "Don't be a quitter if you want to be a winner."

The time had come for my closing remarks. I looked down at my notes:

> The race has now been run. The hopes, the dreams, the anticipation of a year's waiting has now been altered, transformed, and cast into solid reality by the running of the sixty-first 500 mile race. . . .

> Very soon our microphones will record only silence and the reporting job will be complete. For me, it is a conclusion of a month that was filled with mixed emotions from the grief of the loss of one of my closest friends, Sid Collins, to whom we

dedicate this broadcast, to the excitement and elation at being able to broadcast an Indianapolis 500 mile race. It has been my life's dream. . . .

To me, this is more than a race of 500 miles. It is a group of dynamic men operating at the pinnacle of their achievement. It is a proving ground of character.

Until next May, this is Paul Page from the Master Control Tower at Indianapolis wishing you good morning, good afternoon, or good evening, depending upon where in the world you are right now. We are at the Indianapolis Motor Speedway, the world's greatest racecourse. Thank you, and goodbye.

With that, I collapsed into a chair. I had stood the entirety of the race.

I lingered in the booth thanking my colleagues for their great work: Freddie Agabashian, Donald Davidson, Jack Morrow, and John DeCamp. I was exhausted but felt a profound sense of accomplishment. As I left the track, heading to the Iron Skillet restaurant to join friends and family, I wondered if I would get to do it again.

Janet Guthrie invited me to a small party with her crew at her apartment. I stopped by after dinner. Despite a disappointing exit on lap twenty-seven due to a timing gear, they were in high spirits. At the door, a crew member informed me it was a team-only party, and I could stay only if I were properly initiated. Before I could respond, he put a pair of scissors to the rather expensive silk tie I bought especially for the big day. Left with half a tie, I was raucously welcomed onto the team.

The next night I chatted with Tony Hulman at the Victory Dinner. He said, "I understand you did a nice job." I couldn't bring myself to ask about next year.

As the summer wore on, I had no inkling of whether I might return as the Voice.

During the Hoosier Hundred at the State Fairgrounds, I worked the public address system and interviewed drivers. Right before the start of the race, Tony Hulman climbed out of a pace car, stepped closer to me, and asked, "Are you getting ready to do next year's race?" I said, "Yessir." He gave me a big hug and added, "You did a beautiful job. We're all so proud of you."

Tony was a gentleman. He loved the fans. He handed out garage and pit passes as he walked the grounds. He wanted a modern track hospital for both drivers and spectators. If fans needed assistance, the track hospital provided care at no charge. They could return to the stands rather than spend the day at the city hospital. When anyone thanked him, he would always say, "This is our party. This is something for all of us."

Tony's kindness touched nearly everyone he met. Sam Posey took a lot of heat for a cheating scandal when his team tried to re-qualify the same car. He ended up bumped from the field and out of the race. Sam was devastated. Out of the blue, Tony called and asked Sam to join him for a day of public appearances across southern Indiana. It was clearly intended to take his mind off his troubles. Sam recounted it in his autobiography, *The Mudge Pond Express*:

> He treated me with the utmost kindness and hospitality and introduced me as a man who had had a little trouble at the Speedway this year; he said he hoped it would be soon forgotten and that I would enjoy coming back to the Speedway next year.

Before that day, Sam had met Tony only once to shake his hand.

Whenever Tony hit on an idea for improving the track, he would say to Joe Cloutier or whoever he was with, "Wouldn't it be nice if we—." It would be done immediately. And it was always intended to make a better experience for the fans. If a smaller team on a shoe-string budget needed a part, Tony would often buy it. He might even quietly sponsor the team.

Every year in October, Tony threw a party on the grounds of the Speedway Motel for everyone who worked at the track during May. Called "The Sportsman's Dinner," the menu was "duck thumpins" for appetizers and steak for dinner. Tony banned anyone from giving speeches. I last saw Tony at that dinner in 1977, as we had our picture taken beside the pace car. It would be Tony's last Sportsman's Dinner.

Just a few days later, Tony had stomach surgery and died unexpectedly from heart complications. Racing lost its greatest friend, the savior of the Speedway.

I sold my race car that fall. Earlier in the year, at Blackhawk Farms in Beloit, Wisconsin, my good friend Rod Feree parked his camper near my trailer. Rod raced a Formula Vee. The next day, I stood only a hundred feet away when he spun out and hit the wall, bursting into flames. I ran over with the safety workers who only carried fire extinguishers. They were insufficient for the flames. I kept turning around looking for the firetruck, but it never came.

When the flames died down and we got Rod out of the car, he didn't have a pulse. I performed CPR as we rode in the hearse/ambulance to the hospital. Rod died, perhaps of a heart attack before the crash. There was no autopsy.

I was angry. At this level, there shouldn't have been a fatality. Under the rules, every race was supposed to have a firetruck on standby. I wrote the SCCA board a long report on Rod's accident.

I later learned races could avoid the firetruck requirement, and many others, by giving notice to the participants. I'm sure Rod would have raced anyway, but that notice wasn't included in the materials.

I returned to Blackhawk Farms later that season. As I began to unload my race car, track owner Tito Nappe confronted me. He told me I wasn't welcome. He accused me of trying to start a boycott with my letter and told me to leave. I talked to the stewards, but they worried Tito was hot enough to chain the gates and cancel the race if I didn't go.

I left the track and sold my car. It was time. Any hopes I had of becoming a professional driver died long ago.

In 2019, I was the honored guest at Road America in Elkhart Lake, Wisconsin, for the fiftieth anniversary of the Formula Ford. A lot of beautiful old Formula Fords were on display. I learned, with some regret, that my old car would be worth about $30,000 now.

On the last day of November, our Operation Life ambulance was dispatched to a farm near Greencastle, Indiana. We found a farmer trapped beneath his overturned tractor, bleeding from several wounds. One was an arterial bleeder, and he was lucky he hadn't already bled out. With the artery under control, we went to work on his leg. It was a grisly two-bone lower leg tib-fib break, also called a skier's fracture. I would see a worse one the next day.

On December 1, 1977, a Thursday, class was in session on the campus of Speedway High School, due west of the Indianapolis Motor Speedway. As the WIBC news chopper continued on its scheduled flight path, the three of us inside felt the pop of the rotors, the sudden drop, and the frightening realization of the inevitable. Unbuckling my safety harness, I felt a split second of relief as I saw the school building go by—at least we weren't taking any children out with us. Then I saw the green grass, and then black.

With my belts off, I crashed through the glass bubble and somersaulted through the air before landing on my left leg. My forehead bore an imprint from hitting the instrument panel on the way out. I returned to consciousness upon hitting the ground, and I saw helicopter parts still bouncing around me. I heard the pilot asking over and over, "Paul, what happened?"

In the sky above me, the mangled main rotor blade dangled from the chopper. Lying on my back on the cinder track that rimmed the football field, it occurred to me I must be alive.

I still felt detached from myself—almost disembodied. Every moment of the crash seemed like a slide show. Years later I talked with Mike Mancuso, the world champion aerobatic pilot, about his plane crash. He felt the same detachment—almost a view from above.

Instinctively, probably from my military and paramedic training, I made a clinical assessment of myself. I felt the warmth of blood running over my face. Vague sensations in my left leg told me it was broken. I knew better than trying to sit up to look at it. I felt little pain. I figured I was okay.

Then I sensed the suffocating fumes of aviation fuel. The helicopter's fuel tank had cracked open, and pooling gasoline began soaking my down-filled jacket. Any spark would set a bonfire. The only thing most drivers fear is fire, and I could see the fear in the firefighters' faces as they watched the pool of fuel spread wider into the field.

The brave firefighters from the Speedway fire station next door to the high school arrived within seconds. I saw them risk their lives for me, running into danger with hoses in hand. It's something I'll never forget.

The Medic 1 ALS ambulance arrived. I could hear someone arguing with a school official that didn't want the ambulance and firetrucks driving over the grass of the football field. I can only imagine how angry he would have been if the helicopter touched down at the fifty-yard line instead of the running track.

I knew the paramedics of course, and I knew the drill. I became suspicious when one said, "You have a bloody nose is all," but no mention of my leg. "But we need to start an IV," he ordered.

"No way; I'm fine. You're not sticking me!" I told him. "Have it your way," he demurred.

As they went about their work, I learned John Connolly and Ed Moss were going to make it. I felt elated and almost lucky. I just survived a fall from five hundred feet with only a bloody nose and a broken leg. Or so I thought.

Siren screaming, we passed the main gate of the Speedway on our way to Methodist Hospital. The closer we got, the more sensation returned. When we bumped over the railroad tracks at 16th and Stadium Drive, all sensation—and I mean pain—returned at once. The ambulance's interior grew warm, then hot. "Turn the heat down," I told them. "It's way too warm."

"No, it's not. You're going into shock," came the reply.

"That's ridiculous," I argued, "I can't go into shock from a bloody nose and a broken leg."

The medic responded, "Here, see for yourself."

I sat up, and they pulled back the drape from my left leg. It revealed an open tib-fib fracture, and it was definitely a different vantage point as a patient. Both bones stuck out of my leg, and my foot rested alongside my knee. Half my leg dangled by tendons. I tried hard to relax and not move.

Dr. Henry Bock and his team waited for the ambulance. I was relieved to see my old roommate and colleague. I asked him for morphine. Henry said little as he looked at my leg and ordered meds. With the drugs, I felt less pain, but I started to worry more. Henry told me the surgeon for the Indianapolis Fire Department, Dr. John Seltzer, was on his way. They considered me a brother first responder.

John was another friend, and he didn't say a word as he examined me. After a quick consultation with Henry, he leaned over and said it might be better if he turned me over to someone else who could keep a professional detachment.

That caused the worst-case scenarios to enter my head. Am I going to survive this? Will I lose my leg?

They called in Dr. Bob Brueckman, the city's top orthopedic surgeon. He barked at his assistants as they started to move me, "Let's put him under first." Just as gruffly, he said, "Paul, I don't think I can save your foot, but I'll try." I smiled—I liked him immediately, and then lights out.

I awoke in the morning in a double room with my pilot in the next bed. Neither of us was in any shape to talk. The next day brought another surgery, and I discovered my leg dangling from a rope connected to a bar over the bed. Dr. Bob made his rounds with a couple of residents in tow. One of them was Dr. Terry Trammel—everyone just called him Trammel. Dr. Bob told me he saved my foot. I'd be here a while, but I should walk again.

Trammel later removed drains from my leg wounds. Two went fine, but the third did not. In a rookie mistake, he yanked, and the tip of the tube got hooked on an orthopedic pin. Part of the drain was stuck inside my leg, and it wouldn't be coming out easy. The next day Dr. Bob asked me to join him for a meal in the doctors' dining room. I stared daggers at Trammel as he sat across from me, squirming. Dr. Bob began to laugh. As are the twists in life, Trammel went on to play a huge role in racing, and we became close friends.

One of the greatest things about race fans is their kindness. Hundreds of well-wishers sent me handwritten notes, raising my spirits each day. Racing and journalism are tight-knit communities, and I had so many visitors: journalists, broadcasters, owners, crew members, 500 winners; even a US senator and a governor.

To bring peace to the hospital and rest for me, the nurses declared "no more visitors." Two FBI agents breached the embargo when they appeared behind a very serious-looking nurse. They had flashed their badges and requested privacy, saying, "This is an investigation." As soon as the door closed, they produced a bottle of scotch. It was of course my old pals Bob and Arch.

I slowly recovered my strength. To break the tedium at the hospital, I occasionally worked shifts in the ER. During the Blizzard of '78, Henry Bock needed lots of help as several nurses couldn't make it in. I received some strange looks in my surgical gown and white coat as I sutured patients from my wheelchair.

Those months in the hospital became a sabbatical: a time to stop and think. Every moment of my life, I was on the move. In those endless days of recovery, I had to face my thoughts and emotions. I needed to grieve.

I grieved the loss of Sid Collins. It's a hard burden when your lifelong dream comes true through the suicide of your mentor. Like in racing, Bob Sweikert always felt like he didn't deserve the win in 1955 when Bill Vukovich was killed. Somehow you feel guilty for being happy and feel like an imposter at the same time.

I also realized how angry I was at Sid. He died alone with no family at his side because of his stupid pride. It defeated him. Pride is a double-edged sword. His commitment to excellence in his work propelled him to greatness. But he confused his life with his livelihood. For me and many of us who follow our passion, if we're not careful, we set ourselves up for the same emptiness of success. This was the last lesson I learned from Sid.

Somehow, I also felt cheated. On that special day when I became the Voice of the 500, a hundred million people tuned in. But the three people I wanted to be there most were gone: Uncle Harry, my mom, and Sid. As time went by, I made peace with it.

Near-death experiences bring life into focus. In the words of Sid, death comes for us all, and at the rate of sixty seconds every minute.

I felt like the stopwatch timing my laps had stopped, and the Great Timekeeper wound it back. I had been granted a second chance.

Whatever time I had left, I resolved to follow my passions, to seize what opportunities might come, and to be grateful for all of it. I hadn't yet left my mark on the world. This was only the beginning.

CHAPTER 9

Onto the Small Screen

It's a contest for high stakes . . .
to decide who is the best. It's that basic.
—*Bobby Unser*

Before the crash, I pitched the IMS Radio Network on a way to broadcast the whole Indy car series, not just the Indy 500. NASCAR had a similar network. It presented a big logistical puzzle: dedicated lines at every track, road equipment, reserved frequencies, and selling it to stations. It wouldn't be a moneymaker, but the PR for the series and the Indy 500 might make it worthwhile.

The day before the first race, Dr. Brueckman cut off my cast. It was only a brief reprieve, but I'd take what I could get. I bought an oversized pair of tennis shoes and caught a plane to Phoenix.

I chose Bob Jenkins to work color commentary for me. Jenks had a similar story—a radio guy who loved racing. He fell in love with the Speedway as a kid. When his dad told him to mow the lawn, a ten-year-old Jenks pretended he was mowing beside the track at the Speedway. Rounding out our team were Tom Allebrandi, our engineer, and station coordinator Gloria Novotney.

On a shoestring budget, we hired local talent to report from the pits and turns. Sometimes they flaked out, as happened the day before the race at Ontario, California. For a replacement, I called Gary Gerould out of the blue, and he booked a flight within minutes. Working as a sports reporter in Sacramento, Gary's television station sent him to Indianapolis every May, but we had never met. With no warm-up and finding his spot just minutes before the broadcast, Gary was rock solid. That race marked the first of our many great adventures in broadcasting, and the beginning of a life-long friendship.

At Phoenix the roof of the timing tower, four stories up, served as our broadcast booth. With no railing, I spun in place as the cars went around, bum leg and all. The mic and headset cords coiled around me with each lap, threatening to trip me. I literally had to unwind during breaks.

It's difficult to describe the closeness among the owners, drivers, teams, and press in those days. Life on the circuit was half family reunion and half traveling carnival—like the month of May in Indianapolis extended to eight months. I loved every minute of it.

On a flight home from Houston, I sat with Bob Jenkins, Robin Miller, and Dr. Steven Olvey in first class. A couple of the first-class flight attendants were on their farewell flights, one of whom was a bride-to-be, and the whole crew was in a celebratory mood. Robin hijacked the cabin microphone and heckled the drivers and USAC officials back in coach. Some moments must be lived to the fullest. Months after rising from the ashes of my crash, I found myself doing what I loved most, and I was euphoric on that flight.

After the race in Trenton, New Jersey, I dropped off Dr. Bruce White at the local airport so he could catch the USAC chartered flight. Bruce sat on the USAC safety team, and he was one of my closest friends. He offered me a seat on his flight, but I declined. With my leg still in bad shape, the little plane would be cramped. I had a flight out of Philadelphia and dinner reservations at Bookbinders before that. I told Bruce I'd still beat him back to Indy.

Bruce's flight hit severe weather with 100-miles-per-hour winds. The plane crashed southeast of Indianapolis, killing the pilot Don Mullendore and all eight passengers. USAC lost a lot of talent: technical directors Frankie Delroy and Ross Teeguarden, communications director Ray Marquette, starter Shim Malone, typographist Judy Phillips, sprint supervisor Don Peabody, and registrar Stan Worley. Their deaths hit all of us hard.

As May arrived in 1978, the whole front row qualified north of 200 mph with Tom Sneva on the pole for a second year in a row. Mario Andretti took time off to win an F1 race in Belgium on his way to becoming a World Champion that year. A. J. Foyt took advantage of a rained-out practice weekend to place third in a NASCAR race.

With the 500 dedicated to the memory of Tony Hulman, we debated whether to use a recording of Tony reciting the command. In the end, Tony's widow Mary chose to pick up the torch and continue the tradition. With Janet Guthrie back in the field, Mary chose to say, "Lady and gentlemen, start your engines." It became the standard command for races with women behind the wheel.

On Race Day, Al Unser Sr. led 121 laps. With twenty laps to go, he bent his front wing, causing him to lose speed. Tom Sneva gained each lap, but Al Sr. held him off for his third checkered flag. He went on to win at Pocono and Ontario, becoming the only driver to claim the triple crown of Indy cars. Janet Guthrie, in spite of an agonizing broken wrist that she hid from the officials, secured a formidable ninth-place finish in her no longer green car.

Johnny Rutherford drove Al Sr.'s winning Lola at the Goodwood Festival of Speed in England decades later. The handling was terrible, but he knew the car was set up correctly by the restoration team at the IMS Hall of Fame. When J. R. got back in the States, he called Al Sr. and told him how rough it had been. Al Sr. felt vindicated. Back in the day, no one believed him when he complained about the handling. Sometimes it takes a beast to win at Indianapolis.

Victory Lane is a special moment in history, and photographs are displayed for generations. Chester Ricker, the long-time chief of timing and scoring, liked to play a little trick in the panoramic shot of Victory Lane—then taken in multiple phases. In his distinctive riding britches and circular black rim glasses, Chester would stand on one end and race to the other end as the camera moved along. As a result, he appeared on both sides of the photograph.

As Lou Palmer interviewed Al Sr. in Victory Lane, I noticed out of the corner of my eye something out of place. A reporter with press credentials leaned into the car. He held a microphone, but the end of the cord flopped disconnected on the ground. We later discovered the credentials were issued to Movietone News, which hadn't existed in years. Crashing Victory Lane was this guy's way of getting his face in the pictures.

Gate-crashing is an age-old tradition at the Speedway. Generations of scofflaws have schemed to avoid the admission fee as a matter of principle. This might be accomplished by scaling fences, hiding in sheds, or climbing trees. The most famous gate-crasher was One-Eyed Connelly. Back in the 1920s, he was so bold as to have embroidered on the back of his green flannel shirt:

All gates I've crashed,
I'm here to tell.
I'll crash St. Pete's
And then crash H—.

Other common gate crashers are rabbits and dogs. Bobby Unser once got an extra chance to qualify when he hit a bird. Al Unser Sr. hit a rabbit during the 500 in 1988. Normally that wasn't worth reporting, but it flew up and hit Rick Mears's windshield, bringing out a caution. Without giving me a head's up, my producer replayed the footage of the rabbit in slow-motion. So how do you narrate that? I said, "Here we have a rabbit in his last moments." I emceed the Victory Dinner the next night and arranged something special for Al Sr. When he came up to claim his envelope, I had a state conservation officer meet him at the podium. For hunting rabbits out of season and without a license, he handed Al Sr. a faux ticket.

I never returned to my job as a reporter for WIBC after the crash. I decided to go into television reporting and signed with Channel 13 as a feature reporter. I got a truck and a cameraman and free reign to choose my stories. With my newfound fame from calling the 500, and the sensationalism of the helicopter crash, doors opened for me. Having learned another lesson from Sid Collins' mistakes, I wouldn't turn down an opportunity I might regret.

CBS called and offered me a spot as a pit reporter for the USAC Texas World Grand Prix in College Station. Driver Duane "Pancho" Carter Jr. and I caught the same flight and split a rental car. I wanted to look my best, so the afternoon before the race I went to a barber. At his suggestion, I got curls put in. When I met Pancho for dinner, he pointed to my hair and said, "You look like a tumbleweed with eyes."

After a trip to the pharmacy to pick up hair straightener, I felt ready for my debut on network television. Barely a minute into the broadcast, I heard shouts in my headphone, "Get off it. Get off it. The Pope is dead." They cut away from me and switched to the Vatican on the death of Pope Paul VI.

Leading late in the race, A. J. Foyt waited until the last minute to pit during a caution. The pace car began to accelerate for the restart. A. J. realized he waited too long and would lose a lap. He pulled up to the driver's side of the pace car as it was about to head down pit lane and started wildly pointing at the pace car's wheels. Distracted, the driver of the pace car missed the pits and took another lap; A. J. hit the brakes and swerved into the pits for fuel and tires. A. J. kept the lead and got the win. Johnny Rutherford told me that wasn't the first time A. J. pulled that kind of move.

In the victory circle, I kneeled on the sidepod of A. J.'s car, waiting through the commercial break to interview him live. Driver Steve Krisiloff walked right up and called A. J. a cheater for his stunt with the pace car. A. J., still standing in his cockpit, threw a lunging punch. It barely nicked Steve and almost connected with me. A. J.'s bear of a mechanic Big John Fisher hoisted Steve up before a real fight could start. The camera went live and caught Big John carrying Steve off. We did the interview like nothing happened.

It was an emotional moment for A. J. His mother was ill in the hospital, and he dedicated his win to her. The tough old veteran choked up a bit during the interview.

After the race, Pancho drove toward the airport with a bit of a heavy foot. A trooper pulled us over not far from the track and asked, "Who do you think you are, one of these race car drivers?"

Pancho answered, "Yeah, I finished third." His honesty was not met with leniency. We followed the trooper to a justice of the peace and paid a fine.

CBS invited me to the suite for the 1979 Daytona 500, the first live national telecast of that race. It started to rain and looked like a loser for the network. A lot of well-wishers in the hospitality suite began to leave, but I stuck around and drank beer with CBS Sports president Neil Pilsen. The track dried out, and it became a fantastic event.

Watching the duel between A. J. Foyt and rookie Dale Earnhardt Sr. would have been worth the price of admission alone. Then came the final lap. Leader Cale Yarborough and Donnie Allison started trading paint before they took each other out in a wreck, putting Richard Petty on his way to a car-length win in front of Darrell Waltrip. In the meantime, Donnie's brother Bobby stopped at the wreck and a fistfight broke out between Cale and the Allison brothers. Gary Gerould gave a play-by-play of the fight for the MRN radio broadcast. NASCAR had arrived in the national spotlight.

NBC also called and put me in as a pit reporter at the Michigan International Speedway for the Norton Twin 200 USAC stock car race. I felt like a bit of an outsider. I wasn't nearly as prepared as I was for Indy cars. Producer Don Ohlmeyer reminded me all you have to do is walk up with a mic—these guys want to be interviewed.

Having passed my "auditions" for both networks, I had to make a choice. It just happened both offers arrived on the same day. I went with NBC. I already worked for the local NBC affiliate. They guaranteed I could be in Indy for all of May and continue as the Voice of the 500. I would also cover Indy car races for NBC's *SportsWorld*. I hit the big time and could keep the best of both worlds.

Back in April of 1978, I flew to Boca Raton, Florida, to give a speech for IBM. Still hobbling, I caught some fresh air on a walk along the beach and ran into Tyler Alexander of McLaren Racing. He raved about the "White Paper," something Dan Gurney wrote. Dan wanted to create a competing Indy car racing series operated by the team owners. It soon became a reality: the Championship Auto Racing

Teams (CART) series. It was an open rebellion against USAC and the Indianapolis Motor Speedway.

The split was a long time coming. Since 1909, the American Automobile Association (AAA) had sanctioned the races at the Speedway. In 1955, two crashes rocked the headlines: two-time champ Bill "the Mad Russian" Vukovich's fatal crash at the Indy 500, and the carnage at the 24 Hours of Le Mans where a car flew into the stands, killing the driver and eighty spectators. Politicians and editorial boards across America demanded an end to motorsports. The AAA buckled under the pressure and abruptly abolished its racing arm, the Contest Board.

Tony Hulman convened a steering committee tasked with replacing AAA. He asked a local magistrate judge to chair the discussions that led to the formation of USAC. This new body retained most of the same officials and rules from the AAA system.

USAC worked well when the "Championship Trail" remained a series of small events that kept the drivers busy, and only the Indy 500 purse really mattered. That began to change with series sponsors and broadcast rights. Growth in racing led it to be billed as the "Sport of the Seventies." The magnificent Ontario Motor Speedway, a near replica of the Indianapolis Motor Speedway with modern luxury suites, opened in 1970. It helped propel the concept that the series could be bigger than its biggest race.

By the late '70s, racing was no longer just a hobby for rich sportsmen owners like Al Dean, Lindsay Hopkins, and Bob Bowes who sponsored their own cars. They did it for the love of racing and didn't expect a return on their investment. With big companies like Marlboro, Gatorade, and Viceroy spending hundreds of thousands of dollars to have a car carry their name and logo, the team owners now expected to make a profit.

Sponsorship money didn't ensure a profit, but it did ignite an arms race: the cars became more expensive, the crews bigger and more sophisticated. And no money is free. The sponsors wanted more control: viewership, placement, message.

USAC tried to keep everyone happy. The thirty-two-member board had appointments reserved to team owners, drivers, track owners, sponsors, and even fans. It became unwieldy. Too often members spent board meeting lunch breaks running to a phone to ask a big sponsor or supplier which way to vote on something.

Dan Gurney believed the solution to rising costs could only be rising revenues. Dan blamed the track owners' piecemeal promotion of the series and USAC's lack of business savvy for starving the teams. He wanted to force track owners to open their books and let the teams decide the size of the purses. The White Paper declared war on the track owners, including the Indianapolis Motor Speedway:

> It appears that a 'show down' with the Indianapolis Motor
> Speedway is or should be the first target. They are the ones
> who can afford it. We should re-negotiate the TV contract
> (our rights—not theirs) and we should double the purse.

The original proposal would have maintained USAC as the sanctioning body. USAC had an able leader in Dick King, a tall and imposing man with a reassuring smile. He had a way of turning his head toward you with a sly grin when he was amused. Dick worked hard to keep it all together. But he didn't have the gravitas of Tony Hulman. The plane crash left him even more shorthanded.

In the fall of 1978, the Speedway loyalists on the USAC Board rejected Dan's proposed changes. At the Penske Christmas party in Detroit, some of the most powerful teams split and formed CART, including Penske, Gurney, McLaren, Patrick, Foyt, and Chaparral. Like most other professional sports, the team owners would purchase franchises and then share in the revenues from television and other rights.

CART's PPG Indy Car World Series became a reality. It also marked the first shift to "Indy car" in describing the series.

Men like Penske and Patrick fight to win, and CART waged a brutal assault on USAC's race schedule. They pressured Phoenix to switch sides and handed CART the first race of the season—I worked that race for NBC. Penske owned the Michigan International Speedway, and he canceled its two USAC races. Penske leased Trenton, striking two more. He rescheduled the Trenton CART races for the same days as the televised USAC races in Milwaukee and the Texas World Speedway. Pocono got a competing race as well. Because the television contracts required participation by fifteen of the top twenty drivers, USAC could lose their broadcasts entirely. Ontario saw the writing on the wall and also switched to CART.

Perhaps uneasy with the tactics, A. J. Foyt returned to USAC, blasting the other CART owners. While negotiations continued, the Speedway had enough. In late April of 1979, USAC rejected the Indy 500 entries for six of the CART teams. It banned nineteen drivers, including stars like Johnny Rutherford, Al Unser Sr., Bobby Unser, and Gordon Johncock. Another twenty-five CART drivers were accepted. Johnny Rutherford blamed A. J.:

> Let them have their chicken-feed race. Let Foyt win his fifth Indy. Then maybe he'll announce his retirement in Victory Circle. Then we'll be rid of him.

Vicious rumors circulated, even suggesting CART was just a gambit by Roger Penske to force the grieving Hulman family into selling the Speedway to him.

Challenging the lockout, CART sued USAC, its board of directors, IMS, IMS president Joe Cloutier, and other owners and drivers, including A. J. Foyt. It sought an injunction forcing the Speedway to honor their entries for the 500.

Like any business, the Speedway found itself in court on occasion, usually after a spectator got hurt. In one of those cases, a lawyer had Tony Hulman on the stand. The lawyer couldn't resist asking him to disclose the most closely guarded secret in motorsports. He asked, "How many people actually attend the Indianapolis 500?"

Tony thought for a moment and replied, "A lot." When asked if he could be more specific, he paused a little longer and responded, "A *whole* lot." On the third try, the judge sustained an objection to the line of questioning. All of us in the public seats chuckled and let out a sigh of disappointment.

At the injunction hearing, Dan Gurney, Johnny Rutherford, and Al Unser Sr. explained that their livelihoods depended on racing at Indy. Their team sponsorships required them to race in the 500. Without the purse at the 500, the season would be a loss for the teams and drivers. Judge James E. Noland ruled on the third day of May that the drivers had a right to work and the CART teams' entries would be honored. But the judge wasn't blind; he noted the "considerable evidence that the owners tried to coerce the IMS management into rule changes." A countersuit from USAC alleged the same types of violations of the antitrust laws that CART alleged against USAC. It was shaping up to be a hot May in Indy.

In May of 1979, USAC officials received complaints that teams were violating the rules by adjusting their pop-off valves (the mechanism used to limit the boost pressure in turbochargers). The next week, officials disqualified three cars for the same types of adjustments that weren't cited the week before. As qualifying continued, USAC offered a clarification that certain adjustments were permissible. It brought more protests because cars bumped in the meantime didn't have the advantage of making those adjustments. USAC reversed and banned the adjustments once again.

USAC earned a black eye over its handling of the rules. CART took advantage of it in the press, challenging USAC's competence to run the series. On the Saturday before the race, officials allowed eleven cars affected by the controversy to make qualifying attempts. With two hundred thousand people usually attending qualifications in those days, it seemed eerily quiet as I watched the closed qualifying session. Two cars made the cut, creating a Field of 35 and an additional Row 12 with two cars.

The mythical Field of 33 was not etched in stone and handed down by the gods of racing. The first Indy 500 had forty cars, and the field expanded and contracted over the years until 1934. The number thirty-three actually came from a AAA safety regulation issued in 1911 that limited race entrants to one car per four hundred feet of track, or thirteen cars on a one-mile track, and the same interval for larger tracks. The Speedway is 2.5 miles, or 13,200 feet, and if divided by four hundred, equals precisely thirty-three.

For Race Day 1979, the Speedway officials scrapped the old Electro Pacer light system. Instead, a pace car would come out on cautions, and the cars would be allowed to bunch up behind it as they awaited the green flag. New to the team, I hired Bob Jenkins to cover the backstretch for the IMS Radio Network.

Second year driver Rick "the Rocket" Mears started on the pole, but the Unser brothers led 174 laps. Al Sr.'s yellow Chapparal had transmission problems at the halfway mark, and Bobby's gearbox hobbled him with twenty laps to go. Rick found the front again, and a caution with eight laps to go allowed A. J. Foyt to creep up to second. But A. J. needed to pass fifteen cars to get to Rick. A. J. charged with everything he had until his engine gave out on the last lap. He coasted to second place. Rick got the checkered flag. In retrospect, it's very fitting that Rick's first win came from edging out the veteran four-time champ.

By 1980, USAC sanctioned only the Indy 500 and Pocono races. CART later leased Pocono as well. The Speedway hired John Cooper as president, replacing Joe Cloutier. John's efforts at reunification, including the joint sponsoring of five races with CART under the

Championship Racing League, were fruitless. After a short tenure, John left and Joe returned.

While continuing to regulate sprint cars and midgets, USAC lost the first open-wheel racing war. It would govern one Indy car race, not a series.

The series sponsor PPG hired Jim Chapman, an impressive marketing and PR man. Jim once represented Babe Ruth. Always dressed to the nines, Jim brought the catered hospitality tent for the teams and sponsors—a huge step up from the track concession stands or NASCAR-great Frank Mundy making sandwiches for Team Penske. Success kept Jim traveling constantly, but he had a golden rule: always be home on Tuesdays for dinner with family.

With Dick King at USAC and Jim as a backchannel to CART, they mostly kept the peace during the years that followed. In 1983, the rift further narrowed when the Indy 500 became a point-earning event on the CART series.

CHAPTER 10

A Sportscaster in Full

That's what scares me, actually. Not dying. Losing.
—*Al Unser Sr*

I could barely contain my excitement on my flight to Japan to cover sumo wrestling. I felt honored to tour the sacred arenas and training complexes, called stables. We recorded a segment barefoot on the clay floor of the ring. I found it inspiring that, at the end of sumo wrestlers' careers, they remain in training at the stables as they return to a healthy weight. Other sports could learn from this ancient tradition, caring for its athletes as they head into their next phase in life.

The culture shock hit me on my next trip driving through snow-covered Eagle River, Wisconsin, on my way to the Ski-Doo World Championship snowmobile races. Like a lot of these sports, we shot the intro and the ending on location. The announcing all happened at 30 Rock, NBC Burbank, or the famed Glen Glenn Sound where we narrated in front of a big screen.

During the 1981 Major League Baseball players' strike, NBC frantically searched for content to fill its gaps in scheduling. My air miles rocketed. I flew to Budapest on short notice, and without a pre-approved visa, to cover weightlifting, duckpin bowling, and a Rubik's Cube championship. It made me a bit nervous when two guards demanded to know why I was there and traveling alone. I had some difficulty completing my visa application on a typewriter with Cyrillic keys.

The Rubik's Cube World Championship was held inside the breathtaking Budapest Opera House. When the players only take fourteen seconds to solve the puzzle, it's similar to announcing drag racing. The network had not done its homework and expected each competitor to take several minutes.

When NBC assigned me to fencing, cycling, and judo for the 1980 Summer Olympics in Moscow, I felt over the moon. I covered the fencing Olympic trials at Princeton—quite a different world from dirt tracks in the Midwest. No doubt these guys were talented, but it was a far cry from a movie sword fight. Whether a touch counts depends on who has the "right of way," meaning if you stabbed the other guy first, you didn't necessarily score. In saber, you can score with any part of the blade to any part of the body, but almost all points come from tapping the top of a knee or the bottom of an elbow. However genteel the sport might be, the after-party I attended with some of those athletes rivaled the Snake Pit.

As it came to pass, President Jimmy Carter decided to punish the Russians for invading Afghanistan by crushing the Olympic dreams of hundreds of young American athletes with his boycott. Like many of those competitors, I never got another shot. I did get credit for announcing the 1988 Winter Olympics in Calgary, but that was just voiceover work at a studio in Indianapolis.

The cloak-and-dagger feel of traveling behind the Iron Curtain at the height of the Cold War was real. When I traveled to Odessa in Ukraine to cover World Championship Weightlifting, a minder followed me everywhere I went, keeping a short distance away. After a while, I started telling him where I was going. On the last night, I invited him to the wrap party at the hotel. He joined us and suggested a very nice brand of Mockba vodka. Several rounds in, each served in a frozen glass, I asked to see his KGB badge. When he set it on the table, I offered him a hundred-dollar bill for it on the spot. He accepted, proving that capitalism will always conquer communism.

When I started at Channel 13, a young reporter took pity on the poor radio guy in a leg cast who knew nothing about television. Sally Larvick taught me the ropes and helped type my teleprompter material. Sometime along the way Big John Fisher, with Foyt Racing, became friends with Sally. John knew Sally loved disco dancing, and he suggested I come along to the Teller's Cage in the Bank One Tower downtown. It was a favorite watering hole for folks in the news business. In addition to dancing, Sally went shot for shot with Big John that night. She was funny and whip-smart; the type of spitfire you might expect from an Italian family.

While the network sent me around the country and the world, Sally moved up to an anchor position in Nashville, Tennessee. When I flew American Airlines, I made sure my connecting flights came through its hub in Nashville. Our friendship grew. We shared the same biting and sarcastic sense of humor. We both had a passion for journalism.

Sally had blazed her own trail in broadcasting. She earned a degree from Bradley University in journalism and minored in sociology and psychology. In 1969, right out of college, she became a reporter at a Peoria, Illinois, television station. At first, she could only cover fluff pieces. She was told the viewers didn't want to hear the high pitch of a woman's voice delivering serious news. So Sally wrote the hard news for the male reporters—a woman told the story—but the people didn't hear her voice.

When none of the male reporters were available, Sally covered the start of a gruesome murder trial—a fourteen-year-old boy killed his sister and her friend with a shotgun. The station expected complaints. When no one made a fuss, they kept her on the story. She worked her way up to the anchor desk before coming to the larger Indianapolis market. Beautiful and brilliant, everyone noticed her immediately.

As we grew closer, our careers paths did not. We got engaged, and Sally inquired about positions in Indianapolis, but Channel 13's slots were full, and the other stations weren't interested in someone whose spouse worked for a competitor. Management in those days thought only single women took the job seriously—getting married turned it into just a hobby while waiting for the first baby to arrive.

In May of 1980, I asked Johnny Rutherford to be the expert for my station's daily updates from the Speedway. J. R. would have a very good month with a very good car.

Based on innovations in F1 cars, John Bernard perfected the "ground effects" on the Chaparral 2K. The concept is to channel air under the car through a narrow opening in the front and then out through a larger opening in the rear. As the air spreads out, it creates a vacuum that pulls the car to the ground. The downforce of these "underwings" or "Venturi tunnels" is superior to bolt-on wings. This cutting-edge technology put J. R. and his Yellow Submarine on the pole.

At the other end of the spectrum, rookie Roger Rager showed up with a stock-block Chevy in a used Wildcat chassis. The engine came out of a school bus. It had 250,000 miles on it, just the right "seasoning" for the mechanics to do brilliant work. Roger put the Carpenter School Bus Special on the inside of Row 4.

Rookie Tim Richmond, a young gregarious bear of an athlete, claimed the fastest unofficial speed for the month. I set up an interview with him for Channel 13. He showed up late and missed the segment. A bit hot, I explained that the station lost the story, and he lost the publicity. He needed to understand that you're only the new hotshot once; it's the relationships with fans, sponsors, and media that make a career. He genuinely apologized, and the conversation sparked a close friendship.

On Race Day, shortly before climbing into his car, Johnny Rutherford noticed a ladybug land on his shoulder—a sign of good luck. So it was. Leading 118 laps, J. R. took his third checkered flag at Indy on his way to winning the series that year. Tom Sneva, who started thirty-third, ripped through the ranks to finish in second place—his third time as runner-up in four years. Tim Richmond ran out of fuel on the final lap. While taking his victory lap, J. R. asked Tim if he needed a lift. Tim grabbed the rollover bar and perched on the side pod, in the first two-man lap at the 500 in many decades. The fans roared for the victor and the rookie favorite on their way to Victory Lane.

In attendance at my bachelor party were drivers, friends, my brothers, and even my stepfather. As is customary, someone booked a gorgeous and by all accounts talented dancer for the evening's entertainment. Her routine involved neither full nudity nor lewdness. However, a gross violation of decorum occurred when some of the attendees took photographs. Tim Richmond collected the film for safekeeping.

I had soon forgotten all about the photographs. Sally and I got married in the fall in front of both a Presbyterian minister and a Catholic priest.

About a year later, I caught up with Tim during a practice day before NASCAR's Charlotte National 500. Tim wrecked out of several Indy car races during his rookie year, and he switched to

NASCAR before the end of the season. As part of a rehearsal for my NBC crew, we sent a cameraman down to Tim's pit.

My producer noticed Tim showing something to his crewmates and told the cameraman to zoom in on whatever Tim was holding. Tim began displaying to the camera a stack of photos from my bachelor party. It provided all of us in the truck with an explicit recap of the dancer's performance. Our crew cackled with laughter. I think someone started narrating the action. It was all in good fun among our circle of friends on the broadcast truck.

Or so we thought.

Suddenly the phones in the truck started ringing. Angry words from the racetrack's management sent us all into a panic. Unbeknownst to us, the feed from the truck, which wasn't supposed to be going anywhere, went live on the closed-circuit feed for the track: the little TVs in the suites and the giant TVs in the stands. Our circle of friends included several thousand fans who were treated to pictures of a not-entirely-clothed dancer.

Though I can laugh about it now, it was unbearably embarrassing and could have gotten me fired. We firmly believed we were about to be ejected by track president Humpy Wheeler. He ran that beautiful and family-friendly venue with an iron fist, and he was not amused. After a considerable amount of conversation explaining the circumstances, and a thousand apologies, the uproar died down. Tim took the blame, though it wasn't his fault.

Nicknamed "Hollywood," Tim grew up wealthy. His star looks and larger-than-life persona roughly inspired the lead character in the *Days of Thunder* movie. Unfortunately, at the peak of his career, Tim contracted HIV and developed AIDS. His health declined to the extent he couldn't race.

The last time I saw Tim, rumors of his condition were swirling. I bumped into him in the lobby of the Hilton in Daytona Beach, and he asked me to come up to his room so we could talk in private. I saw a Tim Richmond I had never seen before. Gone was his smile, his bright and aggressive outlook, his competitive spirit. He was broken. He told me he had contracted the disease from a woman who was unaware of her condition. Tim felt trapped. Few people understood the disease back then, and it held a very negative social stigma.

When his health rebounded, Tim attempted a comeback, but NASCAR banned him after testing positive for over-the-counter drugs. Tim took another test and passed, but the damage was done. Tim sued, alleging the NASCAR doctor falsified his records. The doctor left NASCAR, and Tim received a settlement.

On August 13, 1989, the Rookie of the Year for the 1980 Indianapolis 500 died at age thirty-four. A friend made a public statement suggesting he died of injuries related to a motorcycle accident. Tim's family held a news conference to make sure the truth was told.

In that heartfelt conversation in Daytona Beach, Tim asked me not to speak of it to anyone, and I kept that promise until now. Later inducted into the International Motor Sports Hall of Fame, NASCAR named Tim one of the fifty best drivers in NASCAR history.

Johnny Rutherford branched into sportscasting at NBC, and we traveled to Italy to cover bobsledding. Fearless on the racetrack, J. R. refused to ride the bobsled for a promo. He thought it looked too dangerous. Back then, the networks often paid for spouses to come along. In the Golden Age of network television, people and family mattered. It all ended too soon when the execs sent in the accountants to squeeze every dime.

Betty Rutherford made the trip to Cervinia, on the backside of the Matterhorn. Every night we played Scopa, a card game, and drank espresso. Sally joined J. R. and me on another trip, along with Betty and their kids, for the motocross race at Farleigh Castle in England. We stayed at a stately manor house from the 1800s.

J. R. and Betty have a true racing romance. At my first race in 1960, J. R. also sat in the stands while Betty, a nurse, attended to spectators injured in the scaffolding collapse. When J. R. returned as a driver in 1963, he sat in his race car before the final phase of his rookie test. He noticed two young ladies by the fence. One of them winked at him. Betty denies winking and says she waved. Either way, it must have been quite a distraction because J. R. botched his final set of laps.

When he came to a stop, J. R. hung his head, fearing he had just washed out. Harlan Fengler wandered over and told J. R. he could try again in the morning. Elated, J. R. walked toward the garages where he crossed paths with Betty. He asked her out on a date for that night.

Betty's father was a bit skeptical when he learned she was seeing a race car driver. The first thing he asked her was, "Is he married?" Betty soon brought her folks to the track to meet J. R. Just as J. R. shook her dad's hand, the public address speaker boomed: "Johnny Rutherford, your wife and children are at the gate." Everyone froze for a second. J. R. looked over and saw drivers Chuck Hulse and Bobby Marshman rolling on the ground laughing just outside the phone booths.

J. R. soon proposed and they married that July. After women were allowed in the pits, Betty worked on J. R.'s crew for twenty years, wearing a headset and tracking laps. She had great words of wisdom like, "Don't fret over the things you can't do anything about." The two would celebrate more than fifty years of marriage.

While J. R. may have come from Texas dirt tracks wearing a T-shirt, he walked into 30 Rock in New York City wearing a tailored suit, his Daytona and Indy 500 rings, and a Rolex. My favorite dinner with J. R. was at Le Chanteclair, the restaurant owned by Rene Dreyfus.

A Frenchman and winner of the 1930 Monte Carlo, Rene enlisted in the army when Germany invaded, but his government sent him to the Indianapolis 500 in 1940 to engender goodwill. He failed to qualify, but he did take the wheel as a relief driver. When the Nazis overran Paris, Rene stayed in America. As a Jewish driver who often taunted the German drivers, he would be a target. Rene eventually joined the US Army and served in Europe.

At a table with Rene, J. R., and David Hobbs (a British Indy car driver and NBC announcer), the racing stories came one after another, late into the night. In the low light of that iconic restaurant covered in racing photographs, I soaked it all in. I had to listen to a thirty-minute-long joke from Hobbs, but it was worth it.

Gary Gerould said I acted like the mayor of 30 Rock as I made the rounds, schmoozing with my colleagues. That title probably belonged to Bryant Gumbel, who held court at Wolf's in Rockefeller Plaza. When Bryant visited Indy, I took him around the Speedway in my red Ferrari 308 GTSi at somewhere near 130 miles per hour. Bryant went into a total panic. It still makes me chuckle when I think of him as a young man, forever poised, losing all composure as we headed into Turn One.

I made certain I never missed out on a trip overseas. At 30 Rock, I overheard my assignment for bobsledding in Italy might be canceled due to a snowstorm. I rushed to the airport with Gary Gerould, telling him to ignore any pages over the speakers so we wouldn't get a message from the network pulling the plug. We made it on the flight and called in after we touched down in Rome. As I expected, the network sent us to the resort since we were already abroad. We landed in Turin and made our way to Cervinia. By morning, snowfall blocked the mountain passes and canceled the event.

"Trapped," we spent five nights like extras in a James Bond movie at the Grand Cristallo Hotel. When the roads cleared, we drove through the Monte Blanc Tunnel to Geneva where we "suffered" through three days of sightseeing. After another three days in London, we headed home. That was quite the paid vacation without a single minute of broadcast work—and Gary's first international assignment.

If my standard commercial flight out of London was booked on British Airways, which also operated the Concorde, I always went straight to the Concorde desk. I would threaten to take an earlier flight on a competing airline if they didn't find me a seat on the supersonic jet. Because the tickets had a cash value in those days, the airline never wanted to lose the money. It worked every time. As Jack Arute would say, this was one of my little scams. I considered it a moral imperative to take advantage of an opportunity to break the sound barrier on my way home.

In May of 1981, Bobby Unser captured the pole. A. J. Foyt got into a fracas with sportswriter Robin Miller. He smacked Robin in the back of his head and discussed removing a couple of his vital organs. In response, Robin wrote an article listing numerous alleged instances of cheating by A. J. In retaliation, A. J. sued Robin and his newspaper for libel. The days of that feud are long gone, and the two are close friends. A. J. still calls him "Poison Pen," now as a term of endearment, and Robin sincerely considers A. J. to be a living national treasure.

On Race Day, I watched a scary moment in the pits as a small reddish whirlwind swirled above Rick Mears's car as he leaped out—the invisible methanol flames caused very visible pain to Rick and two crew members. Danny "On the Gas" Ongais, aka "the Flyin' Hawaiian," slammed into the wall in Turn Three. I feared the worst. He survived with severe leg injuries. It was one of several horrifying crashes Danny survived over the years. In the closing laps, Bobby Unser edged out Mario Andretti by a solid five seconds to win his third Indy 500 at forty-seven years of age.

Hours after the race, Jim McKay and Jackie Stewart narrated the ABC tape-delayed broadcast. They made a big deal of one of Bobby's pit stops. None of the Speedway officials or my radio crew noticed, but in Jackie's opinion, Bobby broke the rules when he picked up a couple of spots coming out of the pits on a yellow.

While passing on a caution is against the rules, how a driver "blends" back into the race after a pit stop is less cut-and-dry.

Besides, that yellow flag came out for Gordon Smiley's wreck almost sixty laps before the checkered flag fell. Jim and Jackie already knew Bobby had won it when they remarked on Bobby's blending. Obviously, they were ginning up a controversy.

Partly prompted by ABC's telecast, Patrick Racing filed a protest on behalf of Mario. Chief Steward Tom Binford reviewed the footage late in the evening and posted the official results at eight the next morning. He handed Bobby a one-position penalty and declared Mario Andretti the winner.

Tom's decision was the equivalent of changing the winner of the Super Bowl on Monday morning on the grounds that a ref should have called offensive pass interference back in the third quarter.

As a matter of policy, Tom intentionally refused to tell drivers what penalty might apply to a particular violation—he didn't want drivers weighing whether cheating would be worth it. In this case, he should have thought long and hard about it. Tom later admitted if Bobby had received a one-lap penalty at the time of the violation, the odds were that Bobby would have still won it. But that never caused Tom to doubt whether he handled it the right way.

Questionable officiating has been a part of the Speedway from the very beginning. In a race in 1909, Lewis Strang's car caught fire and, unsolicited, crew members from other teams helped put out the flames. Speedway officials disqualified Lewis because it was against the rules to accept help from another team to fix a car. The officials relented, but Lewis fell five laps behind while he argued his case. At stock class races in 1910, officials disqualified the victorious Chevrolet brothers for violations announced a week later. The controversy irked Carl Fisher so much he decided the first Indianapolis 500 would be an open class and subject only to a maximum displacement of 600 cubic inches.

Team owner Roger Penske appealed Tom's ruling. The whole thing disgusted Bobby, and he wanted nothing to do with the appeal or the Speedway for that matter. He had been accused of cheating, and his win was taken away. After nineteen consecutive appearances, Bobby never raced the 500 again.

I had a front row seat during the appeal proceedings. In Bobby's corner was Jimmy Binns, who looked and acted the part of a big Philadelphia lawyer and former boxer. He hammered on the fact that Mario was guilty, to a lesser extent, of passing cars on that same yellow. His closing argument was the most compelling: even if Bobby broke the rule, the penalty must fit the crime.

On the other hand, Bobby's recently published autobiography bragged about cheating during cautions, including pitting twice during a yellow to get a half lap ahead of his brother Al Unser Sr. and into second place behind Johnny Rutherford in 1974. That well-known attitude about cautions made it a harder sell.

Finally, on the eighth day of October—138 days after the checkered flag fell—the USAC appeals board announced the winner of the Indianapolis 500. David Atlas, a spokesperson for Team Penske, assumed the worst and handed out a press release announcing the decision would be appealed to the courts. He hadn't realized they won. The board voted 2-1 to reduce Bobby's penalty to a $40,000 fine and reinstated his win.

Back at the Victory Dinner, Mario had his night in the spotlight. The Speedway kept the check and the keys to the pace car. Mario held a grudge against the Speedway for some time afterwards. They handed him a win, and then they took it away. He never became bitter, but he still has the ring.

One of my favorite moments with Mario took place on a private practice day with only the media and drivers. It rained and ended up a complete washout. Mario just felt like driving. I hopped into his rental car, and we coasted around the oval for an hour. We talked and talked about racing. He pointed to little spots on the track that had significance. He explained the tiny shift out of Turn Four you could use to your advantage. That little notch made all the difference before the walls were renovated. One surprising thing every driver at Indianapolis mentions: though perfectly identical on paper, each turn is completely different.

Mario loves pigs and he keeps them as pets. On ABC's opening before a race, we used an iconic picture of him as a young child in Luca, Italy, holding the tail of a pig. I narrated, "We don't know the name of the pig. The little boy is Mario Andretti." At his home in Pennsylvania, Mario and I took a couple of his Ferraris out for a cruise around the countryside. And yes, even a veteran motorsports reporter like myself can mispronounce a word like Countach. I flubbed that one as I started to climb into Mario's Lamborghini to go for another spin. Michael Andretti heard me too and couldn't stop laughing. Neither of them will let me forget it.

Some years later, in iconic footage that made it into a documentary, Mario and I walked along the yard of bricks. He said to me, "You know, I always said I hated this place." After a pause, he added, "I lied."

Networks frequently use the pit reporter slot to audition new talent. Jay Lawrence, who previously worked at the Racing Station KPRC in Los Angeles, joined our coverage in Trenton. At dinner the night before, I began to mention something I wanted him to do. Jay jumped atop his chair, ripped his shirt open—popping the buttons—and declared, "I'd do anything for you!" He had a flare for the dramatic.

During the race, Gordon Johncock spun out and touched the wall just hard enough to put his car out of the race. Unhurt, Gordy jumped out and jogged back to his pit. Jay rushed over, embraced the grizzled veteran with a big hug, and exclaimed, "Thank God you're alive!" We all cringed in the booth.

While the big three networks reigned supreme, the real boon for motorsports came from an unexpected place: cable television. Hungry for content, all kinds of obscure races and contests would find a national audience. I had a front-row seat.

In 1979, a former colleague from NBC called. He needed someone to produce the coverage of a sprint car race only a week away at the Eldora Speedway. He asked me if I could do it. As I hung up the phone, I thought, "ESPN? Isn't that the Connecticut sports cable network that hasn't even made the air yet?" I called Bob Jenkins. He shared my skepticism, but I said, "We take the money and run. It's twenty-four-hour sports. How long can it last?" I lined up Larry Nuber, another race fanatic who did a lot of public address work. Larry later helped guide Jeff Gordon to success.

Track owner Earl Baltes, known as the Earl of Eldora, greeted us at the gate and took us to the Eldora Ballroom, his office and broadcast booth. The track, located in Rossburg, Ohio, is cut into a big terraced hillside where spectators park their cars and trailers overlooking the track. It resembles a drive-in theater and almost a real-life version of something you might see in a Disney *Cars* movie. We worked out of a truck rented from the Christian Broadcasting Network. We might have used some words not previously heard in that truck.

Our on-camera rehearsal revealed a problem: Jenks was much taller than Larry. I sent out for a cinder block to raise Larry up shoulder to shoulder with Jenks. The two worked at ESPN together for years, and Larry always brought a special, height-enhancing briefcase on tour with him.

The production went great: unloading, warm up, hot laps, qualifying, and racing. It was the full USAC Sprint Car experience with hours of good old American racing. ESPN hit the air in September of 1979, and sports changed forever.

When TNN started American Sports Cavalcade, it covered every imaginable motorsport. John Mullin, an excellent director, put me on the headset for drag racing, sprint cars, supercross, tractor pulls, and even swamp buggy racing, where I was thrown in the "sippy hole" in Naples, Florida. As a gearhead, I loved every minute of it. These lesser-known competitions are full of the most wonderful athletes, mechanics, and fans. They still have the can-do, make-it-work spirit that is unrecognizable in the big leagues.

Every sport has its own culture, and somehow that crosses nations and languages. An early trip sent me to a World Championship motorcycle race in Belgium. The Spa-Francorchamps road course snakes around hills and valleys for 4.3 miles. Its corners have names like Eau Rouge, Le Source, and Blanchimont. In America, only a few of the tracks have names for their corners: Road America has its Hurry Downs and Canada Corner, and Laguna Seca has its Corkscrew. I used a photograph with the Raidillon Eau Rouge in the background on my media passes for years.

My NBC mentor Charlie Jones taught me the ropes of network broadcasting on that trip to Belgium. The European format wouldn't work for American television, but the satellite feed automatically converted the format. We did lots of editing in London and beamed it all back home.

I liked the challenge of learning a new sport. In my first taste of karate at the heavy weight championship in Brussels, I worked with Mike Stone, Elvis Presley's former personal karate instructor. Due to the Belgian television network replaying a move at the very moment of the match-winning knock down, the event never made the air. My favorite event that never aired was the World Championship Great Arcata to Ferndale Cross Country Kinetic Sculpture Race. Obscure events, like the water-skiing championships on a river in England, were fascinating. I met so many interesting and oddball personalities.

I hosted the America's Cup yacht race in Auckland, New Zealand. We observed the race from another vessel. On board was

Sir Edmund Hillary, the man who led the first expedition to climb Mt. Everest with Tenzing Norgay. I felt starstruck and broke a big rule of professionalism: I asked him for an autograph. He said, "Sure, give me a fiver." I thought he was being a little cheap by charging me for it, but I pulled out a New Zealand five-dollar bill. He signed it and handed it back to me. Looking more closely, I realized Sir Edmund's picture is on the five-dollar bill. That's when you know you're a big deal.

As I traveled around the world, I met a lot of F1 fans. While my heart will always belong to Indy cars, I genuinely enjoy them both. I first covered F1 for the Long Beach Grand Prix radio broadcast in 1978 and 1979. The monitors caught action on and off the racecourse. The wide pans of the cameras caught the apartments and buildings along the way. During each day of coverage, in the distance, a free-spirited couple intentionally appeared in *flagrante delicto* on a balcony within the camera frame.

In preparation for NBC's coverage of Caesar's Palace in Las Vegas, a road course literally built on top of the casino's parking lot, I attended the F1 race in Montreal. As I chatted with F1 chief Bernie Ecclestone during a practice session, he noticed a lot of sponsors and non-crew people in the pit areas. Bernie called the race promoter over and asked, "What are all of these people doing in the pits?" The promoter shrugged him off, saying, "I have to take care of my clients." As the drivers prepared for their runs, engines revving, Bernie walked down pit lane and gestured to cut them off. He left no doubt who was in charge, and the pits cleared.

In Las Vegas, I had another conversation with Bernie beside the Caesar's Palace swimming pool. Bernie and the rest of the visiting F1 contingent could be identified by their European-style swimsuits.

Roger Penske joined me in the broadcast booth at Caesar's Palace. We had spent time together in the studio for the *Month of May* reports on Channel 13. Roger brought a three-inch-thick binder with all kinds of F1 information assembled by his right-hand Dan Luginbuhl. I told him he would never have time to look through it after the race started—he would be too busy. Roger ignored my advice. That may have been the only time when I was right and Roger was wrong.

During an Indy car race at Nazareth, long-time F1 announcer Murray Walker stopped by the booth and kindly put on a headset. Murray loved Indy cars as well as F1. His first comment was, "You know Paul, in the past few minutes I've seen more passes on this racetrack than in the entire Formula One season." I'm sure he got a lot of grief from F1 fans over that one. The biggest dig on F1 racing is that it turns into a long day of follow-the-leader with very few passes or lead changes.

At Silverstone in Great Britain for World Championship bikes, I noticed Murry's one-page chart. I adopted that format for my own. Not as thorough as Roger's, but much more functional.

I've met a lot of F1 greats, and I have to admit I've liked every one of them, from Jimmy Clark to Nigel Mansell to Juan Pablo Montoya. I worked with Jackie Stewart a few times calling Indy car races. He arranged the most extravagant plans to beat the crowds to the exits. He might hitch a ride on an ambulance or have a golf cart waiting by the gate to run him to his car parked at a filling station down the street. And if you rode with him to the airport, he drove like he was chasing a checkered flag.

Among drivers like Nigel Mansell, Eddie Cheever, and Derek Daly, whose careers included both F1 and Indy cars, they all insist F1 is the "pinnacle" of racing. But they also admit F1 has nothing comparable to the Indy 500. The giant crowds and stadium seating along the track, the welcoming fans all over town, the history, the month-long journey; it's one of a kind. They all agree the Indy 500 is the greatest motor race in the world.

CHAPTER 11

A Family Business

Racing on the edge is not a death wish.
It's living to the max.
—Johnny Rutherford

On Pole Day 1982, speeds pushed drivers to the limit. As Gordon Smiley climbed into his car, he announced, "If the Whittingtons can run two hundred, so can I." He did, but lost control, hitting the wall in Turn Three at a speed of 200 miles per hour. His vehicle disintegrated and pieces bounced off the catch fence and back down the track. Though it never aired, I viewed the tape of the accident—I'll never forget seeing his helmet rolling down the track. In his twenty-five years as CART medical director, Gordon's wreck was the worst Dr. Stephen Olvey ever encountered.

Venturing into the macabre for a moment, track medical teams often hesitate to declare a driver's death—even if it appears that the injuries are fatal. Declaring a death at the scene of the wreck might trigger an investigation by the coroner, halting the race for hours if not canceling it. The vague diagnoses at the track often obscure whether a driver died instantly or not.

The medical team didn't hesitate with Gordon. I knew Gordon and his beautiful wife Barbara quite well. Almost a decade had passed since I last felt the sting of losing a close friend on the track. Speedway president Joe Cloutier asked me to give the eulogy at Gordon's funeral. We flew to Texas on the Speedway's private plane. I recited my favorite quote from Teddy Roosevelt:

> It is not the critic who counts; not the man who points out how the strong man stumbles, or where the doer of deeds could have done them better. The credit belongs to the man who is actually in the arena, whose face is marred by dust and sweat and blood; who strives valiantly; who errs, who comes short again and again, because there is no effort without error and shortcoming; but who does actually strive to do the deeds; who knows great enthusiasms, the great devotions; who spends himself in a worthy cause; who at the best knows in the end the triumph of high achievement, and who at the worst, if he fails, at least fails while daring greatly, so that his place shall never be with those cold and timid souls who neither know victory nor defeat.

On that trip, I got to know Joe personally. Joe would say he had only two bosses his whole life: Tony Hulman and Tony's father before him. He started keeping books for the company as a teenager, worked his way up the ranks to the very top, and stayed there past eighty years of age. At the Speedway, Joe was the one who called you on the carpet. Unvaryingly calm and collected, it made him even more intimidating.

Joe had a quick wit, though he usually kept it to himself. He once spoke at a breakfast for the American Auto Racing Writers and Broadcasters Association (AARWBA)—often referred to as "Aruba." I introduced Joe and teased him by remarking that everything about the Indianapolis Motor Speedway is false advertising: the track is in the City of Speedway, not Indianapolis, and the cars are propelled by engines, not motors. Without missing a beat, he pointed to the banner with the acronym for our organization and said, "Huh—you get 'Aruba' from that?"

Lots of things about the Speedway are misleading. There is no gasoline in Gasoline Alley, no carburetors can be found on Carb Day, and the Brickyard has very few bricks.

On Race Day 1982, five sets of brothers took the field: three Whittingtons, two Bettenhausens, two Snevas, two Mearses, and Pancho Carter and Johnny Parsons Jr. (half brothers). With Rodger Ward as my color commentator in the radio booth, the bigger-than-life winner of my third Indy 500 race had become a friend and colleague.

The booth's windows in the old Control Tower cast a terrible glare. At some angles, you had to press your face against the windows to see the action on the track. As Rick Mears, the pole-sitter, brought the field down on the green flag, Kevin Cogan swerved right, bounced off A. J. Foyt, and then into Mario Andretti. Anticipating the action and the glare, Rodger, the spry old fighter pilot, flattened me against the glass so I wouldn't miss a thing.

Poor Kevin took out the two biggest fan favorites on the first lap. It brought out the red flag and delayed the race nearly an hour. People heaped more grief on him than he ever deserved. Mario's hot take: "This is what happens when you have children doing a man's job out front." A. J., who was able to return to the race, said "Coogan" had "his head up his a——." The prior year, Kevin finished fourth (yet Josele Garza, who crashed out, took rookie honors). This year Kevin broke the track record with his qualifying run, and only Rick Mears topped him. Kevin earned his spot at the front. I liked spending time in Kevin's garage. You always found great conversation and often a movie star hanging around.

Rick controlled the race and led seventy-seven laps when Gordon Johncock snatched the lead with forty left to go. Both cars pitted a couple of laps apart, but Rick had a slight collision with Herm Johnson in the pits and handed Gordy an eleven-second lead with thirteen laps to go. With each lap, Rick gained a second or so, putting him only two seconds behind on lap 198. On the white flag, Rick kept charging alongside, aggressively looking for a window to pass. Unfortunately, ABC decided a shot of Rick's wife was more important than the race, and the fans at home missed the move by Gordy that broke Rick's momentum.

On the radio, our team caught it all and did some of our finest work. Out of Turn Four, Rick drafted Gordy and gave everything he had to slingshot to the front. Gordy countered with a subtle weave at the right instant and crossed the yard of bricks in a photo finish just 0.16 seconds ahead, the closest ever at the time.

I couldn't have been happier for Gordy—I still considered him a teammate from my days with Patrick Racing. With the Victory Dinner canceled and his teammate Swede Savage in the hospital, Gordy missed the full 500 victory experience the first time around in '73. In '77, he lost a nail-biter to A. J. Foyt. Finally, the veteran relished the pomp and ceremony he richly deserved.

As I traveled the world, Sally stayed busy with two young children at home: Brian and Marlo. Travel is never easy on young families. Whenever I left on a trip, she'd pull me in close, kiss me goodbye, and say, "Come back to me."

Sally left Nashville and her job as an anchor when we got married. She found work at PBS and other local stations, but not as a full-time reporter or anchor. Russ Arnold asked Sally to join the IMS Radio Network, and she became the first woman reporter on the network.

Growing up in Chicago Heights, Sally followed the Sox and the Bears, not racing. Though she did fall in love with a car. Her senior year of college, she pinned to her wall a picture of the '69 Camaro. When she got her first job, her folks bought one for her, brand new, and Sally made the payments. Hugger orange with a white top and a small block under the hood, she still has it today.

Even without a motorsports background, Sally succeeded because she approached it as a professional reporter. She learned what she needed to know to do her job. If she didn't understand, she asked questions until she did.

In her first year, she interviewed celebrities and dignitaries in the Tower stands. Sid would have laughed—I was too full of myself to interview Evel Knievel, and now my wife got her foot in the door by doing the same job. Sally shared my sentiments about celebrities. She enjoyed interviewing the handsome actor Tony Curtis in his white suit and fedora, but she wanted to report on the real action at the Indy 500.

The next year Sally reported from the hospital and anywhere else she was needed. She took on more responsibility each year and soon moved to Chuck Marlowe's slot in the pits. None of it was easy. As she prepared all month long, the garages often became awkward and quiet when she entered. Worse, people questioned whether she only got the job because she was married to me. Even Chris Economaki's *Speedsport News* took a dig at her. They didn't do any research. Very few racing reporters, if any, had a degree in journalism or a decade's experience as a television reporter and news anchor when they took the mic at their first race. Betty Rutherford wrote a scathing letter to the editor of *Speedsport News* in support of Sally.

Even after several years as a pit reporter, the yellow shirts singled her out to prove her credentials on her way to the garages or Victory Lane. Other times, it seems they thought she should make way for the male reporters. When Sally interviewed Roberto Guerrero, the runner up, at the end of a race, a yellow shirt started pulling on the wires to her headset and microphone, trying to physically pull her away. He told her she needed to leave so a television reporter could interview Roberto. Sally gave him hell and finished her interview.

No one in this business is invulnerable to pranks or dirty tricks. Someone in racing once gifted Sally a pretty pink ball cap with the words, "Pit Lizard." She wore it often, thinking it was cute and girly and a token of being accepted. A friend pulled her aside and asked if she understood what it meant. Teams used the term to describe female groupies, but it was ugly: a variant of "lot lizards," the hookers who work the parking area of a truck stop. Sally tossed the hat aside and kept doing her job.

But Sally knew how to handle herself. When Vince Granatelli wouldn't let Sally, or any woman, in his pit or garage, she gave him a piece of her mind during a shouting match. As I've seen among Italians before, the blowup actually bonded them, and Vince became a bit more inclusive.

Sally pursued her career in racing so we could live our lives together. When the drivers' wives came along on the series, it worked out. Betty Rutherford joined J. R.'s team. Theresa Fittipaldi sold her jewelry line on the tour. Sally saw firsthand the role Kathy Penske had in her husband's successes. She knows the part these women play. Sally always says, "There is a strong woman standing beside every successful man, *not behind.*"

In 1983, the Italian Teo Fabi, a rookie, announced himself on Pole Day by rocketing to the front of the line at 207 mph. With ever higher speeds, even veterans found the wall. Johnny Rutherford lost it twice, and the second wreck put him in the hospital.

In the final eleven rows, all but one car had a turbocharged Cosworth. The March chassis filled eighteen spots. Unfortunately, the March design poorly protected the drivers' legs in an accident. The first chassis designs for ground effects moved the drivers way up front with their legs extending beyond the front axle. Few drivers escaped this era without severe leg injuries.

On Race Day, a big storyline centered on the first father and son to make the same field at Indy: the Unsers Sr. and Jr. Rookie Al Jr. turned that storyline into something no one expected. During a late caution, Al Sr.'s splash-and-go pit stop put him in the lead, just ahead of Tom Sneva. A few cars behind, but five laps off the leaders, Al Jr. floored it before the restart, passing both his dad and Tom. It earned the young Unser a two-lap penalty. While up front, Al Jr. let his dad pass, but blocked Tom. After several laps, officials gave Al Jr. the blue flag, ordering him to make way for Tom's faster car. He ignored it. On lap 190, Tom finally passed Al Jr., and a half-lap later he rounded Al Sr. to take the lead.

On his tenth try, Tom Sneva finally found Victory Lane. It also gave ole George Bignotti his seventh win, a new record as the winningest chief mechanic in Indy 500 history.

After leaving WIBC, I moved into television production work, including the *Month of May* program covering the 500. I won the New York Film Festival Silver Award for my *Horses of Steel* documentary. For a guy who did only radio for his first fifteen years in broadcasting, I considered the honor a big accomplishment.

Sally and I started our own company, Page Productions. We operated out of the same office building as WIBC—even on the same floor. The parking lot backed up to our neighborhood, and Brian and Marlo, when they got a little older, could walk over. With most races on the weekends, Sally and I could usually both be home with the kids after school.

We bought the radio rights to broadcast the CART Indy car races for one dollar. We eventually lined up some big sponsors like K-Mart, Toyota, and Klein Tools. While I took the headset on occasion for races that NBC didn't broadcast, Lou Palmer usually sat in the booth with Sally in the pits and Gary Gerould in the turns.

For our first race in Portland, we lined up a local production company. Instead of proper two-way IFB communication equipment, they brought walkie-talkies to communicate with Gary. The radios kept overheating and shutting off. Gary had to run to the pit directly across the track from our booth and vigorously wave to get our attention. I would introduce him and wave back for his cue. Surprisingly, we had a flawless broadcast.

On occasion, our radio coverage of CART races directly competed with my network coverage on television. Sally usually chased down drivers for interviews first because radio is faster—a television reporter must wait for the camera crew to set the scene. At Michigan, Sally interviewed Mario Andretti while retired driver and ESPN pit reporter Jon Beekhuis waited. In the ESPN truck, our producer Deb Luginbuhl shouted over my headphones, "Sally's in the way! Get her out of the way!" Deb expected me to do something. I said, "I'm just calling a race here." ABC Sports president Howard Katz happened to be in the booth right beside me, and he nodded and smiled at my awkward position. Howard hired Sally for *SportsNite*.

As Deb counted down to his live feed, Jon started shouldering Sally aside. Bad move. Sally didn't budge and finished her interview. Jon and Sally were friends, but she let him have it afterwards: "Don't you ever do that again!" He didn't.

With the radio network, our family went on tour with the CART series. Marlo and Brian grew up playing in the dirt outside the Penske motor coach. Too young to be around the garages, we corralled the kids among the trucks and trailers in the broadcast paddock. Lou Palmer and his wife Cal and Gary Gerould and his wife Marlene became favorite "aunts and uncles." Our kids' extended family included the many reporters, spotters, videographers, and production assistants.

The kids liked the hotels with swimming pools. They loved staying on the Queen Mary. Marlo enjoyed traveling but not getting up early in the mornings—the day started off cold and she had little to do. As she grew, I would give her a headset so she could listen to the broadcast. Even then she couldn't believe I could concentrate with all of the shouting behind the scenes from the pit reporters and producers. Marlo told me she learned several of her first curse words listening to Don Ohlmeyer on the headset.

The kids spent spring break in Phoenix every year. Brian knew his birthday would be celebrated at Long Beach. As older children, they looked forward to dinner at a nice restaurant after the wrap—usually a place we returned to every year.

The family spent a lot of time together at the Speedway in May. Sally once co-chaired the fashion luncheon for the women's Championship Auto Racing Auxiliary with Kathy Penske. Marlo remembers modeling at about five years old. We had lots of visitors to the house. As a tot, Marlo clung to Johnny Rutherford. Whenever he sat on the couch in our living room, Marlo would climb on his shoulders.

Every year, Brian and Marlo watched the Indy 500 from the stands with my brothers Chuck and Tracy. Uncle Tracy always made up flash cards and spent the whole race quizzing them as to the names of the drivers and the colors and numbers of their cars. Uncle Chuck brought a cooler full of drinks and Aunt Diane's fried chicken. Afterwards, we had dinner at the Iron Skillet.

In May of 1984, a record 117 entrants assembled at the Speedway under the shadows of the new Hulman suites. With the best teams buying new rides every year, a lot of cars with life still in them could be bought on the cheap. The garages, fields, and parking lots filled with ragtag longshot entries hoping to be the next Cinderella story.

Underdog stories are great. Frank Fiore, an airline machinist, invested in an old Vollstedt for the 1971 race. He picked up rookie driver Denny Zimmerman on commission. They placed eighth and pocketed a tidy little profit. For someone who spent a lifetime dreaming of fielding a car at the Indy 500, every moment at the Speedway meant something beyond words. That gamble also earned Denny the Rookie of the Year title.

A formidable rookie class arrived in 1984: Roberto Guerrero, Michael Andretti, and two-time World Champion Emerson Fitti-paldi—Emmo couldn't be missed in his Barbie-pink fire suit and livery. Returning champion Tom Sneva broke the 210-mph barrier and captured the pole.

On Race Day, the Speedway's two scoring computers, a primary and a backup, somehow failed. We scored the race using pen and pencil. In the old manual days, the Speedway assigned a scorer for each car. Based on a master clock, the scorer wrote down the time when each car passed the start-finish line. The scorers also sat in thirty-three chairs assigned by starting position. In a fantastic mani-festation of Musical Chairs, they physically switched seats as the cars changed positions.

By the end of the race, all the contenders had piled into the pits with car troubles, leaving Rick Mears clear for his second victory.

Later that season, Rick Mears suffered severe leg injuries in a wreck at Sanair Speedway in Quebec. He recovered in Indianapolis at Methodist Hospital. I visited him as often as I could. From my heli-copter crash, I knew the pain of recovery and the confusion from the drugs. The first worry is whether you'll survive or be poisoned by the trauma of the horrible breaks. Next it's whether you'll keep your legs or ever walk again. Finally, the monotony of those months of "sheet time" wears on your spirit.

Derek Daly also experienced a devastating crash that season at Michigan. He injured his left leg and hip, lost a toe, lacerated his liver, and suffered third degree burns on his arm. I would drop by his room at Methodist in the evenings after his family left. Sometimes we would talk, but more often I would just sit with him. He looked so frail.

Getting back after a wreck is both physically and psychologically difficult. Wrecks happen so fast that there is no fear in the moment. As Johnny Rutherford said, it's when you have time to think about it that it gets scary. Many doctors comment on how quickly race car drivers heal. J. R. attributed it to the burning desire to get back into the competition.

Bobby Unser's autobiography, *The Bobby Unser Story*, has a visceral description of losing a wheel at full throttle, and ending up in a fiery wreck:

> Spinning, the car and I hit the wall backward, bounced down across the track and over the tops of some sharp steel plates that ripped through the floorboard—just missing my balls—then right through the fuel tank.

That might make you think twice about strapping in again. But nearly all the greats have had horrible wrecks and injuries and yet only thought of racing again.

In the hospital, some drivers—not Rick or Derek—received unexpected guests to alleviate the loneliness. Bobby Unser brought an amorous young lady from the Speedway to visit an injured driver in the hospital. They opened the door to the patient's room and found the driver's wife and mother bedside. Bobby and the woman made an awkward excuse and bolted. For a different driver, a couple teammates snuck a gal into his hospital room in a nun's habit. Unnerved by the costume, the patient couldn't bring himself to accept her affections.

My friendship with Derek grew as he endured at least a dozen surgeries, and we treated him like family. When work prevented me from attending Marlo's daddy-daughter dance for the Brownies, Derek went in my stead. Marlo doesn't remember the dance, but she does recall having her first little-girl crush on him.

Even without a race car, I raced whenever an opportunity came along. The Speedrome, a great old 1/5-mile track on the Eastside, held a figure eight three-hour endurance race, and they put me in a Datsun 240-Z with an inline six. I quickly got the hang of the crisscrossing traffic. When you're at the top of the eight, you just look at the other end of the eight to see if you're likely to meet a car in the intersection.

Unfortunately, I didn't watch for a car coming out of the pits, short of the top of the eight, and I got T-boned and plowed fifty yards past the starter's stand. The remaining cars bumped and swooped by until a yellow finally came out many laps later. I still earned the rookie honors.

I also participated as an embedded driver for NBC's coverage of Brock Yate's One Lap of America. Brock was a friend who organized the original, and highly illegal, Cannonball Runs in the 1970s. We started in Detroit, headed through Portland, Oregon, and down to LA for the traditional, and only, night's rest at the Portofino Inn. Then we headed east over the Angeles Crest at seven thousand feet above sea level, and passed through Great Bend, Texas, on the Rio Grande, on our way to Florida. After a hard turn north to New England, we rounded back to Detroit—around the country in just eight days.

I raced a Ford SVO Mustang in the Mid-Ohio Showroom Stock 24 Hour Race. On my team were Lyn St. James, driving school owner Bob Bondurant, World Championship motorcycle legend Kenny Roberts, and Olympic Decathlon gold medalist Bruce Jenner—since she identified as Bruce rather than Caitlyn back then, I'll refer to her as Bruce. Our team wore through a dozen sets of brake pads, and that time in the pits kept us out of contention.

Bruce tried his hand as a driver in the International Motor Sports Association (IMSA) circuit. I got to know him when he worked as a pit reporter for several NASCAR and Indy car races. We became good friends, as did Sally and Bruce's then-wife, Linda Thompson, an actor and previously Elvis Presley's long-time girlfriend. In Vegas, Linda pointed out a hotel to us and announced, "That's where Elvis took my virginity."

Around 1981, Bruce invited me along to a call-back audition for a sitcom about a washed-up football player who became a bartender. Bruce didn't get the part, but I figured out later he was almost Sam Malone from *Cheers*. The original script had the lead as a football jock. When the slim Ted Danson was cast, the story changed to a former pitcher. Bruce's acting career never really took off, but I did attend the premier party for *Gramblings White Tiger*, a made-for-TV movie with Bruce as the lead.

Linda openly mentioned that Bruce liked to wear women's clothing on occasion. It wasn't a sensitive subject; just part of his personality. When Bruce married into the Kardashians, his first Christmas card featured Bruce and his boys in black leather, the Kardashian girls in white leather, and a Santa on a Harley in the middle. They were building a brand from the very beginning.

I've worked with a few celebrities over the years. I produced a video called *Road to Indy* with Jim Brolin as the talent. An impressive and consummate professional, he also joined us for dinner at a tiny Italian restaurant in Indy, Rudy & Rosa's. Jim's presence caused a bit of a stir, and he graciously signed autographs and entertained the whole restaurant.

Paul Newman fell in love with the Speedway when he filmed *Winning*. Johnny Rutherford stood in as his driving double, and he noticed how Paul tore off after every shoot to come around the track for the next take. He tried his hand in racing, and J. R. considered Paul the best amateur driver he ever saw.

Paul and his team partner Carl Haas could often be found playing backgammon and quietly chatting. Carl is from my old stomping ground in Highland Park. He owned the Lola distributorship. Carl had a pre-race habit of walking around the team's race cars and touching, or blessing, every part of the car. At a Road America race, the cars were covered with tarps due to the rain. He blessed the wrong car, but no one had the heart to tell him.

I'll never forget catching a ride with Paul on his brand-new jet on our way from Lime Rock Raceway to Michigan International Speedway. Always a generous host, he personally served drinks and sandwiches. When Marlo was about sixteen, I brought her to the Indy car race at Laguna Seca. As we walked by the motor coaches, Paul greeted us and remarked on what a beautiful and charming young lady Marlo had become. He graciously invited us inside to visit with him. Naturally, the attention she received from the debonair older man flattered her. As we walked away, Marlo looked at me and asked, "So, *who* was that?"

I sighed and told her, "The salad dressing guy."

Everything Roger Penske does is done first class. When he owned the Michigan International Speedway, we usually got a Cadillac pace car for the weekend. The real treat was an invitation to the steak dinner. On the southeast end of the property sits an unremarkable little white house, no doubt predating the track. In that simple farmhouse, Roger hosted some of the most powerful people in racing. I remember a dinner with Teddy Mayer, who ran McLaren for many years, and Les Richter, a NASCAR exec nicknamed Coach from his time in the NFL.

Coach pointed to a photograph on the wall showing the giant crowd at Michigan for the NASCAR race. He bragged about its attendance compared to Indy car and F1. Teddy said he wasn't surprised that NASCAR would attract bigger crowds than an F1 race in Detroit. NASCAR was almost more about drivers' personalities than racing. It was entertainment, and NASCAR pandered to fans in a way F1 never would. Coach just kept referring to the crowd size as the only measure of success. Teddy retorted that F1 was the most-watched sport in the world and yet remained pure racing. Roger kept his thoughts to himself. I sat back and enjoyed the show.

Roger "the Captain" Penske has been a successful businessman and team owner for so long that people forget he was a great driver who captured USAC road racing and SCCA titles. His motto is "Effort equals results." He is known for being hands-on in all aspects. He often talks his drivers' ears off during races. When the team's radios went out during a race, the writing on Penske's chalkboards got so long that it took Al Unser Jr. three laps to read it all.

Like many who have achieved success, Roger established habits for time management. He would buy several of the same suits and white shirts, so he had less to consider when getting dressed. At corporate headquarters, Roger demanded that everyone end the day with a cleared desk. He had the same expectation with his garages. I chatted with Rick Mears in the garage one of his early seasons, and when Roger walked in, Rick picked up a broom and started sweeping the floor.

Sam Posey described the discipline on a Penske team as Prussian and what you might expect on a German U-Boat. There's a reason Team Penske has won the most Indy 500 pit stop competitions (not to mention the most Indy 500s). When Gary Bettenhausen raced a Silver Crown car at Syracuse against team rules, and got hurt in a wreck, Roger fired Gary while still laid up in a hospital bed.

Uncompromising in his expectations, Roger is always a gentleman and makes everyone feel comfortable. He kindly accepted an invitation to dinner at our home. Sally's Italian fare is always amazing, and he raved over her Cherries Jubilee. He sent us crystal glassware from Tiffany's in memory of the occasion.

On Pole Day 1985, Pancho Carter found the fastest four laps in the Buick pushrod—a fast but unreliable engine. Speeds increased, and for the first time, every car in the Field of 33 was brand new.

Every May, I invited the radio network audience to write and tell me where they would be listening from on Race Day. The letters became part of my opening. People wrote from all over: Ireland, Papua New Guinea, Japan, Antarctica. Fans said they would be tuning in while working on the Alaskan pipeline in Prudhoe Bay, vacationing in a cabin in Ontario, or staying in an off-the-grid hut in the jungles of Costa Rica. Most amazing, I learned a priest in Africa, hiding from rebels, expected to listen in on a portable short-wave radio out in the bush.

On Race Day, I had great color with Gordon Johncock and Rodger Ward in the booth. By the halfway mark, Mario Andretti had led seventy-five laps, and Danny Sullivan moved up into second. Due to a garbled radio message, Danny mistakenly believed only twelve laps remained. On lap 120, he charged at Mario, pressuring to find a way to pass. Danny dove low in Turn One in a daring move on the inside. He caught the apron and began to spin out right beside Mario. Threading the needle, Mario got clear as the younger driver spun around backwards. Danny continued spinning, nearly 420 degrees total, until he straightened out facing the right way. Somehow Danny kept control and continued to race like nothing happened—perhaps the greatest save of all time. The officials were so certain of a crash they dropped the yellow flag.

Twenty laps later, Danny tried the exact same pass again in Turn One. This time he made it. He fended off Mario for another sixty laps to claim the checkered flag. The third-year driver bested the veteran, and Danny's incredibly good luck, and skill, added more evidence to the Andretti curse. In Victory Lane, Lou Palmer called it the "Spin and Win." Moments like these are why the Indianapolis 500 is and will forever be the Greatest Spectacle in Racing.

CHAPTER 12

A Televised Race Day

We are not Formula 1. We should not prostitute
ourselves or our sport by going to places where
speeds are of a routine highway variety.
—*Pat Patrick*

With one exception, the IMS Radio Network provided the exclusive live coverage of the Indy 500. In the late '70s, the network learned from one of its affiliates that radio pirates tried to sell a competing broadcast. During the race, our engineers Tom Allebrandi and John Royer used special equipment to pinpoint a signal emanating from a house near the track. An FCC agent knocked on the door and the jig was up. They found the announcer in the grandstand "penthouse" and two reporters in the paddock. They must have elicited some confused looks from the ticket holders around them as they gave a play-by-play in the stands.

Live television first arrived on local WFBM (now WRTV 6) in 1949 and 1950. After that, everyone had to wait weeks for the abbreviated "Speedway International" showing. From 1964 to 1970, MCA produced a live closed-circuit broadcast of the Indianapolis 500 at select movie theaters across the country. Charlie Brockman, a local Indy sportscaster for Channel 13, hosted the coverage. Early on he worked with Sid Collins as an analyst on the radio broadcast. The old control room for MCA still hangs under the Turn One grandstand.

In 1965, ABC's *Wide World of Sports* aired a week-delayed and compressed version of the race. Color came in 1967, and the first same-day television broadcast in 1971. After 1985, the IMS Radio Network lost its monopoly on live coverage. ABC's telecast of the Indy 500 went live—and put the IMS Radio Network on the back bench.

In May of 1986, Rick Mears found the pole. New concrete garages with steel overhead doors replaced the iconic wood garages with their gaping barn doors. The Speedway Museum preserves one of the garages as an exhibit. Over the years, the new garages, additional bleachers, and other buildings eliminated a sizable chunk of the Snake Pit. As the Speedway tolerated less of the excesses of the infield, the rowdiness moved across Georgetown Road to the Coke Lot. The large field to the northwest of the track is part of the Coca Cola bottling plant property. Covered with a grid of tents, trailers, and RVs, the party on that grassy plot never stops. On the Saturday evening before a race, I liked to walk down Georgetown Road beside the Coke Lot to take in the mood.

Because the new garages faced inward, it eliminated the fence-row where generations of fans could see inside and line up hoping to meet a driver and get an autograph. The route from Gasoline Alley to the pits became the place to see drivers in person. Yellow shirts clear the way for the golf carts and tow trucks, but the Alley Cats are the rowdy masters of that domain. Whenever the track is open, this loose collection of rambunctious superfans congregates along the path, with beverages in hand. They cheer the drivers who are generous with fans and heckle those who aren't.

On Race Day 1986, the racing gods did not smile on the changes to the garages. It rained all day Sunday and again on Monday. Officials rescheduled the race for the following Saturday. The gamble on better weather paid off with a beautiful day and enormous crowds.

Bobby Unser joined me in the radio booth. He had a rough start; I asked him a few softball questions so he could find his footing. Soon we found our stride.

The folks on ABC were still finding their sea legs going from tape-delayed to live broadcast. With three laps to go, they decided to have Sam Posey radio an in-car interview with Kevin Cogan. Kevin led the race with Bobby Rahal and Rick Mears right behind him. With the green flag about to fall any second, Kevin said, "I'm kind of busy right now Sam, I'll talk to you afterwards."

Bobby Rahal bolted ahead on the restart, flying out of Turn Four and powering past Kevin on the straightaway. Bobby blazed around at 209 miles per hour. Kevin and Rick kept pace for the closest three-car finish to date. Bobby took the checkered flag and went on to take the series.

The rain delays canceled the Victory Dinner. Instead, a small group of drivers, sponsors, and insiders gathered for a private reception on the patio and lawn by the golf course. Though not the typical big gala event of the year, it was very special. No long speeches, just a beautiful evening on the grounds of the Speedway.

The night had a somber note because Jim Trueman, Bobby's mentor and team owner, was suffering through late-stage cancer. He was only fifty-one. Jim had a great saying: "Let people succeed on their own terms." Due to his illness, he barely made it into the pits on Race Day. I made sure Bill Donaldson in the PR department understood the urgency of the situation, and he asked the jeweler to rush the victory ring. Jim was wearing it when he died eleven days after the race.

Bobby filled the fiftieth and last spot on the original Borg Warner Trophy. When the company expanded the base of the trophy for future winners, they added the face of a non-driver in striking gold against the sterling silver trophy: the face of Tony Hulman.

The trophy is kept under lock and key these days in a way it wasn't in the '60s and early '70s. I would like to tell a story about joyriding around town with the Borg Warner Trophy in the back of my green Fiat Spider convertible, and how I know it can hold six gallons of beer, but I'd rather not incriminate my accomplices.

Throughout the '70s and '80s, the civic leaders of Indianapolis promoted the city as the "Amateur Sports Capitol of the World" and lured the governing bodies of sports organizations to headquarter here, including the NCAA, USA Gymnastics, USA Track & Field, and USA Diving. In a crowning moment, the city hosted the 1987 Pan American Games with Mark Miles at the helm. The Walt Disney Company produced the epic Opening Ceremonies on the main straightaway of the Indianapolis Motor Speedway, and eighty thousand people attended. Then Vice President George H. W. Bush opened the ceremonies, and Indianapolis native Oscar Robertson lit the torch.

In reinventing Indianapolis as a sports and convention hub, the leaders took risks. They built a football stadium before they had a team, based on the theory: "If we build it, they will come." No one should have been surprised when Indianapolis received rave reviews for its hosting of the Super Bowl. The city had been putting on the super bowl of racing for over a century.

Events like the Indy 500 and its Parade and Mini-Marathon require thousands of volunteers. Little things, like locals crocheting scarves for every ticket holder at the Super Bowl, make an event unforgettable. This spirit of hospitality permeates the culture of Indianapolis, as demonstrated by the ubiquitous banners that spring up every May in front of gas stations, restaurants, stores, and private residences: "Welcome Race Fans."

During our time in the booth, Bobby and I became fast friends. Life would never be the same. In a sport full of colorful characters, Bobby Unser will forever be one of a kind. As a boy, he dreamed of racing the Pike's Peak Hill Climb. The "Race to the Clouds" is a twelve-mile timed course that rises from an altitude of nine thousand feet above sea level up to fourteen thousand feet and traces along bare cliffs and 156 hairpin curves. His dad and uncles were the first to climb in motorcycles and then cars. Uncle Louis Unser held nine victories. Bobby went on to win it thirteen times.

A. J. Foyt took it upon himself to show Bobby how to set up his sprint car when he raced Ascot the first time. Just as he planned it, A. J. came in first, Bobby second. I could not overestimate how many drivers A. J. helped along the way. He quietly provided financial help to hundreds of drivers' families. A. J. is fiercely competitive, and yet exceedingly generous.

Bobby joined me at Eagle River to cover the World Snow Mobile Championships for a local television station. It's a hardcore sport. They race fastest on the smooth ice of the lakes, and the treads have fierce spikes for traction. The mechanics work in the back of unheated trailers, wearing special gloves that allow them to function in the cold. In 1980, "Uncle" Jacques Villeneuve, also an Indy car racer and namesake of the younger F1 and Indy 500 champ, won the first time I called the race at Eagle River.

For years, Bobby hosted a promotional snowmobile ride for Ski-Doo and brought along Rick Mears, Big and Little Al Unser, and me. I chased after Bobby on a ride across the lake, and he kept swerving close to these mounds of snow on the ice—which I instinctively avoided. When I asked about them afterwards, he laughed as he explained they were chunks of ice removed by ice-fishermen that had frozen solid to the lake. If I had hit one, I would've been done. That's a good illustration of Bobby's sense of humor.

I tagged along for Bobby's photoshoot at the Ski-Doo headquarters in Valcourt, Quebec. Just to take a load off, I sat down sidesaddle on the back of Bobby's snowmobile. The next thing I knew, Bobby gunned it. Foolishly I tried to hold on, finally tumbling off into the snow at about 20 mph. That's an even better illustration of Bobby's sense of humor.

A little later in the day, Bobby shot off through the woods in one of the brand-new show models. I followed along at a slower pace. When I came around a corner, I saw Bobby standing beside a not-very-new-looking snowmobile. He had hit something hard, and the cowling and a few other parts were pitched across the snow. I laughed as he jammed the pieces back together as best he could. Nonchalantly, Bobby rode back to the shoot, giving everyone a wave. He hit the brakes, and, right on cue, his snowmobile fell back to pieces.

In May of 1987, Al Unser Sr. made the trek to Indianapolis without a ride. After four years, Team Penske cut him loose in the off-season. In life and racing, it's always best to not burn bridges or hold grudges. When an injury sidelined Danny Ongais—one of twenty-five accidents that year—Roger Penske asked Al Sr. to come back. He signed on, but Roger didn't yet have a car for him. The new PC-16s substantially underperformed. Team Penske had no choice but to ditch them and scramble to find older replacement Marches. The car they found for Al Sr. was sitting on display in the lobby of the Sheraton Hotel in Reading, Pennsylvania.

Mario Andretti took the pole. Veteran George Snider suited up for the twenty-second time, the most by any driver without a win.

Parnelli Jones joined me in the radio booth. One of the most iconic photos from the Speedway is Parnelli diving out of his beloved Calhoun while at speed exiting the pits during the 1964 race—the fuel tank had exploded, setting the car ablaze. With only seven races and just one checkered flag, Parnelli still earned his place among the most legendary drivers to suit up at Indy.

On Race Day, Mario Andretti led 170 laps and everyone, except for maybe a few A. J. Foyt diehards, rooted for the old favorite. Tragedy struck when Tony Bettenhausen lost a wheel—it launched off Roberto Guerrero's car and into the stands, killing a fan, Lyle Kurtenbach.

Loose wheels can be deadly. In 1931, a wreck sent a wheel over the Speedway's fence and into the neighborhood across the street. It struck and killed eleven-year-old Wilbur Brink, who was playing in the front yard of his home at 2316 Georgetown Road. After two horrific incidents where lost wheels killed spectators at Michigan and Charlotte, wheel tethers became mandatory in 1999.

With twenty-five laps to go, Mario's car began to flounder. Roberto took the lead until his car locked gears on a pit stop—a result of damage from the collision with the wheel. A caution dropped, allowing Roberto to catch up to leader Al Sr. With four laps to go, the green flag unleashed the front-runners in a furious final sprint. Al Sr. held off Roberto and found his fourth victory. He was just five days away from his forty-eighth birthday. Bobby Unser, as part of the ABC telecast, interviewed his brother in Victory Lane as he tied A. J.'s record of four wins.

The brass at ABC realized they needed someone who could capture the excitement of the Indy 500 in a live broadcast. ABC offered me the role of chief announcer. I called Mari George about the opportunity, and she said, "Take it. We need someone who understands who we are." It meant leaving NBC and the IMS Radio Network, but radio had lost its place at the top. Only in the television booth could I play my biggest part in the 500. ABC also assigned me a role on *Wide World of Sports* and steady work on ESPN.

Lou Palmer became the next Voice. Having covered the turns since A. J. Foyt's rookie year, he was certainly ready for it. At ABC, my color commentators were a true odd couple. You couldn't find two retired drivers with less similar backgrounds than Bobby Unser and Sam Posey. Sam first met Bobby as a rookie. I would like to tell the story of when Sam first shook hands with Bobby, but some things in racing just aren't fit to print.

Bobby and his brothers grew up in the desert outside of Albuquerque. They caught live rattlesnakes because of a rumor that people would pay for the venom. Bobby dropped out of high school to race, and he roughed it as his own mechanic. If he was short on cash, he wasn't above siphoning gas to get to the next race. He once "borrowed" an alternator cap from a spectator's car in the parking lot to put in his race car, leaving a note. The owner came by afterwards to retrieve it, quite amused to have a story to tell the boys at work.

Sam grew up in an eight-story home with an elevator in New York City before the family moved to a place overlooking Central Park. He spent much of his childhood at his family's ancestral country estate in New England. Sam was just an overweight teenager when he bought his first race car, brand new, and hired a mechanic on retainer to travel with him to his amateur races. Sam also studied art at the prestigious Rhode Island School of Design. He was by far the most talented writer I ever worked with in the booth.

Fans loved their banter and humor, and they took sides. Some favored Sam with his eloquent and detailed analysis over Bobby's often inarticulate gut reactions. Others wondered why anyone would listen to Sam—he had only one Indy 500 appearance compared to

Bobby's nineteen. Keeping these two in line was a constant struggle. Jack Arute bought a striped referee shirt for me to wear at production meetings. In a subtle message, I painted the door to the booth with the words, "ABC Broadcast Booth, Paul Page: Star. Bobby Unser and Sam Posey: lesser stars."

My producer Don Ohlmeyer insisted on perfection. He pioneered the televised broadcasting of Indy car racing. He was determined to open my first year with the best racing montage ever assembled. Don must have spent thirty hours in the trailer editing the footage. Today it would take no time at all, but back then it was still linear tape-to-tape editing. Don picked the theme music from the Chuck Norris movie *Delta Force*. Based on his video, I chose the words and voiced the narration. The end product was a hit.

The *Delta Force* opening montages became known as "Paul Page Indy 500 Teases." It gained a bit of a cult status. To this day, YouTube has a large catalogue of people's own versions. I brought the *Delta Force* intros back when I returned to the radio broadcast.

On Pole Day 1988, Rick Mears took the pole, proving the power of the Chevy Ilmor V-8 and challenging the dominance of the Cosworth. Ilmor Engineering was formed by two former Cosworth engineers, Mario Ilien and Paul Morgan, in a deal Roger Penske brokered with Chevrolet. Team Penske took the entire front row. Unlike the prior year, the new PC-17 chassis performed up to Penske expectations.

On Race Day, a bad start caused Scott Brayton to spin out in Turn Two and head into the wall, taking out Roberto Guerrero and Tony Bettenhausen on the first lap. Mid-race, Rick Mears didn't like the handling of his new "flush disc" wheels and asked his crew to switch back to the old ones. It wasn't a small request. The crew would have to dig the wheels out of storage before hauling them into the pit. The team trusted their driver. With the change in wheels, Rick controlled the race for eighty-nine laps during the second half and earned the checkered flag for a third time.

Our coverage gained a lot of attention. We were rewarded with an Emmy for Outstanding Live Sports Special. My intro also earned an Emmy nomination for writing. I felt like I won the Indy 500 as a rookie.

Life with Bobby Unser is an adventure. Everyone calls him "Uncle Bobby," and he calls me, and anyone in charge, "Father." During our broadcast, he always had to have the last word, usually a loud, "Sam, you're dead wrong." To get him to shut up, the crew told Bobby I had a switch that cut off his mic every time he finished a comment. It worked. I didn't let Bobby know the off switch was a bunch of bull until he left the network. He's still hot about it.

You had to keep a wary eye on Bobby for shenanigans. Once when I didn't have an earpiece, Bobby gestured at me to do a mic test, so I did. He told me to do it again, and I did another. Then he said, "Your mic's not coming through, they want you to sing." He could barely keep a straight face, and I didn't take the bait.

Much to my surprise, the Pike's Peak hill climb champ is deathly afraid of heights. Unfortunately for Bobby, to get a good view of the tracks for our introductions, we filmed from the top of the grandstands. In a race at Milwaukee, I took advantage of his fear of heights to break him of his cue card habit—his delivery became very stilted when he read his lines. From the roof of the grandstands, I told a crew member to let go of the cue card as he was mid-sentence. The wind took it right off the roof and over the side, leaving a speechless Bobby with a slight case of vertigo. I let him think we were live (we weren't).

Perhaps the only time I ever got even with Bobby for his never-ending antics was at Long Beach. Our broadcast booth was a scissor lift. I took him all the way up, pausing at about every ten feet so he could really feel the height. When we topped out at seventy feet, the fearless race car driver was uncontrollably shaking. And I didn't feel one bit sorry.

On Pole Day 1989, the Nigel Bennett PC-18 helped Rick Mears earn a back-to-back seat up front: a record-breaking fifth pole. He also smashed the 220-mph barrier. Danny Sullivan broke his arm in a crash during practice but still qualified while wearing a cast. The Lolas began to dominate with only four drivers in the field sitting behind the wheel of a March.

Prior to May, the Speedway repaved the entire track. The newly graded safety lane became level and adjacent to the track. Drivers could take a new line, cutting below the white line in the turns. Chief Steward Tom Binford would receive 1,700 reports of drivers illegally crossing the white line over the course of the race. As best explained by Mario Andretti, "If you don't want me to race there, don't pave it." The Speedway fixed it in the off-season by separating the track and safety lane with a strip of grass and adding speed bumps beneath the white line.

On Race Day, Bobby Unser drove the pace car and gave a live report during the pace lap. Emerson Fittipaldi dominated most of the race, but Al Jr. passed him with six laps to go. Over the next four laps, Emmo fought back and hoped he had enough fuel to go the distance. The racing spoke for itself, and I avoided too much narration that might break up the video. With two laps to go, Emmo and Al Jr. both went low to get around traffic with Emmo on the inside. Their tires touched and sent Al Jr. spinning into the wall. We jumped in hard to narrate the crash. As Emmo came around on the next lap with the white flag waving, Al Jr. looked furious as he marched back toward the track. In the booth, our producer scrambled to find a camera angle that might obscure a rude hand gesture. To our surprise, Al Jr. gave Emmo two thumbs up.

While many believe Al Jr. intended the more forceful set of hand gestures, it's not true. Angry at first, Al Jr. realized he and Emmo both had to head into that turn to win. One might make it out, and one might be dead. Those are the stakes at the highest echelon of racing. You have to push your chips all in and see how the cards play out. Neither would have had it any other way. When Emmo came back around, Al Jr. was overcome by his love of the Indy 500 and genuinely cheered Emmo's victory.

When the Speedway replaced portions of the wall in preparation for the Brickyard 400, Al Jr. wanted the eighty-foot section from the spot where he crashed out. He shipped it back to Albuquerque on a flatbed and set it in front of the Unser compound.

Emmo won the first million-dollar winner's purse. I thought, "Why not have the top prize on display in cash at the Victory Dinner?" When I proposed the idea to Speedway President Joe Cloutier he said, "Sure. Just go to the concession vault. It will be there."

Nearly all gate and concession receipts were cash in those days. With a couple hundred thousand people in attendance, it shouldn't be surprising that millions of dollars of cash would be on hand. But it is. And it's fantastic that the Indianapolis Motor Speedway has its own vault, a veritable Fort Knox right on the grounds. Another ornate vault from an earlier era can be found in the Speedway Museum and Hall of Fame.

As it turned out, the million dollars was a less impressive pile than we expected. They went back and brought out more cash. Shortly before I called Emmo up to the podium at the dinner, Bill Donaldson panicked because he forgot the keys to the Pontiac Trans Am pace car, which are traditionally presented to the winner. Bill improvised, and I handed Emmo an Indy 500 fob with the key to Bill's room at the Hyatt.

Our coverage won the Emmy again. Two Emmys in a row for this category had never happened before. I felt like I won the Indy 500 back-to-back.

Press junkets are a wonderful job perk. Derrick Walker of the Porsche Indy car team arranged an event at the company's headquarters in Germany. He invited me along with Jeremy Shaw as the American contingent. The highlight was the chance to drive an Indy car around the Nürburgring F1 course. Lined up at the track were all nine of Porsche's domestic models. The hardest part of driving an Indy car is getting it going. The transmissions don't have low gears—that's why the crews help push them out of the pits. As I headed down the pit road in the Porsche-March, I fishtailed and nearly wiped out all nine of those brand-new Porsches.

After I found my bearings, I felt a real shot of adrenaline when I saw my speed pushing 185 mph. The brakes were incredible. While I didn't get to drive the Old Ring, which meanders along castles and the idyllic European countryside, it was a big step up from the time I drove an Indy car around a Meijer grocery store parking lot.

I compared my telemetry results to Teo Fabi's run. He had no hesitation when he hit the throttle. Back in racing school, they taught us to ease into the throttle. I guess Teo went to a different school.

They also let us drive the Porsche street models at the company's test track. As I started to get into one of them, the Porsche test-driver, Gunther Stekkonig, shook me off. I asked if he thought it was too much power. In a thick German accent he explained, "No. Not good car. Only for doctors and lawyers in America."

My trip to Germany happened to coincide with the historic days when the Berlin Wall came down in 1989. At the time, no one knew if Russian tanks might halt the free travel between East and West Germany. I heeded caution and returned home without witnessing those heady days in Berlin. I've regretted it ever since.

May of 1990 arrived with a new face in charge of the Speedway. After the death of Joe Cloutier in December, thirty-year-old Tony George took the helm. The golf course, renamed Brickyard Crossing, reopened after an overhaul by Pete Dye, the Hoosier and legendary golf course designer. On the IMS Radio Network, Bob Jenkins succeeded Lou Palmer as the next Voice of the 500.

New rules required diffusers on the ground effects of older chassis in an effort to slow the cars. A lot of the drivers blamed them for problems with handling and wrecks. The rules didn't slow down Emerson Fittipaldi, who claimed the pole and broke the 225-mph barrier.

On Race Day, Emmo led a record ninety-two consecutive laps, but tire troubles stalled him and others. Late in the race, Arie "the Flying Dutchman" Luyendyk, who had never led a lap in any Indy car race, found the front of the pack. Bobby Rahal gave chase, but Arie broke the average race speed record to take the checkered flag. The crowd roared as long-haired Arie punched his fist in the air on his victory lap.

In an interview, Rick Mears said he would have been a Navy aviator if not a race car driver. That sparked Deb Luginbuhl at ABC to organize a promotional shoot with Rick taking a flight off the USS *Roosevelt*. Rick's arrangements went through Captain Bill "Bear" Pickavance, who set up a flight for me as well. I went through training at NAS Pax River: the parachute harness, the helicopter dunker, the fighter jet dunker, and worst of all, the survival swim. Dropped into a large pool with a full flight suit, boots, and helmet, you must swim three lengths. I felt fine until I rolled over to do the backstroke on the last lap. My helmet filled with water and I sank. Choking, I made it to the side and looked up at the petty officer supervisor, who yelled, "Go back and start over." As I caught my breath, a pilot leaned over and whispered a tip: "When they aren't looking, blow air into the G-suit and it will give you some flotation." It worked.

At Cecil Field I strapped into the full-dome flight simulator where you can "dogfight" with the pilot in the other dome. It's so realistic that even seasoned pilots get vertigo. I got the real thing in a two-seater FA-18 with the Gladiators VFA-106. My pilot put on quite a demonstration, including getting us "parked" where the jet is pointed straight up, balanced on its thrust, and just hovering. After my flight on the Roosevelt, I could attest that there is no thrill like being catapulted off an aircraft carrier. You never feel more alive than when you're at Mach speed in a Navy FA-18 Super Hornet.

I returned to the Roosevelt with Danny Sullivan during Desert Storm. We flew to Italy after the race at Phoenix along with Emerson Fittipaldi, Scott Pruett, and cameraman Ken Heinniman. Emmo hosted us at his favorite restaurant in Rome before wishing us luck on the ship. Stationed in the Mediterranean, the crew of the Roosevelt had been at sea for over six months with no hope of shore leave while the mission was underway. The sailors were ecstatic to meet Danny. To pass the time, the crew held remote-controlled car races on the flight deck. They asked to me to be the announcer, and I had a ball barking out the play-by-play for these young sailors.

After the Long Beach Grand Prix, a group of us toured and stayed overnight on the USS *Nimitz*: Parker Johnstone, Scott Pruett, Christian Fittipaldi, Jeff Krosnoff, motorcycle champ Eddie Lawson, Paul Morgan, and several others. Parker brought his wife Sharon, a fireball of energy. Eddie brought his girlfriend, the actor Crystal Bernard from the sitcom *Wings*. We used her to distract the crew while we prowled the ship.

When my son Brian considered attending Annapolis for college, I scheduled a visit so he could do his interview aboard the *Kitty Hawk*. Sally joined me on another trip, and she says being launched off the Roosevelt in a C-2 Greyhound was the most fun she's ever had. Altogether, I've had a chance to trap and launch from five aircraft carriers: *Roosevelt, Nimitz, Constellation, Stennis*, and *Kitty Hawk*.

Strapped in the Blue Angel 7 as NAS Pensacola, the pilot caught me by surprise and pulled enough Gs that I passed out. At NAS El Centro, a Blue Angel took us low enough for the wing vortices to kick up dust on the ground. While inverted, we passed over a dune buggy out on a trail. You can't hear an FA-18 coming, and I'm sure the driver got one heck of a shock from our flyover. I saw it bouncing along in the rearview mirror.

The most unusual aircraft I ever boarded was the Goodyear Blimp. The near silence, even at full throttle, surprised me. They let me take the controls. Without warning, they shut off the engines. It scared me more than any other flight. It was the only time I flashed back to the helicopter crash. Just for an instant, it seemed like a free fall, and it hit me hard.

Many Indy car drivers are pilots. Rodger Ward flew P-38 fighter planes in the Second World War. Johnny Rutherford flew acrobatics in his P-51 Mustangs from the same era. Bobby Unser got his pilot's license so he could reach more races. Dick Simon was a competitive parachute champ before his racing days—the FBI actually interviewed him as a D. B. Cooper suspect. I once bought an ultra-light aircraft from Rick Mears with the ridiculous notion of flying it from the north side of Indianapolis, where I lived, to the Speedway. Not one of my better ideas or investments

In May of 1991, Rick Mears claimed his sixth pole position (not to mention four poles out of the last six 500s). The veteran Gary Bettenhausen, however, posted the fastest qualifying speed for a spot in Row 5. Four Andrettis joined the field: Mario, Michael, John, and Jeff. Willy T. Ribbs became the first African American to qualify.

Willy drove his first laps at the Speedway in 1985 when boxing promoter Don King lined up a sponsorship. He realized he needed more experience and raced for Dan Gurney in the IMSA GT circuit. He needed two tries for NASCAR as well. He lost his first shot in NASCAR due to an unauthorized drag race with a law enforcement officer. Days before the Charlotte 600, Willy mistakenly drove the wrong way down a one-way street. A squad car attempted pull him over for the infraction. Seated in an official pace car, Willy raced off and got away. The police tracked him down and charged him, causing his team to fire him.

In Indy cars, Willy experienced one of the hardest things for a driver. At Vancouver, driver Ross Bentley stalled in a blind right-hand corner. The corner crew, who were volunteers, lined up to push-start Ross. After the engine fired, the crew began to cross the track to their station. Three were hit by Willy's car. One worker, Jean Hein, suffered fatal injuries when he was sucked under the left rear wheel of Willy's car.

Racing is dangerous. To look the monster in the face, and survive, is part of the allure of racing. Going out in a blaze of glory doing what you love isn't the worst thing imaginable. Even when an error injures another driver, those are the stakes. The guilt that follows hurting a bystander is completely different. That accident left deep scars on Willy. I reached out to him at the time—I hope he found some comfort in my thoughts.

On Race Day 1991, the seventy-fifth Indy 500, Michael Andretti controlled the first half and then dueled Emerson Fittipaldi until Emmo's gearbox grounded him late in the race. Rick found his way to the front, but Michael roared back after a restart, taking the lead on a gutsy pass in Turn One. Rick returned the favor on the next lap in the exact same spot. Rick raced through the pain of a broken foot sustained in a wreck during practice. When he weakened, he pushed down with his left foot on top of his right to keep the throttle down. He kept his edge on Michael, who slowed down late due to the car's handling. The Rocket joined Al Unser Sr. and A. J. Foyt as the third four-time winner.

For years I emceed the Victory Dinner. The evening always included a montage featuring candid shots of drivers throughout the month of May. Footage of a driver sitting in a golf cart with a big smile got me in hot water one year. The editors didn't realize the young lady seated beside the driver was his girlfriend—his wife and family were a bit embarrassed at the dinner. It became a standard part of the editing process to identify the women in the shots to avoid such situations.

This year I learned at the last minute that Jay Leno would replace me as the host. No one thought it through, and a conflict between the networks prevented Leno from appearing on television. No one at home saw the car-loving funny man or the drivers' remarks at the podium. They got a series of driver interviews backstage.

Among other Indy 500 side gigs, I announced the national broadcast of the 500 Festival Parade with personalities like Willard Scott, Gary Collins, and Florence Henderson. That parade was tough on the horses—the black squares on the checkered carpet in front of the VIP stands looked like deep holes to a horse. They bucked and reared and stumbled their way across.

On the Borg Warner Trophy, each of Rick's portraits is unique, unlike A. J. and Al Sr. who elected to use the same portrait for each win. It's hard to imagine Rick started off as an off-road racer—his mom hoped switching from motocross to four wheels would be safer. Bill Simpson discovered Rick and convinced him to switch to open-wheel racing. Roger Penske and Rick met while they participated in Wally Dallenbach's Colorado 500, a charitable dirt bike race through the ghost towns outside Aspen that has continued for decades.

We all expected Rick would become the first five-time winner. Having great cars and starting in the front helps. In the first one hundred Indy 500s, pole-sitters went on to take the checkered flag twenty times, reflecting a twenty percent chance of winning from the pole. Rick delivered on fifty percent of his starts on the pole, way ahead of the curve. Rick's Indy 500 strategy was simple: keep pace with the leaders, and then go for it during the last fifty miles. When he went for it, Rick gambled as fiercely as any competitor.

At age eleven, I built a TV studio in the basement. Uncle Harry built the camera and the mic is a bud vase.

S.N.B.S

CHANNEL 9

My uncle Harry set this photo up with the fiftieth Anniversary Golden Thunderbird Pace Car. I didn't have a driver's license yet!

OFFICIAL CAR
'500'
Festival
MAY 28-30

It was thrilling being inside the Indy 500 radio booth with the great Roger Ward.

Mickey Thompson showed me around the garage while I interviewed him.

1965 was the first year I had a credential. Mike Hiss's team gave me this cool hat. I watched Mario Andretti pull of his rookie stripes.

I used my Lotus 51 Formula Ford #11 to get my National License.

Robin Miller and I both started in Formula Fords. Art Pollard and I helped with Robin's first test drive at the 5/8ths oval at the Indianapolis Raceway Park (now Lucas Oil raceway). *Courtesy of Robin Miller*

Sid Collins holding my son Brian weeks after he was born.

The great writer Brock Yates and I at the start of the One Lap of America.

This is what was left of the WIBC Traffic helicopter after we crashed at Speedway High School in 1977.

This was my official photo from 1977. *Courtesy of IMS Photo*

My first time anchoring on the IMS Radio Network was A. J. Foyt's fourth win. We took this photo together the morning after. *Courtesy of IMS Photo*

The whole gang took a flight home from Houston together in 1978. Frankie Delroy, me, Robin Miller, Pancho Carter, Steve Krisaloff, a flight attendant, Johnny Parsons Jr., Dr. Steve Olvey, Bob Jenkins, and Stan Worley posed for a photo. Robin conducted a ceremony for a flight attendant who was about to be married.

At Texas World Speedway 1978, we created the first IndyCar series-long radio network. Tom Allebrandi, the engineer; me; and Bob Jenkins posed around the pace car. Not pictured is Gloria Novotney, the station liaison.

I always enjoyed interviewing Roger Penske, the winningest team owner and the future owner of the Speedway.

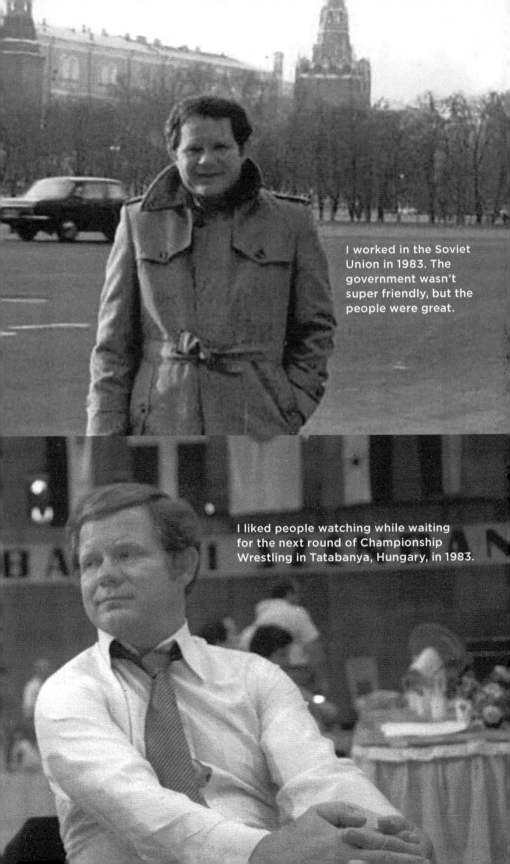

I worked in the Soviet Union in 1983. The government wasn't super friendly, but the people were great.

I liked people watching while waiting for the next round of Championship Wrestling in Tatabanya, Hungary, in 1983.

Since the public couldn't get up to the booth in the early years, I had the booth door painted to tease Bobby and Sam.

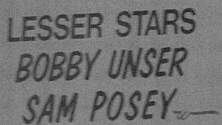

ABC
BROADCAST BOOTH

★ MAJOR STAR ★
PAUL PAGE

LESSER STARS
BOBBY UNSER
SAM POSEY

Lou and I were at the Lone Cyprus by the Lodge in Pebble Beach, California, working for the CART Radio Network.

Interviewing Rick "the Rocket" Mears was always a treat. This was at Phoenix in 1987.

Sally worked as a reporter for ESPN, NBC, ESPN 2, CBC Canada, Prime, USA Network, the IMS Radio Network, and our CART Radio Network.

I took this awesome photo on the flight deck of the USS *Theodore Roosevelt*.
Courtesy of the US Navy

Pac West was silly enough to let me drive one of their IndyCars. I gave it back unscratched to owner Bruce McCaw. *Courtesy of Bruce McCaw*

I taught some great shooters at the Indiana State Police when I was an instructor. Here they are ready to go out on the final test.

This official photo from 2004
was from my last race for ABC.
Courtesy of ABC Sports Publicity

I met with Helio Castroneves just outside Victory Lane when he won his third 500. We hugged for the win and the fact his battle with the IRS was over, both victories! *Courtesy of IMS Photo*

Steve Schunk, Juan Pablo Montoya, Robin Miller, and Bobby Unser must have liked my joke when we attended the Borg Warner Party. *Courtesy of Steve Schunk and Borg Warner*

Alexander Rossi and I posed for a photo the morning after his incredible rookie win at the one hundredth Indy 500.
Courtesy of IMS Photo

From all my years at the track, I've accumulated quite a collection of media passes

My great uncle Harry Geisel helped support my passion for the Indy 500.

CHAPTER 13

Living the Dream

A. J. Foyt did not make the Indianapolis Motor Speedway.
The Indianapolis Motor Speedway made A. J. Foyt.
—A. J. Foyt

A fter the IROC at Daytona, Bobby Unser brought me along to the Best Damn Garage in Town to visit the owner, Smokey Yunick. It may have been the best thing he ever did for me. Smokey and Bobby were old friends, and he broke open a case of White Lightning in Ball canning jars for the occasion.

Smokey's genius was legendary. For the 1959 race, he engineered the Reverse Torque Special, sending the RPMs counterclockwise to have the car lean left when it revved instead of right, for better balance into the left turns. His novel design in 1964 set the driver in what amounted to a floating motorcycle sidecar rigged alongside the engine. It didn't qualify, but only because Bobby Johns wrecked it.

In NASCAR, no one could find his changes and adjustments— what some might call cheats. For a lover of motorsports, it doesn't get any better than listening to Smokey and Bobby swap stories about cheating whilst sipping moonshine straight from the jar.

Smokey knew a lower car is a faster car: the less distance between the bottom of the car and the ground, the better. Early on, he stuffed dirt clods in the coil springs of the suspension to pass the height requirement at inspection. The first time the car cornered at speed, the dirt would crumble, lowering the car. Once officials got wise to the mud, he started lifting the car and freezing the shock absorbers with CO_2 from fire extinguishers. The car passed inspection, but it lowered as the suspension thawed. Those tricks led to NASCAR requiring both pre-race and post-race inspections.

Most memorably, Smokey found ways to hide fuel. One year during an inspection, officials removed his car's fuel tank. They kept pulling off parts until only the drivetrain remained. Finally, Smokey had enough. He hopped in, started the car, and drove away—with the fuel tank still sitting on the floor.

Smokey also had a knack for identifying talented drivers. In 1963, he called Johnny Rutherford out of the blue and asked him to come down for the Daytona 500, just days away. They had never met, but Smokey had watched J. R. race sprint cars a couple times. New to NASCAR, J. R. blazed Smokey's black and gold number 13 to set a new track record and claim the pole. J. R. won the 100-mile qualifier race and had a great showing in the Daytona 500. Smokey asked him to stay on the series, but J. R.'s heart was already in Indy.

With Frankie Delroy as head of technical inspections at the Speedway, few teams dared to cheat. The rotund little man with his signature white cowboy hat was as sharp as a whip. When Sam Posey had a hard time qualifying, his team switched out the serial number plates to get a new set of runs. As they started to head to the track, Frankie wandered back and said, "I wouldn't do that if I were you. I always put my mark on each car." He knew it wasn't a new car.

Every now and then someone tried a blatant cheat, like when Jerry Sneva's car had a bolt welded to keep his pop-off valve closed.

More often it was a bending of the rules. George Bignotti built a turbocharger so powerful that it overwhelmed the pop-off valve, rendering it useless. A more recent innovation was a flex-steel column for the wing that flattened at speed, lowering the wing and reducing drag.

Technically, a cheat must be against the rules. When A. J. Foyt distracted the pace car at Texas World Speedway, A. J.'s crew had been listening to the USAC officials' radio to determine when the pace car would come in. But the officials changed the frequency to keep off eavesdroppers. A. J.'s crew lost the signal, and that's why A. J. had to "improvise" to keep the pace car out for another lap. The rule book did not expressly ban eavesdropping or distracting a pace car driver. Sometimes teams had "accidents" rather than cheats, like when Jerry Grant accidentally overshot his pit and stopped in his teammate's when his own pit might have been out of fuel.

Sometimes teams leave before getting caught. Famed mechanic Carroll Shelby entered a couple of turbines at Indy in 1968. When officials came by to inspect an alleged violation, the garages were empty. A hasty press released indicated the cars had been withdrawn for "safety" reasons.

Another type of cheating was espionage. In the early '70s, a British guy named "Chalkie" wandered Gasoline Alley and somehow always got the drawings to everyone's cars. His real name was Eamon Fullalove, a master fabricator who came from F1 and worked for Foyt Racing. His primary accomplishment was driving a car into the motel pool across from the Speedway. That feat has been copied often since then.

The one thing that Bobby and Smokey completely agreed on: everyone else was doing the same thing. You can't be a winner unless you're willing to push the envelope as much as your competition.

The last story from Smokey I'll never forget was about NASCAR legend Glenn "Fireball" Roberts. Glenn bought a helicopter and needed a minimum of forty hours of training to get qualified on it.

He hired an instructor who guaranteed the license after the minimum airtime. At the end of the forty hours, the instructor told Glenn he needed more practice. Glenn insisted on the instructor honoring his guarantee. Ready or not, Glenn got his license.

Glenn didn't like his nickname—it actually came from his days as a AAA pitcher. Though it proved prophetic: he suffered severe burns from a fiery wreck at Charlotte, just six days before Eddie Sachs was killed in Indy. He succumbed to his injuries several weeks later.

In May of 1992, Roberto Guerrero blew through the 230-mph barrier to take the pole. Crashes brought heartbreak once again: rookie Jovy Marcelo wrecked in Turn One on a practice lap and suffered fatal injuries—ten years to the day that Gordon Smiley was killed.

While no one knew it at the time, fans saw the end of an era: the last race for A. J. Foyt (thirty-five consecutive), Rick Mears (fifteen consecutive), Gordon Johncock (twenty-four total, twenty consecutive), and Tom Sneva (eighteen total, seventeen consecutive). A record ten past winners qualified. Lyn St. James became the first woman to start since Janet Guthrie in '79.

Fifty-degree temperatures on Race Day resulted in cold tires, bad traction, and lots of wrecks and injured drivers. Pole-sitter Roberto crashed out on the parade lap. Dr. Terry Trammell rode in the ambulance to Methodist Hospital with Rick Mears and Mario Andretti. Trammel had to triage his patients as Jeff Andretti arrived with even more severe injuries. Methodist Hospital admitted nine drivers that day.

In the midst of this, Trammel tells the story of a young boy in a leg cast crying his eyes out in the ER. It turned out the tears were not from physical pain but from missing the Indy 500. Trammel wheeled the young fan over to Rick and Mario who signed his cast. The boy learned he wasn't the only one in the hospital missing the race.

Michael Andretti seemed poised to beat the Andretti curse, leading 160 laps. But on lap 189, he lost fuel pressure and was out. Al Unser Jr. took the lead while Scott Goodyear, who started thirty-third, trailed close behind. They ran the final seven laps neck and neck at 224 mph. Both said they never lifted. As they rounded Turn Four under the white flag, we knew it would be a photo finish.

Back then, the television broadcast booth sat on top of the grandstand roof. Because the room sat back a bit from the edge, you could barely see the yard of bricks. As they came around, we pushed our monitors out of the way. Standing on the table, leaning against the glass, I wasn't sure who won. I said generically, "He's done it." Even Jack Arute, standing in the pits at the finish line couldn't tell who won. I looked at the scoring monitor, and Al Jr. found the yard of bricks just 0.043 seconds ahead of Scott, the closest finish ever.

Al Jr. may have led by a little more than that at the finish line. Back then, the placement of the transponders wasn't uniform. With Scott's device set in the nose cone and Al Jr.'s in the sidepod, Scott had a virtual head-start. You can imagine the controversy if the photo finish and timers showed different winners.

Don Ohlmeyer usually shot the finish from the Turn One camera because the angle foreshortened the field and made the cars appear closer together. Obviously, this race didn't need it, and the audience at home couldn't tell who won either. After the race, Don inserted into the tape a new shot from the control tower camera above the finish line. At the next production meeting in Milwaukee, he apologized for "ruining the good job" we had done on the race. Don was that much of a perfectionist.

On his tenth try, Al Jr. found Victory Lane. Overcome by emotion, his eyes filled with tears as he uttered those unforgettable words, "You just don't know what it means to win here at Indy."

Derek Daly joined me in the broadcast booth for ESPN. I first met him when he switched from F1 to Indy cars. When I learned he got his start racing Formula Fords, I knew we would get along just fine.

A native of Ireland, Derek came up in racing like a lot of the greats, scrapping his way. He converted an old school bus into a mobile home and garage for his race car. He spent six months laboring in a gold mine in Australia to earn enough money to buy a better ride. With the right equipment, he soon made a name for himself.

On the air, I think our genuine friendship came across to the viewers. Derek took his role seriously. He quickly began offering ideas to make the coverage better. Derek noticed it was stupid to use miles per hour as the graphic on a road course; it would be better to use lap time.

On occasion, his injuries came back to haunt him. Shortly before a race at Laguna Seca, he started having horrible back spasms. He couldn't move. We loaded him on a golf cart to rush him from the media compound down to the medical coach. After some great work by the CART medical team, Derek recovered enough to go on the air. I looked over from time to time. No doubt he was hurting, but he wasn't about to give up.

We had a great idea for a television series. Derek would drive and evaluate cars: F1, CART, sand buggies, whatever. I would produce it and put together great shots and audio. In other words, we thought up *Top Gear* long before the BBC. We shot a few scenes and pitched it to ESPN, but it never got off the ground.

One of Derek's finest broadcast moments came at the 2005 US Grand Prix F1 race in Indy, the year of the tire issues. He nailed the story while his producers still couldn't accept so many cars were going to pack it in. He knows his subject and gets it on the air.

May of 1993 saw the arrival of reigning World Champion Nigel Mansell. The former engineer with thirty-one F1 wins had never raced an oval before joining the Newman-Haas team. Ovals are different, as three-time World Champion Nelson Piquet learned at Indy the year before. He crashed into Turn Four during a practice session, severely injuring his foot and missing the show.

Nigel won his first Indy car race at Surfer's Paradise, a road course in Australia. At Phoenix, an oval, Nigel broke the track record on a practice lap. I still have the timing slip from that run. His inexperience caught up with him on another practice run, and he crashed hard, putting a hole in the wall. It knocked him unconscious, and his injuries sidelined him. Another World Champion won that race: Mario Andretti.

But Nigel is no quitter. A few weeks later at the Long Beach Grand Prix, he took the pole. As Nigel stood in the cockpit for a live interview, I put my arm around his back to help him stand. I realized his back was in full spasm. He had back surgery right after his third place finish at Long Beach.

The international press descended on Indianapolis in force. Michael Knight, VP of Communications for Newman-Haas, kept order by requiring all interviews to go through him. Sally was friends with Michael, so she could always walk right up for an interview with Nigel.

On a practice lap, Robby Gordon crashed into the wall. It caused another driver to quit: Robby's teammate and team owner, A. J. Foyt. Super Tex shocked everyone as Tom Carnegie announced his retirement as a driver. A. J. coasted around the Speedway in an impromptu farewell lap for one last checkered flag.

Gary Bettenhausen suited up for his last Indy 500 (twenty-one total). He ran most of those races with a partially-paralyzed left arm. Gary always lands high up the list of best drivers who never won the 500. Unlike some drivers, winning wasn't everything to him. While in eighth place in 1971, Gary stopped to help get Mike Mosley out of his burning race car. Mike had suffered a broken leg in the wreck and needed help.

Rick Mears, who had surprised us all when he announced his retirement the prior December, tried a stint in the booth. He had terrible stage fright; his hands shook. He gave up any ambitions in television.

On Race Day 1993, we sent Bobby Unser over to Turn Two because I wanted to give a greater illusion of speed by covering the race radio-style. Bobby wasn't happy about the location—being up high and away from everyone else. With the collaboration of the yellow shirts, Bobby smuggled up tables, chairs, umbrellas, and an entourage of pals and young gals, plus a full spread catered by Jug's, known for its comfort food.

In a battle of F1 champs, Mario Andretti took control at the half-way mark, leading seventy-six laps before fading late. With sixteen laps to go, Nigel had the lead but lost it on the restart to Emerson Fittipaldi. Two-time World Champion Emmo picked Nigel's pocket and claimed his second checkered flag.

Emmo broke tradition by refusing to drink the quart of milk in Victory Lane, instead promoting orange juice from his native Brazil. The fans were not amused by the breach of tradition. Someone persuaded Emmo to later drink the milk for the photo. In a peace offering, he donated the prize money from the dairy association to charity.

Nigel went on to win the series, proving his dominance in open-wheel racing. We became friends. His wood-paneled home office in Clearwater featured a big brass inset of his signature in the floor, and on the wall hung a Bobby helmet from his time as a reserve police officer on the Isle of Man.

Years later, I had a role in the ceremonies inducting Nigel into the Motorsports Hall of Fame. We checked out the facility's private course, and a Porsche driving school was underway. With the students in the classroom, the instructors lent us a couple cars to take for a run. They asked us to take it easy, and we nodded as I thought to myself, "Not bloody likely."

We slowly rolled out of the pits before hammering it. After several laps, I caught a wild hair and decided to try and pass World Champion Nigel on a corner. I dove hard to the inside, pulling ahead. I realized, "I got him." But when I glanced over, he just smiled as I passed. I knew that was a bad sign. Way too hot to corner, the car pushed, and I skidded off into the gravel as Nigel flew on by. I thought to myself once more, "Me, passing the world champ? Not bloody likely."

Nigel found the gravel a few times himself. As we returned the cars, the instructors were waiting for us. Gravel fell out from the undersides as we braked. For not taking it easy on the cars, they sent us to visit the classroom as punishment. You can imagine the looks from the students when they saw Nigel stroll in and take a seat.

May of 1994 marked the retirements of Al Unser Sr. (twenty-five consecutive, twenty-seven total) and Johnny Rutherford (twenty-four total). Both took farewell laps around the Speedway. It would also be the last 500 for Mario Andretti (twenty-nine total).

The GOAT (Greatest of All Time) debate between fans of Mario and A. J. Foyt may never end. They each have a Daytona, A. J. has a 24 Hours of Le Mans, and Mario has many F1 victories. As for the Indy 500, it's hard to overlook A. J.'s four wins to Mario's one. On the other hand, since 1968, each has only one checkered flag. A. J. scored ten top-five finishes compared to Mario's six and captured four poles to Mario's three. On the other hand, A. J. only really cared about Indy cars, and Mario cared equally about winning the F1 series. His F1 commitments kept Mario out of one 500 (1979) and caused him to start in the back in others (when another driver qualified for him). In total laps led at the Indy 500, Mario had 556 to A. J.'s 555. Great rivalries are part of what makes the Indy 500 so special.

Team Penske arrived that May with a surprise: the Mercedes-Ilmor 500I stock block. Ilmor switched from Chevy to Mercedes and developed a new engine in total secrecy for the sole use of one team. Paul Tracy tested it at Nazareth during the winter to avoid attention. Snowplows cleared the track, and PT dodged the snowbanks lining the groove. It stretched the definition of "stock block."

Roger Penske certainly wouldn't cheat, but he always exploited a loophole to achieve a legitimate yet unfair advantage. When pressurized refueling cans were banned for CanAm races, the only rule was they had to be gravity fed. At Road America, Roger hoisted the fueling tank on thirty-foot-high stilts to achieve a faster fill-up through head pressure. It was legal, though banned the next week. When he ran sports cars, he used acid to burn weight off the frames. That philosophy inspired the title for Penske driver Mark Donohue's autobiography: *Unfair Advantage.*

The Ilmor put Al Unser Jr. on the pole, though Team Penske's drivers probably sandbagged during qualifications and practice. Nigel Mansell returned for another crack at Indy. Lyn St. James found a spot in Row 2. A new scoring pylon replaced the original that was first erected in 1959.

On Race Day, Emerson Fittipaldi had it in the bag, leading 145 laps with only fifteen to go when he approached teammate Al Jr. from behind. Racers have a killer instinct, and Emmo hoped to seal his win by lapping him. Overly aggressive, Emmo came in too low, bouncing along the rumble strips and crashing out. This time, Al Jr. passed by Emmo's wreck on his way to put his face on the Borg Warner Trophy for the second time in three years.

Danny Sullivan joined us on ABC in Turn Four that year, and we covered a lot of races together. In Rio, the temperature hit 108 degrees. To keep cool, we wore shorts rather than slacks below our dress shirts and blazers—knowing the shot would be only from the chest up. In the middle of the segment, I noticed the camera lens turning for a wider angle. The live audience caught our full attire.

Rio did not live up to my expectations. Sewer breaches polluted the famed Ipanema Beach. Due to crime, the hotel requested we wear their signature blue robes on the beach. It made it easier for security to keep watch over hotel guests from the rooftop. I guess the rest of the beachgoers were on their own.

Leading up to the IROC at Michigan, Danny coached me as we climbed the high banks in a Dodge Avenger. On the road course, the former cab driver kept saying "fast is slow." He wanted a gentle trail braking: a short hard brake at first to get the nose down followed by easing off the brake, all while keeping the steering wheel as steady as possible. Just turning the wheel slows the car. The smoother the turn, the less speed lost. Ideally, on an oval, you never lift in the turns, keeping the rev up all the way into the straightaway.

I went through Uncle Bobby's driving school before the IROC at Watkins Glen. With Bobby riding shotgun and hollering instructions at me, I about lost it on the first turn. On the long straightaway into the boot, he kept at it, yelling at me to stay on the throttle: "Now, Father, you have it all wrong. You ain't a race car driver, and I'm the best driver ever." He put his foot on top of my foot and held down the pedal, flooring it into the curve. So continued my driving lesson.

Later in the day, I took a practice lap alone, and believe it or not, I followed Bobby's instructions. Another car quickly closed in on me from behind. As I swerved into the pit to get out of the way, it pulled in behind me. Worried I had done something wrong, I kept the net up. Dale Earnhardt Sr. stepped out and said, "That's pretty good," and walked away. No doubt the best racing compliment I ever received, but I still hate it when Bobby's right.

The IROC series ended too soon. Founded by David Lockton, developer of the Ontario Speedway, along with Roger Penske and Les Richter, they wanted to bring together the champions of different racing disciplines to see how they fared head-to-head. In the '80s, NASCAR legends Dave Marcis and Dick Trickle tested the cars, with Dick always smoking a cigarette in an open-faced helmet as he charged around the track. After a while, the team owners didn't want to share their stars with another race promotion, or risk a driver getting hurt, and the series closed. It's a shame—no other contest offered such a battle of pure skill among the best of the best.

At Michigan, Roger Penske offered me a ride on his helicopter to fly to Brian's graduation from summer camp at Culver Military Academy, a prestigious boarding school in northern Indiana. In his youth, Roger attended Culver's summer camp, and he joined the Drum and Bugle Corps—as did Brian. Roger greeted us as we returned. Known for being reserved, Roger has a deadpan demeanor even when he's on the headset telling his driver they've just won the Indy 500. I had to chuckle at Roger's excitement as he gushed to Brian, still in his marching uniform, about his days at summer camp.

Mario Andretti and Jim Williams, Roger's long-time partner in racing, underwrote the expenses of Father Phil, the chaplain at the Indy car races. On Sunday mornings, Father Phil held several masses around the paddock in a team's trailer or a broadcast truck. His thirteen-minute mass, including the homily, had the feel of a race.

Sally and I went to Italy for our twenty-fifth anniversary. Father Phil, then at the at a church on the Piazza Navona, gave us a private tour of Rome. In Amaseno, the ancestral home of Sally's family, he made arrangements with the parish priest who led us through the narrow streets up to a second story apartment. Inside were Sally's cousins, aged ninety-seven and 103. Anglicized into Larvick when her grandfather immigrated to the US, Sally's surname was originally "la Vicari," As we drank espresso together in that tiny room, Sally found her roots in the Old World.

In the summer of 1994, for the first time since 1916, the Speedway hosted two races. NASCAR arrived at the Grand Old Oval for the inaugural Brickyard 400. I had the honor to serve as host and call the play-by-play with Bob Jenkins and Benny Parsons for three Brickyards.

The first race exceeded all expectations, selling out and becoming the most attended NASCAR event ever. A. J. Foyt came out of retirement to compete on the hallowed track one more time. Shortly before showtime, a power failure knocked out every camera except the one in front of me. In a few stressful moments, I prepped for a one-man show. Thankfully, the power came back just before we went live. Local boy Jeff Gordon, in his second season, made the storyline come true and claimed the checkered flag.

The tradition of kissing the bricks at the Speedway started with the 1996 NASCAR race. Driver Dale Jarrett and his crew chief Todd Parrott wandered off from Victory Lane and over to the yard of bricks. They kneeled down and kissed the bricks. When asked by reporters about the pavers, no doubt flavored with burnt rubber and motor oil, Dale said, "They tasted like victory."

When I covered NASCAR, Benny Parsons usually shared the booth with me. His great smile and infectious enthusiasm kept the show running smooth. A chance encounter at a gas station launched his racing career. A customer showed up towing a race car, and he invited Benny to the racetrack. When the driver didn't show, the owner let Benny, a Detroit cabbie, take his place.

Benny had an amusing piece of racing memorabilia—a NASCAR poster featuring the drivers competing in the 1987 Winston, a race comprised of only the drivers who scored a first place in the prior season. The first version of the poster caught a prank by Tim Richmond. I'll just say it resulted in an overexposure. When officials realized the gag, they collected the posters and issued replacements. Benny had an original, and I located another one for my own collection.

Atlanta 1993 is one NASCAR moment I'll never forget: the Blizzard of Atlanta. Rusty Wallace qualified for the pole in an uneventful run-up to the race. The next day, the snow started falling—in Atlanta—and the winds whipped up as high as 50 miles per hour.

For a panoramic shot of the snow-covered track, my director asked me to stand on the grandstand roof between the race control room and the booth. Just as I stepped off the walkway and onto the ice-covered roof, a gust of wind pushed me toward the edge. My cameraman's eyes widened as I slid. I reached out and grabbed the window frame of the booth to catch myself. I stood there motionless, trying to figure out how to get to safety. With my cameraman pulling my microphone cord like a lifeline, I edged back in. We taped the report from the safety of the booth.

Unfortunately, the most dangerous part of the weekend was yet to come. The ride to the hotel was complete chaos. None of the locals had any concept of how to drive in the snow. I have no idea how we made it in one piece.

Dark clouds gathered over Indy car racing in 1995. No longer content to rest in the shadow of his grandfather and namesake, Tony George had big plans for big changes.

Shy by nature, Tony struggled giving speeches in his younger days. We attended a racing school I arranged in Monterey and became acquainted. On occasion, I would help with a speech. No longer uncertain of himself, Tony grew in confidence and set a course that would lead to a great rift in open-wheel racing.

Over the years, Tony proposed a number of changes to CART that he thought were necessary for the long-term viability of Indy car racing. He eventually resigned from its board of directors. During May of 1995, Tony announced the Indy Racing League, a new series in direct competition with CART, starting in 1996. Everyone knew a split would be disruptive and should be avoided, but negotiations proved fruitless. The fifteen-year truce in the open-wheel racing war came to a sudden end.

In May of 1995, I moved our booth down to pit level for qualifying, to get a better feel of the action. Scott Brayton, in his fourteenth start, found the pole for the first time. The field was surprisingly fast: the slowest qualifier that May would have been in Row 2 the year before. Derek Daly and I covered some very tense days with Team Penske on the ropes. Al Unser Jr. couldn't make the cut, and Emerson Fittipaldi sat on the bubble on Bump Day.

USAC reduced the boost for all engines, sidelining the dominating Ilmor from the year before. The new PC-24 chassis, with a less powerful badged Ilmor, handled slow in the turns. Penske abandoned the PC-24s and borrowed Lolas from Bobby Rahal. Time ran out. Emmo got bumped. When the shot rang out at six o'clock, ending Bump Day, Team Penske failed to qualify a car, ending a twenty-six year streak. Returning champ Al Jr. and two-time winner Emmo missed the show. After eleven consecutive 500s, Emmo would never race at Indy again.

A few minutes later, Tim Cindric, then on Rahal's team, sent a note to the public address shack. The loudspeaker blared, "Paging Dr. Kevorkian to the Penske garage. Dr. Kevorkian, please report to the Penske garage." Roger doesn't hold a grudge—Tim went on to run his racing operations.

On Race Day, Stan Fox lost it on the first lap, igniting a nasty wreck collecting three other cars. I correctly called the drivers involved, including Stan's purple car, but I never mentioned Stan again as the race progressed. It was a mistake. Many fans wrote me harsh letters for ignoring Stan, or perhaps mistaking Stan's car for another. That brutal wreck ended Stan's racing career, and he deserved more.

Jacques Villeneuve, in his second Indy 500, caught an early two-lap penalty, but Bobby Unser still predicted the baby-faced Canadian would win. Rookie Eliseo Salazar, who started twenty-fourth, made some of the most amazing passes to move up to the leaders. Jacques crept up behind leader Scott Goodyear during a caution with ten laps to go. Scott saw the green flag and gunned it, jumping the pace car and drawing the black flag. Scott and Steve Horne, owner of Tasman Motorsports, chose to ignore the black flag and finish the race, hoping any penalty would be recalled.

Officials upheld Scott's penalty, and Jacques got the win. Adding in the laps stricken by his early penalty, Jacques completed 505 miles, winning the hard way en route to claiming the series title.

As for Scott's infraction, some say the pace car unexpectedly slowed. In any event, it was a very minor violation. I'm not sure it warranted a forfeiture for the driver in the lead with five laps to go. After reviewing the tape, Scott's team chose not to challenge the ruling.

Tony and Roger's disagreements over the rules drove the wedge deeper, as illustrated by the striking results in 1994 and 1995. Every May after 1996, CART teams had to invest in Indy-only engines and chassis to comply with USAC's rules for the 500, an expensive proposition for a single race.

In the first open-wheel racing war, the CART teams sued to race in the Indy 500, telling the judge they needed it to survive. This time, the titans of CART thought they could get along just fine without the Indy 500.

CHAPTER 14

Casualty of the Open-Wheel Racing War

I'm a race car driver risking my life at all those other races so I can run in the Indianapolis 500, not so I can run in St. Louis . . . because of some political battle.
—Al Unser Jr.

In 1996, the battle for American open-wheel racing supremacy blew wide open. The Indy Racing League commenced its inaugural three-race season at Walt Disney World. Buzz Calkins Jr. won it, and he gave me his helmet from that race. For the Indy 500, the Speedway reserved twenty-five spots for drivers with the best points standings in the IRL. That left only eight slots for the twenty-some regular drivers on the CART series. In retaliation for the 25/8 rule, CART boycotted the Indy

500 and scheduled a competing race for the same day: the US 500 at Roger Penske's Michigan International Speedway.

Both sides called in the lawyers. A couple of years earlier, CART changed its name to IndyCar, a trademark owned by the Speedway. The Speedway revoked CART's license to use its trademark, prompting CART to seek an injunction. The IRL filed an antitrust suit against CART alleging interference with sponsors. It felt like a bad acid flashback to the late 1970s.

The split brutally divided the drivers and fans. David Letterman, remaining loyal to CART, invited Paul Newman onto his show as a guest, and they both said they would be in Michigan on Memorial Day Weekend. Mario Andretti aptly called it "racing's Russian Roulette."

Sally expected to work the 500 radio broadcast as she had the last thirteen years. But her invitation to the annual network breakfast never arrived. When she inquired, she learned she was off the team. Our production company's radio broadcast of the CART series became a liability. The brass at the Speedway felt like Sally was "working for the enemy." Questioning her loyalty doubly stung because Sally turned down an offer from ESPN to join their coverage of the competing US 500.

By then, Sally had established herself as a network motorsports reporter. In 1987, she became the first woman pit reporter for Indy cars on NBC when she replaced Bruce Jenner on NBC's *SportsWorld*. She also worked as a pit reporter for the Canadian Broadcast Company. Rudy Martzke, the sports reporter for *USA Today*, often singled out Sally's reporting in his weekly "Best in Sports" kudos.

Sally appeared on ESPN's *SportsCenter* and featured regularly as the motorsports expert on ESPN2's *SportsNite*, with Keith Olbermann and Suzy Kolber. The inaugural live broadcast of ESPN2, aka "the Deuce," featured the Indy car race at Laguna Seca; Sally and I covered that race together. She also worked on *RPM2Night*, *This Week in CART* on the Prime Network, and other shows like *Super Chargers*. It was the Speedway's loss, not Sally's.

To add insult to injury, CART ended our contract and took the radio broadcast in-house. Sally and I really felt like we got it coming and going in the open-wheel racing war.

Many people ask me *why* Tony George did it—why did he form the Indy Racing League? I think the answer is control and protection against a boycott. CART had around twenty-two cars in the series. If CART teams withdrew, perhaps in order to force concessions, the Indianapolis Motor Speedway would be in a bind. For the Indy 500 to maintain its reputation as the Greatest Spectacle in Racing, it couldn't just be the biggest race on the CART circuit.

When Johnny Rutherford went to work for the IRL, he wanted to save the sport. The top CART owners had financial interests in the engines and chassis that the other teams had to buy or lease to be competitive. In other words, the best teams profited off the smaller teams. Ever-escalating costs from badged engines and technological innovations made racing all about finding sponsorships. The corporate sales guy closing on sponsors had become more important to the team than any driver or mechanic.

J. R. hated that teams were choosing sponsored drivers over the best drivers. CART drivers were expected to pay their way onto a team, and talented young racers without sponsors were heading to NASCAR. If CART continued on its course, could American open-wheel racing and the Indianapolis Motor Speedway survive?

Others, like Robin Miller, could find no excuse for what Tony George did. He believed the split was the worst thing that ever happened to the sport, setting it back forty years. He blamed Tony personally for turning the Indy 500 into the equivalent of AAA baseball. If you ask him who won the open-wheel racing war, Robin's response is NASCAR. Many believe Indy car racing would have remained above stock cars through the 1990s and 2000s without the split. That's my view too.

While I think Tony George had the best of intentions, he and J. R. offered no compelling plan to fix the system. When Robin

Miller crewed for Bill Finley in the '70s, the team had three seasonal employees. When I worked for Pat Patrick, a large team, we had maybe four people for each car. Pat used semitrailers, but smaller teams towed their race cars on flatbeds or box trucks. No one had today's semis with mobile offices and computerized garages. Large teams have twenty employees traveling with each car, and a full-time staff of 150. Most of these costs would never go away.

Perhaps Tony genuinely believed he could force a quick and mutually beneficial merger that protected the Speedway. CART's decision to become a publicly traded company certainly complicated the issue. Control began to shift to shareholders obsessed with short-term profits rather than team owners who loved racing and the Speedway. Wall Street would sell off anything for a dime. Both sides dug in deeper. The battle raged for more than a decade.

In May of 1996, the Speedway's loyal fans were rewarded with a riveting Pole Day. Arie Luyendyk put up a fast time, knocking Scott Brayton off the top spot. Only thirty-three minutes remained for Day One, and owner John Menard wanted back on the pole. Already in the front row, withdrawing Scott's car risked a much lower slot. In the booth, Danny Sullivan and statistics guru Russ Thompson were floored; they couldn't believe John would try it. It was the equivalent of splitting tens in Blackjack in hopes of catching aces. Rookie Tony Stewart was relieved when he didn't have to "nut up" and requalify. John sent Scotty out again, and he caught the ace, boldly recapturing the pole for a second year in a row.

That evening, officials discovered Arie's car was seven pounds underweight and disqualified his run. The next day, Arie shook it off and shattered the track record with a 237.498-miles-per-hour lap. That's around the track in thirty-eight seconds. His qualifying set of laps broke the record as well. Those speeds still stand over twenty years later.

In this unique era of speed, drivers reached 260 mph on the straightaways and never lifted the throttle in the turns. But every new era of speed seems to require a sacrifice to the gods of racing.

On Friday, May 17, Scott Brayton lost it on a practice lap. He fatally crashed into the wall in Turn Two. Evidently a tire with a slow leak failed on him. Away at Charlotte for the IROC, the news blind-sided me. I knew Scotty well and everyone loved him. The Speedway hosted Scott's memorial service, and mourners sat in the stands along the main straightaway. Tears ran from the faces of hardened drivers and crew members when Carly, Scotty's young daughter, picked up a picture frame and kissed the portrait of her father.

On Race Day, Tony Stewart assumed the pole. Arie stood out as the lone past winner in the field. Seventeen rookies lined up around him. CART fans jeered the Indy 500 as amateur hour, with the professionals all in Michigan. Robin Miller likened it to putting the Toledo Mudhens in the World Series. CART ran ads for the US 500 as "The Real Stars, The Real Cars." But before even reaching the starting line, the pros in Michigan found themselves in a colossal wreck involving twelve of the twenty-seven racers. On the restart, nine drivers sat behind the wheels of their backup cars.

In the ratings war, eight million watched the Indy 500; only two million watched the US 500.

After the green flag in Indy, it seemed like destiny for Tony Stewart: the local-boy rookie phenom gets a win for his fallen veteran teammate. He led forty-four laps, but shortly before the halfway mark, his engine gave out. Buddy Lazier seized the lead late in the race. Buddy hobbled into the Speedway that May with a cane, just two months after breaking his back in sixteen places during a practice lap at Phoenix. His car was fitted with a special seat for his back. As the race wore on, Buddy kept reaching out of the cockpit and up into the airstream to ease his cramping hands and stretch out his back. He pushed through the pain to Victory Lane and his first checkered flag in an Indy car.

Later that season, Buddy told me he felt like he hadn't won the 500 because so many great drivers were in Michigan that day. This isn't uncommon when a driver wins due to the mishap of another racer. Drivers are out there to prove they're the best. Some wins answer that question more definitively than others.

I knew Buddy and his dad Bob very well. We talked a long time. I told him the Indy 500 always has a twist. Indy has its own personality. It doesn't always go to the fastest car or the hottest driver. Those are the facts: lots of Indy 500s came down to a cloudburst, a wreck, or a six-dollar part breaking. Whoever takes the checkered flag is, and forever will be, a champion of the Indianapolis 500.

It seemed to help. I hope so. Twenty years later, Buddy still suited up at Indy, trying to prove himself one more time. He told me, "I'd take all the pain I felt driving that car and double it for another Indy win."

On Pole Day 1997, Arie Luyendyk caught the top slot and kept it this time. When Lyn St. James and Johnny Unser were bumped, despite posting faster times than the slowest eight qualifiers, USAC amended the 25/8 rule (it had already been repealed for future years). Lyn and Johnny were in, rounding out a Field of 35.

The IRL's new rules swept into effect, bringing entirely different cars and engines to Indy. They disallowed turbochargers, and Cosworth, Buick, and Ilmor declined to participate. The normally aspirated engines came from Oldsmobile and Nissan. The spec chassis from Dallara and G-Force banished the Lolas, Reynards, and Penske Cars from the Grand Old Oval.

Tom Sneva joined me in the booth. Tom had an unlikely backstory: schoolteacher turned race car driver. I don't know what he taught those kids. You never knew what he might say. Live in the booth, I asked Tom his thoughts on Gary Bettenhausen. Tom had a number of complimentary things to say about Gary, including the fact that, "Gary knows every place in the country to get a good lap dance." I had no comment. Tom laughed, his eyes sparkling from behind his signature clunky glasses, the only glasses on the Borg Warner Trophy. His two great loves are racing and golf. At his golf course in Arizona, he fitted his golf cart with a motorcycle engine. It can break 100 mph.

A fire at the warehouse destroyed nearly all of the floats for the 500 Festival Parade, but Race Day began with rain. Sunday rained out completely. On Monday, Mari Hulman gave the starting command for the first time, but fans only saw fifteen laps before the rain returned. My producer helped get us out of the booth by prerecording a series of clichéd updates: "Rain is still delaying the Indy 500 but we hope to get running soon," or, "The skies are beginning to clear and we hope the track will soon dry," and of course, "It's stopped raining in Terre Haute."

On Tuesday, the weather cleared and the green flag flew. Arie Luyendyk traded a few cutting passes with Tony Stewart, including Arie mowing the lawn with two wheels in the grass. With six laps to go, Arie found the lead by jumping ahead of Scott Goodyear on a restart. On lap 198, Tony Stewart brushed the wall and brought out a caution as Scott and Arie shot out of Turn Four. Both drivers began to slow. Almost all the way down the main straightaway, the starter began waving the white and green flag while the yellow light still shined. The green light came on seconds later. Both reacted to the flag, but Arie kept in front. Scott gave everything he had, crossing 0.57 seconds behind. Arie won his second Indianapolis 500.

In essence, Scott lost three Indy 500s by less than a second *combined*; two of those by controversy. Though he puts on a brave face, you can still see the pain in Scott's eyes when those three races are discussed. At his home, an empty niche for a Baby Borg Warner, the smaller version of the trophy given to the driver, will never be filled.

USAC earned a lot of well-deserved heat for the blunder of the green flag and the yellow lights. Tensions with the officials remained high at the IRL's next race at Texas Motor Speedway. When Tony Stewart crashed late in the race, a few cars dodged the wreck by darting down pit road. The computers scored A. J. Foyt's driver Billy Boat in first place. I kept Barb Hellyer on my staff to score laps manually in case the computers went down. She started tapping her pencil on the leader's boxes on her chart. According to her notes, the officials had all three of the top positions wrong. Barb was always right—the best scorer, hands down, for any race from midgets to Indy cars. She caught a similar mistake at the NASCAR Charlotte 500 years earlier. I told my producer, but he said we had to go with the official scoring.

Arie Luyendyk won it according to Barb's notes, and Arie reached the same conclusion. He charged the victory circle and announced himself as the winner. A. J. cut him off from confronting Billy and backhanded Arie. I later asked Arie about it, and he said the then sixty-two-year-old A. J. landed a very hard hit. I thought I knew the answer. I just wanted to know if Arie would admit it.

Billy Boat got his moment of victory, and A. J. still has the trophy, but a review declared Arie the winner. The IRL terminated USAC as its sanctioning body; it would sanction its own races. After a half century officiating Indy car races, USAC finally made one mistake too many.

In a cost-savings move, the Speedway shortened the month of May for 1998: six days of practice, two days of qualifications, and Carb Day. For the first time, a rule change allowed cars to be towed to Gasoline Alley for repairs. Previously, any car that left the pits for the garages was disqualified.

On Race Day, Billy Boat started on the pole and the reigning IRL series champ Tony Stewart sat on the inside of Row 2.

Neither car would go the distance. Interviewed live by Jack Arute, Tony vented on being first out, saying, "This has been my number one goal; every year I get s—— on."

In a sign of advancing technology, A. J. Foyt's nephew used a laptop to calculate fuel for Kenny Bräck. A. J. thought the car needed to pit, but he deferred to the computer model, which indicated a couple more gallons in the tank. A. J. regretted not trusting his instincts as Kenny ran out of fuel and coasted to the pits, losing a lot of time. As Kenny drove off, A. J. picked up the laptop and slammed it into the pit stand.

Veteran Eddie Cheever, who started in seventeenth position, battled to the front. Back in 1981 at Caesar's Palace, Roger Penske remarked on the then young driver's skills. A decade later Eddie left F1 for Indy cars. In the closing laps, Buddy Lazier put the pressure on Eddie, nearly pulling alongside, but to no avail. On his ninth try at Indy, Eddie found the checkered flag.

In the midst of the hostilities between CART and the IRL, I became another casualty in the open-wheel racing war. The network decided CART announcers should only do CART races, meaning I would no longer be in the booth for the Indy 500. I couldn't believe it. I had no say in the decision. In the words of Howard Katz, I was just a hired gun.

It's hard to describe how polarizing those days were for drivers, crews, owners, and race fans. In his book *Tales from the Indy 500*, Jack Arute likened it to walking down the middle of a highway and getting hit by trucks going in both directions. Part of the nastiness came with the advent and widespread use of the internet. In the time before registering commenters and "community standards," message boards and blogs offered nearly total anonymity. No one monitored the deplorable levels of vicious rumor, character assassination, and even violent threats. It didn't take long before I decided on the Page Rule for sanity: Don't read the internet. Back then, most publications were still in print. Even today, I think anyone in the public sphere should avoid reading the comments sections.

Parker Johnstone became my color commentator for the CART races. Early in his career when Parker found the pole at the Michigan 500, we interviewed him to start the telecast. With the temperature in the nineties, I asked him if the heat would be a factor. He answered, "No. I dig postholes at my ranch in Oregon in hotter weather." I knew he would be good on television from the start.

In addition to being a race car driver, Parker was an Eagle Scout, a classically trained trumpet player, an aerobatic pilot, and even a stuntman for the movie Speed. He turned down Julliard to earn an engineering degree from the University of California, Berkeley.

We had great chemistry. At a race in Houston, Robby Gordon's car stalled and let out a plume of smoke. Parker asked, "Do you know what that was?" I deadpanned, "Electrical problem." Parker asked, "You sure it wasn't the engine?" When our pit reporter got to him, Robby said, "Must have been an electrical problem." The drivers always called it an electrical problem to avoid badmouthing a sponsor's engine.

During a practice session at Hawthorne, the former horse track in Chicago, a film crew shot footage for the movie *Driven* featuring a scene with Burt Reynolds confined to a wheelchair. Burt kept wheeling back and forth in the pits. After a few takes, Burt stood up and walked away. Parker exclaimed in a televangelist voice, "It's a miracle!" Ben Edwards, a British announcer who was live on the air at that moment, heard Parker and couldn't stop laughing, losing all composure.

Parker has a playful disposition. At Portland while waiting to go on the air, we mimed a circus act for the broadcast truck. With no discussion, it just happened: stools to tame lions, imaginary trapeze landings, a sword dance. We switched off as performer or ringmaster directing the audience to applaud. The show went on for some time to the hysterics of our production crew. Our audience, to our surprise, also included the folks in race control looking through the window next door and most of the crews in the pits directly in front of us.

When the Jackson Symphony Orchestra in Michigan asked me to narrate its tribute to Dr. Martin Luther King Jr., Parker, who once played professionally with the Berlin Philharmonic, wanted to come along to the rehearsal. He realized the conductor seemed to be missing my cues. At the concert, Parker sat in the second row with sheet music in hand. I ignored the conductor and followed Parker, to the amusement of some of the musicians. Levity aside, it was a great honor to be part of the event.

In May of 1999, I found myself on the sidelines for the first time since 1973. Bob Jenkins followed in my footsteps yet again, leaving the radio broadcast to join the ABC telecast. Mike King became the next Voice of the 500.

I called the CART race at St. Louis the Saturday before the Indy 500. Dan Luginbuhl of Team Penske offered me Roger's personal seats for Sunday, and Rick Mears brought them over. They were front row in the upper deck in Turn One, looking up the main straightaway—some of the best seats in the house.

On Race Day, with none of the distractions and demands of the broadcast booth, I blissfully lost myself in the race. Pole-sitter Arie Luyendyk led sixty-three laps before losing it on a low pass and spinning into the wall. Robby Gordon led late in the race and gambled on his fuel. On lap 198, Kenny "the King of Sweden" Bräck chased down the leader on the back straightaway, when Robby ran out of fuel in the short chute. Robby coasted into the pits, leaving Kenny a free path to Victory Lane.

Kenny, a native Swede, received a congratulatory call from the real King of Sweden. As the team needed to head to other postrace festivities, owner A. J. Foyt asked who was on the phone. He shouted to Kenny, "Tell him the King of Texas says it's time to go."

Fontana, just a few miles away from the old Ontario track, hosted the last race of the season on Halloween. I wandered down to the pits to see driver Greg Moore. The day before, Greg injured his hand when a tow cart crashed into his motor scooter, leaving him with stitches and a broken finger. Initially, CART Medical Director Dr. Terry Trammel would not clear Greg to race. Trammel later spoke with another specialist and came up with a splint that might allow enough movement to drive. Greg put up a couple of smooth practice laps, and Trammel cleared him.

Years earlier at Nazareth, I had watched as this skinny blonde kid with glasses stood all day outside the ropes at Penske Racing hoping for a chance to talk to Roger. As the hours went by, he wouldn't give up. Dan Luginbuhl and I couldn't stand it any longer. We asked Roger to come out and talk to the kid.

Greg eventually made his way up to the CART circuit. Greg and his pals Dario Franchitti, Tony Kanaan, Helio Castroneves, and Max Papis became known as the "Brat Pack" for their tight friendships, youthful antics, and late-night carousing. Even at twenty-four years old, Greg looked like a high school freshman.

As we chatted, Greg showed me his bandaged hand—he was amused by it all. He wondered if the Novocain injection might affect his racing in a good way. He had big news that morning: Roger Penske just offered him a spot on his team for the next season. I congratulated him. As I left I said, "Stay safe;" the last words I spoke to him.

During the race, Greg lost it coming off the second turn and hit the berm of an access road. It sent him into a side roll that ended with his cockpit against the concrete wall. I knew instantly it was a fatality. I pushed the talkback button and said to my producer and director off-air, "No replays." The yellow flag came out and we could only wait for the bad news.

The medical team confirmed it was fatal, but we couldn't say anything on the air until his family was notified. There should be no rush to publish a driver's death. The race rolled on as management came up with a worse idea than at Toronto.

At the Molson Indy Toronto in 1996, rookie Jeff Krosnoff suffered fatal injuries when he left the straightway and crashed into a tree. His tire also came loose, killing corner worker Gary Arvin. The families were properly notified, but race officials decided to wait out the race and announce the deaths after the broadcast. I thought it was garbage. The news should be reported as soon as appropriate, not ignored for PR purposes. Brian Williams of the CBC was disgusted as well.

With Greg's death, management decided to do the opposite and make a spectacle of his death. They wanted to wave the caution flag to slow the cars, lower the flags to half-staff, and make a dramatic announcement. We were livid. A tragedy shouldn't be showcased. I looked to Chief Steward Wally Dallenbach through the glass separator between us and race control. I saw the same pain in his eyes that I'm sure he saw in mine. The higher ups insisted.

In the end, it all got bungled: the flags lowered but the caution never came. The flags went back up. By then the families had been notified, so we sent a camera to Dr. Olvey to simply confirm the injuries were fatal, and we were done with it. We just wanted that miserable day to end.

The death of a driver is very difficult; we're all a family traveling together on the series. Greg's death came just weeks after rookie Gonzalo Rodriquez died in a wreck during qualifications at Laguna Seca. Greg's death hit us especially hard. Trammel's decision to seek a second opinion on the splint racked him with guilt for years.

The next night, Parker and I emceed the CART awards banquet at Century City in Los Angeles. Greg secured a top ten spot in the

229

series standings. In one of the most difficult moments in my career, I presented his award posthumously and in memoriam. A few drivers added their own heartfelt remarks. I looked over at Parker, and he had a haunted look in his eyes.

As a member of the safety committee for the Championship Drivers Association, Parker felt a personal responsibility for Greg's death. He thought he failed Greg by not forcing the track to make changes to the exit of Turn Two. Parker felt if he had worked harder, Greg might still be with us.

Greg could have been the next Rick Mears. Tony Kanaan says if Greg had lived, among Dario, Helio, and himself, Greg would have had the most Indy 500 wins.

In the winter of 2000, I covered the Winter X Games in Mount Snow, Vermont. ESPN's Chris Fowler came by to watch us work. Our booth consisted of a small scaffold wrapped in a tarp to block the freezing wind. Several space heaters blasted against the cold. As Greg Creamer and I called the race where Tucker Hibbert got his first pro SnoCross win, Chris stood too close to one of the heaters for too long. His snow pants caught on fire right beside me. I half-tackled Chris to beat down the flames and missed my cue. My producer, Terry Lingner, jumped on me in my headset. Greg hit the talkback button and explained what happened. With the fire extinguished, and Chris unharmed, Terry barked, "I don't care who is on fire. You do the show." I'm fairly sure Terry was joking.

That reminds me of another announcer named Chris with his pants on fire. In the late '70s, I looked down from the south wing of the Control Tower to see ABC shooting a segment with Chris Economaki and Jackie Stewart in the flag lot. They were demonstrating the difference between gasoline and methanol by setting on fire a couple of baking pans filled with fuel. The first take went fine.

But as they say in the business, they did a second take "just for safety." Chris got his mic cable in a tangle, gave it a tug, and dumped the invisibly flaming pan of methanol. It ignited his pants, and Chris immediately panicked as he felt the warmth of the flames. With a champ's reflexes, Jackie dove on Chris, encircling his legs and putting out the invisible fire. In the process, he pulled down Chris's trousers. The very confused crew couldn't figure out why Jackie suddenly tackled and de-pantsed Chris.

I covered the first Winter X Games at Big Bear Lake in California near the Fontana track. I got a kick out of the snow-shovel races. The contest arose out of the long tradition of ski-lift operators sitting in the scoop of a snow-shovel to slide back down at the end of a shift. We actually televised these athletes racing in modified snow shovels. The snowmobile events blew me away. It's absolutely terrifying to see those guys pull off acrobatic moves in those giant, heavy machines.

I went to a lot of beautiful mountains working the X Games, including Aspen. My daughter Marlo, all grown up, came along, and we took rides on the cable cars and enjoyed fine dining. It was a special father-daughter trip.

The ESPN Great Outdoor Games Flyball, or perhaps doggie-drag-racing, featured side-by-side lanes. At the sound of the bell, the pooches ran over hurdles to hit a pad on the machine at the end of the lane. As tennis balls popped up, the dogs chomped on them midair before running back over the hurdles to the finish.

My last X sport was the PRCA Xtreme Bulls league: professional bull riding. With eight-time champion Donnie Gay, who has a great sense of humor, I learned more bull than I ever imagined. And that's something after a career spent around race car drivers. The sport seemed to favor contestants with smaller statures: the lower center of gravity must really help. Maybe I missed my calling.

In May of 2000, the skyline of the Speedway changed with the shiny new glass and steel pagoda replacing the old Master Control Tower. The Goodyear blimp flew over the Speedway for the last time. Firestone had only returned a few years earlier. The first Carb Day rock concert kicked off race weekend.

The CART/IRL conflict began to thaw as Chip Ganassi Racing, having won four successive CART series titles, brought Jimmy Vasser and series champ Juan Montoya to the Grand Old Oval. In a surprise move, Al Unser Jr. switched from CART to the IRL. His sentiments in an interview expressed what a lot of drivers felt:

> All I know is I don't have to convince anybody of my reasoning to come to the IRL, because I don't give a s—— what they think. My heart lies in the middle of Indiana, not at Mid-Ohio. I'm a race car driver risking my life at all these other races so I can run in the Indianapolis 500, not so I can run in St. Louis on Memorial Day Weekend because of some political battle like I had the last three years.

Greg Ray relished catching the pole on his third of four straight starts in the front row: "The four laps of qualifying are the ultimate speed event." Lyn St. James and rookie Sarah Fisher made history with two women qualifying in the same field for the first time.

My whole life, I put the Indy 500 above anything else. But with no responsibilities at the Speedway, I spent the weekend in Georgia for Marlo's college graduation and her move back to Indianapolis. I listened to the 500 on the radio broadcast for the first time since 1968. It was still a fantastic way to experience the race.

On Race Day, Lyn lost it in Turn One taking out Sarah as well. The irony of the lady drivers crashing into each other became water-cooler humor for some time. Juan controlled the race and led 167 laps. Buddy Lazier caught up late but couldn't close the distance.

Juan, the rookie and native of Columbia, found the checkered flag with a leisurely seven-second lead.

One of my favorite memories of Juan is competing for the Automundo Cup. At Road America, Automundo owner Jorge Koechlin proposed an endurance go-kart race at the nearby Briggs & Stratton test facility. The rules allowed one professional driver on the four-person teams. I picked Juan as my pro but also Parker Johnstone (technically a non-pro since he was now a broadcaster). Last, I brought in Jono Klein, son of team sponsor Rick Klein. Jono was still just a kid, but he had mad karting skills.

We blew them away and took the trophy all three years. Some of these racers have a youthful zest for life that never leaves them, and there's something special when one of the world's greatest drivers still loves strapping into a go-kart.

In September of 2000, the Speedway held its first road race, the US Grand Prix F1 race. A series of turns were carved into the infield leading the drivers into Turn One with a right turn up the main straightaway to the north. Opposite the direction of the Indy 500, the right turns seemed very unnatural. To accommodate the F1 teams, the Speedway constructed a row of garages behind the pits.

Try as I might, I came up empty in my efforts to obtain press credentials for the race. I dug deep and called in a favor. The ID I scanned to gain admission on Race Day might have left the impression I was on detail with the FBI.

Fans from all over the world flocked to the city. Some die-hards bring their Ferraris with them when they travel to an F1 race. I gawked at the grid of eighty or so Ferraris in the infield and another grassy parking area full of them across from Georgetown Road. I felt the same awe when MotoGP arrived at the Speedway: beautiful bikes everywhere.

CART scheduled the Firestone Firehawk 600 for April of 2001 at the Texas Motor Speedway. Dan Wheldon, who was not yet an Indy car driver, kindly introduced himself to me. As it turned out, no one would race that day.

After two days of practice, twenty-one out of twenty-five drivers complained of dizziness and disorientation. The much higher banks (twenty-four degrees compared to the Speedway's nine degrees) resulted in vertical and lateral forces exceeding five Gs in the corners. The CART cars were far faster than NASCAR stock cars, and even the IRL cars. Dario Franchitti told me he felt like he couldn't connect with his car. In the turns at Indy, drivers face up to four Gs separated by the straightaways. At Texas, the higher Gs also lasted twice as long without the separation of the short chute. Officials canceled the race. With no race, I invited astronaut Dave Brown to the booth, and he explained to our viewers how increasing Gs can affect astronauts, fighter pilots, and race car drivers.

Ironically, it was also during a race at Texas that my cell phone rang and the caller announced himself as Ed. I asked, "Ed who?" It was astronaut Ed Lu. I didn't expect a call from him because I knew he was on the Space Station—*in outer space*. He called because he knew it was Race Day and he just passed over the track.

I met NASA Flight Director Phil Engelauf when I visited the Johnson Space Center. Like many in his field, Phil loves Indy cars. Particularly in the '60s and '70s, astronauts often visited the Speedway in May. Hoosier astronaut Gus Grissom invested as a team owner. Al Unser Sr. broke his leg racing an astronaut and Parnelli Jones on motor scooters at the Speedway—it kept him out of the show. Phil and I became friends, and we would get together with his colleagues. I was flattered when Dave asked for my help in setting up his personal cameras for the STS 107.

If you can't become an astronaut, the next best thing is the full motion simulator for the *Orbiter*, the real name for the shuttle. I've had three rides with varying success. On the last one, I really botched the timing of the landing and undershot by hundreds of miles. There's no engine, no thrust, you have to just glide back to the runway at Cape Kennedy. Beside me, astronaut John Kelly took the controls and called out: "Orlando International, this is STS 105 on guard, with you in three minutes. Declare an emergency and clear the runway."

On Dave's mission on STS 107, he sent an email from space to a few of us down below. Marveling at the beauty of our planet, he wrote:

> If I'd been born in space, I know I would desire to visit the beautiful Earth more than I've ever yearned to visit space.

In Aspen for the Winter X Games, I fell asleep thinking of Dave. I had watched the launch. The next morning I awoke and turned on my hotel television. It showed the disintegrating remnants of the space shuttle on reentry.

In May of 2001, Roger Penske returned to the Speedway, ending his five-year absence following the split. Fans cheered as old favorite Michael Andretti rejoined the field.

On that cold, rainy Race Day, I sat in the stands with Sally and Brian. The least inspiring pace "car," an Oldsmobile Bravada SUV driven by a rock star's wife, lumbered around the track on the pace lap.

Cold tires took out pole-sitter Scott Sharp in Turn One right after the green flag. Sarah Fisher lost it, causing Scott Goodyear to crash hard. He broke his back for the second time. Bouts of rain caused yellows and finally a halt late in the race. When the track dried, CART veteran and Indianapolis rookie Helio Castroneves battled his Penske teammate Gil de Ferran for the last thirty laps. They brought the fans to their feet as they roared by on the white flag. Helio held on to a 1.7 second lead as the checkered flag fell.

In an iconic moment, Helio stopped his car at the yard of bricks during his Victory lap. He ran to the outside wall and climbed high up the catch fence to the roars of the crowd. It created a new tradition. Helio's Spiderman routine wasn't spontaneous—he always climbed the fence to celebrate a win.

After the race, Roger Penske reflected back on the open-wheel racing wars and said: "We redeemed ourselves for the lousy thing we did in 1995." With his drivers finishing first and second at the Indy 500, Roger said it was the best day of his life.

CHAPTER 15

Another Stretch in the Booth

I was no longer an Indy car driver. I knew it was
the right choice, but it rips out part of your soul.
—*Scott Goodyear*

n September of 2001, Sally and I headed to Europe for the CART races in Germany and England. Before the races, we traveled by rail on the Royal Scotsman for a sightseeing trip in the Highlands. During our cab ride in Edinburgh, the driver mentioned the news of a plane crashing into the World Trade Center. At the hotel, we saw the towers fall in real time on Sky News—and the station didn't hide the footage of the jumpers.

As parents, Sally and I had a tense few hours. Marlo worked in Manhattan. Brian had hopped a flight to Germany that morning. An FBI friend tracked down Marlo for us. She walked from her office at 38th and Broadway south to her home in Brooklyn. We eventually telephoned Brian at his hotel. His plane departed before the hijackings.

In Dresden, Germany, the teams, network crews, and fans in town for the race probably made up the largest concentration of Americans traveling outside the US. That might make us a target, and we discussed emergency plans in the event of trouble. The network bosses worried that references to the attacks or even a focus on the American flag might be offensive. They did the same thing during the Persian Gulf War—prohibiting us from using words like battle, fight, or conflict. Despite the network's directive to refer to the attacks as a tragedy, I used the term atrocity.

The race had its own tragedy: Alex Zanardi's brutal wreck. We all gasped as his car sheared in half. We had little hope for him. With both legs nearly severed, Dr. Terry Trammel used his partner's belt for a second tourniquet. Father Phil gave the sign of the cross as the helicopter lifted off and rushed Alex to a hospital in Berlin.

For the tape-delayed broadcast, the network wanted me to record three possible endings, including one reporting his death. I refused. They had already broadcast the wreck and his extrication, which we were promised they wouldn't do.

Parker and I rushed to Berlin after the race. We waited, hoping the best for Alex. Due to the disruptions in air travel following 9/11, Alex's wife, Daniela, didn't make the race. The actress Ashley Judd, then engaged to Dario Franchitti, watched over Alex and organized the visitors at the hospital.

Alex survived, but neither leg could be reattached. When Daniela walked into his hospital room, Alex lifted up his sheet a slight bit, and looked underneath. Then he turned to his wife with an impish smile and made a joke about his "third leg" being just fine.

What indomitable spirits some of these race car drivers have. Days after losing his legs and his career—at the very moment he sees his wife for the first time—he brings Daniela to laughter and tears. A wreck could amputate his legs but not his passion for life. Alex soon raced touring cars and became a Paralympic gold medalist in hand cycling.

Alex was lucky to have Trammel watching over him. He is renowned for his work on emergency rescues from race cars. He developed ways to measure G-forces within a driver's helmet so rescuers can better predict the likelihood of an injury. He's spent a career making racing safer.

The outpouring of support for Americans after 9/11 was overwhelming. Dresden, a city firebombed in the last world war, held a candlelight vigil that passed in front of our hotel on the way to the Cathedral. The Brandenburg Gate in Berlin was draped in black with the words "With Sympathy" in silver. In London, candles, cards, and notes covered Grosvenor's Square in front of the US Embassy.

The CART awards banquet marked a turning point in the open-wheel racing war. ABC/ESPN declined to renew its contract with CART and signed with the IRL. CART announced a self-funded broadcasting arrangement at the dinner. The venture soon caused a cash crunch. Over the years, the aging team owners divested and diversified, unloading their interests in the publicly traded corporation. People should have seen the writing on the wall when Roger Penske sold most of his interest along with his racetracks. Stock values spiraled downward and eventually sent CART into a structured bankruptcy. CART was down but not yet out.

With ABC no longer covering CART, I used all my powers of persuasion to return to the booth. Tony George and others came through for me. I couldn't wait for Race Day.

The Indy 500 never lost sight of its roots as a Memorial Day tradition. Throughout the month of May, the Speedway holds several events recognizing the sacrifices of those who serve in the armed forces. The playing of "Taps" shortly before the race always takes me back to growing up on base. As America found itself at war, other sporting events began to include similar tributes.

The legacy of the Speedway should be remembered. When honoring veterans was considered controversial by many after the Vietnam War, the Indianapolis 500 never wavered. The ceremonies honoring the Band of Brothers, Company E of the 101st Airborne, or the Medal of Honor recipients, like my close friend Sammy Davis, reminded everyone of the reason for the holiday.

After the race honoring the Band of Brothers, I encountered two of the heroes on their way to the parking lot, and one's legs were giving him trouble. He flagged me down on my golf cart and asked if I could give his comrade a lift. Of course, I picked them both up. They still had each other's backs sixty years after the war.

When three dozen new recruits take the oath in front of a couple hundred thousand cheering fans, we can hope they will remember how much they matter to us—especially when they return home broken from the horrors of war.

In May of 2002, the new Steel and Foam Energy Reduction (SAFER) walls lined the track—a huge step forward in protecting drivers. Second-year driver Bruno Junqueira clocked north of 230 miles per hour to take the pole. The Brazilian invasion included Bruno and six other countrymen.

George Mack became the second African American to qualify, punching his ticket on Bump Day after getting cleared from a con-cussion sustained during a practice lap. The excellent collection of stories, *Indy 500 Memories* by Art Garner and Marc Spiegel, contains George's perspective at Indianapolis as a rookie:

> Growing a pair of balls big enough to drive the car down into Turn 1 at 230 mph without lifting was very tough. It gets narrow as you head down into Turn 1 and turns into a tunnel. When you're in the car it's like sitting in a bathtub with wheels. You have no vision. You can only see in front of you, that's it. You're blind. It's a leap of faith.

Sarah Fisher claimed the fastest qualification laps by a woman. It proved to be Arie Luyendyk's last 500 (seventeen total, fifteen consecutive).

For the telecast, Bob Jenkins moved to the host position, and Scott Goodyear joined me in the booth. Scott had never seen the prerace festivities and kept pestering me, saying, "Hey Paul, look at this—." Jenks brought us back from commercials and filled in during the lulls from cautions. After the long roads we both traveled, it was special to work the 500 together.

On Race Day, the hard-charging rookie (to Indy, but not Indy cars) Tony Kanaan led for a few laps until he found an oil slick. Helio Castroneves found the lead late, but Paul Tracy, who started twenty-ninth, pressured at every turn. As they dove into Turn Three on their way to the white flag, a crash behind them brought out the yellow flag. At the same instant, P. T. passed Helio. The radio squawked, "Yellow, yellow, yellow—car three is the leader." After some delay and confusion, officials confirmed number 3 Helio had the checkered flag.

In the booth, it wasn't immediately clear what the officials were doing or how they got there. Our crew on ABC and the team on the radio network thought the officials would look to the order of the cars as of the last time they crossed the start/finish line or a timing line under green, putting Helio ahead. We were wrong. The officials looked to the position when the yellow flag dropped. Our split screen on replay showed the timing of the crash and the pass, but not the yellow lights. We thought we found an angle, but it turned out to be a yellow shirt's jacket as he turned into the sunlight. Helio swore up and down that he saw the yellow light on his dash before the pass.

With the official decision, Helio won back-to-back and climbed the fence again. That feat put him in rare company: Wilbur Shaw, Mauri Rose, Bill Vukovich, and Al Unser Sr. He remains the only driver to win his first two 500s.

Team Andretti-Green Racing appealed the decision for P. T. The officials declared that the track is yellow when the officials say it is. But that begged the question: Is it the moment of the crash? The moment the caution is called in race control? The moment the yellow light shined on the track? At the hearing, both sides used telemetry data—my son Brian worked with a couple of professors to create P. T.'s exhibits—in addition to video footage to prove their points. Team Penske pointed to the rulebook: the positioning of cars at the time of a yellow flag could not be challenged—it was left within the judgement of the officials.

On the second day of July, Paul Tracy learned he lost the appeal. I'm sure the 1981 Unser-Andretti mess weighed heavily in Tony George's decision against changing the winner. For the rest of the season, a television in the Andretti-Green garage ran a nonstop loop of video that sure seemed to show P. T. passing Helio just before the yellow caution lights flashed on. P. T. took it hard and refused to return to Indianapolis for seven years.

Scott Goodyear loves to fly by private jet. He hustled every race to avoid commercial—like a high school underclassman desperate to avoid the indignity of riding home in the Big Yellow Loser Cruiser. It may go back to 1996 when he had a horrible wreck in Rio and broke his back. The team couldn't find an emergency airlift back to the States. Fed-Ex, the CART series sponsor, stepped up and literally Fed-Exed Scott back home on a cargo plane.

One season, Scott kept complaining about running into dead ends. I stopped by Roger Penske's coach and soon had a handwritten note from Roger on his official letterhead offering me unlimited use of his private jet. On Race Day, I left it on the table in the booth where Scott would be sure to see it. I waited so I could see his reaction. He turned to me with his face a mixture of awe and envy. I couldn't keep a straight face and busted out laughing. I told him it was all bull; we were both flying commercial.

Scott might also prefer private flights because of my tendency to antagonize the TSA folks—he was scared to death my antics would get him in trouble. As a personal form of protest, I used to carry stickers that read, "This is a tribute to the success of terrorism." I would surreptitiously affix them to conveyor belts and shoe bins. My feud with airport security dates to 1989 when I received a gift from Porsche: a piston connecting rod from an Indy car. On my return flight from Germany, the screeners tried to seize it as a weapon. I had to raise hell to keep it. I've been reactionary ever since.

Jack Arute is just the character you would expect. Growing up, his family owned a racetrack, and he was a decent driver back in his day. I've known Jack since the '70s when he ran the Motor Racing Network and asked me to work the radio broadcast of the NASCAR race at Michigan.

With all his experience, sometimes things just didn't click for Jack. At Long Beach, he said in a live report, "Wankers are slowing down and bottling up the field." He didn't understand why he couldn't use that word. We had a discussion on its etymology during the commercial break.

I accepted an invitation from Jack to race Legend cars at his family's track. We took a helicopter with Bobby Unser and Gary Gerould. We hit fog, the visibility worsened, and the pilot decided we should land. As he changed directions, Bobby started arguing with the pilot, telling him to just watch the headlights of the cars to follow the road.

Bobby Unser took air travel about as seriously as anything else. He once landed his plane on the main straightaway at Phoenix. He had enough runway to land, but not enough to take off again. He had to disassemble the wings to get the plane out of the track. Once reassembled, he took off from the highway. He also had a habit of putting his plane on autopilot while he wandered to the back to do paperwork or take a nap. He often flew through restricted airspace over the White Sands Proving Grounds as a shortcut to his cabin in Chama, New Mexico. On at least one occasion his plane was intercepted by fighter jets. No matter what trouble Bobby got into, he always seemed to talk his way out of it.

Thankfully, the pilot navigating the fog proved immune to Bobby's powers of persuasion, and I avoided a second helicopter crash.

We finally made it to the racetrack. Right off the bat Jack rammed me and began trading paint at every turn. So I rammed him right back. It lasted the whole race. Another time we competed in the Toyota Celebrity Race. Jack asked if he could take a look in the trunk of my car. I popped the trunk, and he took a quick look and closed it. After the race, I realized a rubber chicken had been hanging out of the trunk the whole time.

May of 2003 really started on a test day in April. As Tony Kanaan recovered from a broken arm, sixty-three-year-old Mario Andretti agreed to test T. K.'s car and qualify it if necessary. Mario quickly reached 220 mph despite a decade's change in technology since he last raced. It caused Mario to genuinely consider a return to racing.

In the next session, Kenny Bräck crashed shortly before Mario followed him into Turn One. Mario's car struck debris that sent him flying up end over end, nearly clearing the catch fence, before landing right side up. Midair, he thought to himself, "What am I doing?" With only minor injuries, he walked away still considering a return to racing. After a good night's sleep, Mario doused any speculation of coming out of retirement.

On a rained-out Pole Day 2003, Jack Arute thought we should have a birthday cake for Helio Castroneves's twenty-eighth birthday. We interviewed Brazilians Helio, T. K., and Gil de Ferran in the studio in Gasoline Alley. As Gary Gerould and Jack chatted with the threesome, T. K.'s eyes kept glancing at the cake. Finally, he picked it up. The camera followed the action. Helio backed away, hoping to avoid the inevitable. He took the cake in his face like a champ. True to form, Helio was mostly concerned about his hair.

The friendship of T. K. and Helio has deep roots. They grew up karting together. Unlike Helio, T. K. grew up very poor. Struggling as a young driver in Italy, he worked at a race shop and lived upstairs, locked in overnight. Hard-scrabble beginnings like T. K.'s should inspire us all.

When the track dried, Helio captured the pole on a windy day under difficult conditions, proving once again his unique combination of daring and skill. Rookies Scott Dixon and Dan Wheldon secured spots in the second row. August Joseph Foyt IV qualified at eighteen years old, turning nineteen the day of the show.

While the war between CART and IRL seemed to be winding down, the damage inflicted on Indy car racing began to show. The Speedway didn't announce a sold-out crowd. For decades, the race sold out in July of the preceding year. The race also had difficulty attracting entries. On Bump Day, nine slots stood open. The challenge became finding enough drivers to fill the field. With less than two hours before the six o'clock gunshot, a full field qualified.

On Race Day, before heading to the booth, I wandered through the garages as usual. On my way back, Tom Carnegie waved, and I heard on the public address system, "Here at the starting line, we have Paul Page." That was Tom's trademark lead-in for an interview. I had never been interviewed by Tom on Race Day. A little embarrassed at the time, I'm grateful I checked off something that had been on my bucket list since my first race.

Helio began to take control on lap 129 with teammate Gil de Ferran soon in second. Gil had recently suffered two concussions during wrecks and wasn't cleared to drive until May. Mid-race, Gil's neck started cramping so bad he almost quit. Helio had the lead when the yellow flag dropped for Dan Wheldon's scary crash—he ended up "wearing it"—late in the race. After the green, Gil snuck around Helio in traffic. They relentlessly battled for the next six laps. With the white flag down, both roared out of Turn Four with Gil reaching the yard of bricks 0.299 seconds in front. The long-awaited three-peat was not to be, and the two friends climbed the fence together.

As a nice diversion for the drivers during race week, I arranged a day at the firing range hosted by the Indianapolis office of the FBI. In the early '80s, the local FBI SWAT commander, Chuck Smith, asked me to help staff their law enforcement training courses. Later, I did the same for the Indiana State Police's Emergency Response Team (ERT). I wasn't paid, but they compensated me with time on the range and free ammo.

I regularly volunteered at the FBI's weeklong courses at Camp Atterbury, an Indiana National Guard base in southern Indiana. With the ERT, we once trained at the decommissioned and abandoned VX gas chemical weapons facility in western Indiana. Crawling through a storm drain deep in the complex, somebody asked, "Anybody smell something?" It still makes me laugh just thinking about it.

A lot of drivers are great shots. Wilbur Shaw's autobiography includes a story of him shooting cocktail glasses off a tray held in the air by his wife. Bobby Unser was a crack shot in the Air Force and competed on the Sandia Base's traveling rifle team. After retirement from racing, Willy T. Ribbs became a professional clay shooter.

The FBI let the drivers shoot almost any gun in the arsenal. Tony Kanaan was an enthusiastic participant. He declared if he wasn't a race car driver, he'd be an FBI agent. I'll just say T. K. should look at his targets more.

I instructed Dan Wheldon on the sniper rifle. The targets were the standard human silhouettes used by law enforcement. Dan and I were laying side by side as I showed him how to adjust the scope and operate the rifle. He suddenly stopped and looked at me. In a whisper, Dan said, "Paul, I can't deal with the thought of shooting a human being, even if it is only a target."

I nodded my head and stopped him from going further. I respected his feelings. Though I was trained to shoot in the military, I told him I never hunted and only kept a firearm for self-defense. We moved on to handguns and some targets not shaped like people. This brash young driver had a very humane and compassionate core.

In May of 2004, speeds dropped with new rules decreasing the size of the engines. Second-year-driver Buddy Rice found the pole. In the off-season, rookie Tony Renna died in a wreck during a test run at the Speedway. The crash sent debris hurtling into the stands. No matter the safety measures, racing will always have its risks for drivers and spectators.

I felt the undercurrents of change at the network as I headed to the broadcast booth. Terry Gannon, best known for covering figure-skating, replaced Bob Jenkins as host. We had six pit reporters, including rookies Jamie Little and Todd Harris. Jack Arute joined me in the booth.

Race Day saw lots of rain, causing hours of delays. After the green flag, Buddy Rice kept in front. At the halfway mark, the constant threat of rain caused the teams to roll the dice on whether to pit or stay out front. After cycling through a series of late pit stops and leader changes, Buddy's timing put him in the lead as rain began to fall, bringing out the yellow flag on lap 174. A real thunderstorm arrived, dropping the red and checkered flags on lap 180. David Letterman's team got its first win. The team ran the tables at Indy, claiming the pole position, the pit stop competition, and the most laps led.

The Victory Lane ceremonies were conducted inside the Pagoda. It was the longest Race Day in the booth: we were live for eight hours and twenty minutes; a record for network coverage of a single-day sporting event. The weather worsened, and officials ordered an evacuation of the track. Unaware of the order, Gary Gerould and I wandered over to the empty ABC catering tent. We ate steak as the rainwater grew to ankle deep—almost four inches fell that day. As the skies darkened and tornado sirens blared, we fled to safety. Tornadoes touched down just a few miles away.

That was the second tornado Gary and I weathered together. Many years earlier, Gary and Marlene attended Marlo's elementary school concert. Weather rolled in with hail banging loudly on the auditorium's roof. When the sirens went off, we all ducked and covered in the hallways.

As the season wore on it became clear the network wanted to boost ratings but didn't know how. In a ridiculous demonstration of their cluelessness, they put us in sportscoats and turtlenecks—that'll boost the viewership.

During the off-season, the network picked Todd Harris to replace me. Todd called ahead to give me a head's up, which was more than my agent did, who also represented Todd. We had become friends working the X Games, and I considered myself a mentor to him. We once barely survived a cab ride in Aspen with a driver who was navigating the mountains while three sheets to the wind.

I also wished the best for Jamie Little, who did motorcycle racing public address work before landing the X Games. With her talent and hard work, she rose quickly at ESPN. Jamie looked up to Sally and even thanked her for being a trailblazer in the profession.

Having spent a career cramming to learn all kinds of sports on very short notice, I can say racing is not an easy sport to pick up. It took years as a pit reporter, crew gofer, amateur driver, and lifelong fan to build a solid foundation of knowledge. Racing in general, and Indy cars in particular, cannot be picked up on the fly. The strategy, terminology, and physics are complicated. I wish someone had written down a brief explanation of these concepts when I first started out, so here's a stab at it:

> For Indy car drivers, a car pushes when the car tends to keep going straight even after you turn the wheels. To recover, you lift off the throttle and slow down. An F1 driver will call it understeer. NASCAR calls it tight. I keep it straight by remembering "push" and "understeer" both have a "u."

> Loose is what you feel when you're driving on ice in a rear-wheel-drive car: a fishtail. As you turn the wheel, the rear tires lose grip and start sliding. To recover, you turn the wheels into the slide until the car straightens out. An F1 driver calls it oversteer.

> Drafting: a speeding race car pushes through the air much like a boat through water. You can't see them, but race cars have bow waves and stern waves. The air turbulence created by a car

at 240 mph is huge—you can feel it fifteen car lengths back. Right behind the car is a vacuum. Drivers can pull into that vacuum and it pulls the rear car forward. In the draft, the driver can lift on the throttle to save fuel. Or the driver can use it as a boost to slingshot around the car in front. When we covered NASCAR events, Bobby Unser called it slipstreaming. It drove the NASCAR fans nuts every time he said it.

Rick Mears told me drafting can also affect the car in front. On a practice lap he thought to himself, "Did I just cause the car ahead of me to spinout without touching it?" He discovered if he moved his car into the right side wake of the car ahead of him, he made the other car loose and forced the driver to slow a bit or risk losing control. The same was true for the left side wake but the car pushed. Rick learned to control the car ahead of him just enough to create an opening to pass.

Another term is aero or wing, as in "adding wing." The aerodynamics from a wing adds downforce. An Indy car, at 1,570 pounds, is very light. The wind pushing down on the car makes it heavier. Like adding sandbags to the back of a pickup truck in winter, the weight gives the tires better traction. The actual amount of tire that touches the ground on a race car is only about the size of a handkerchief. That's not much grip with 750 to 800 horsepower turning the tires.

First came the rear wings, then the front wings, and then the underwings, which create most of the downforce. The front and rear wings became smaller and resulted in less drag. Changing the angle of the wing (adding more or less wing) changes the amount and effect of the downforce.

Theoretically, if a car had large enough wings and enough speed, it could drive on a ceiling upside down. To keep speeds down, the rules limit the size of the wings. Overall, drivers are happier when crews add more wing because it means more traction in the turns. But every tweak changes the car's handling. More downforce may affect the suspension differently, and the driver might feel the car push or become loose and slow down to avoid spinning into the wall.

The driver in the cockpit can adjust the suspension through the roll bars (also called anti-roll bars, sway bars, or stabilizers). They soften or tighten the roll rate—roughly how much a race car tilts to the side as it corners. These adjustments compensate for the weight lost by burning fuel, which is significant as each gallon of fuel weighs a little more than six pounds.

Fans need to understand what the drivers and teams are talking about in interviews. The viewing public is smart enough to understand—announcers just need to explain it in a way that captures the imagination. The role of explaining Indy cars was no longer mine. The irony wasn't lost on me that the big brains at the network thought I was too old for Indy cars, but not too old for the sport with the youngest demographic: the X Games.

CHAPTER 16

On the Outside Looking In

*I love Indianapolis. I love the people. I love
everything about it—the tradition, the history.
I just don't know what to say anymore.*
—*Dan Wheldon*

In May of 2005, rookie Danica Patrick electrified the Speedway. She qualified in the fourth spot, but if her first lap had been as fast as her last three, she would have sat on the pole. Kenny Bräck suited up again, just eighteen months after his near-fatal wreck at Texas Motor Speedway. His body withstood 214 Gs, the most anyone has survived. Fan favorite Tony Kanaan claimed the pole, still on fire from dominating the points standings the year before. Carb Day moved to Friday from its traditional Thursday.

I felt a bit like a veteran driver getting bumped or dropped from a team. Those were the breaks, but the breaks still hurt. On the eve of the race, I joined Dan Wheldon and Andretti-Green Racing sponsor Rick Klein for dinner at St. Elmo's, the landmark Indianapolis steakhouse. The night before the big race is a private time for drivers, and usually a quiet evening reserved for close friends and family. I felt honored to be there.

Midway through dinner, I noticed Rick looking intently at Dan's T-shirt. Rick asked, "Is that one of the team's shirts?" Dan hesitated for a moment or two. Rick went on to say, "That's not the way our logo is supposed to look." Dan sheepishly admitted, "These are my T-shirts, not the team's." He explained that he didn't like the material or the fit of the team shirts, and he had his own tailor-made. The whole table chuckled—it was exactly the kind of thing a fashionista like Dan Wheldon would pull.

The laughter turned into a roar as Rick followed up by asking, "But why is the Klein Tools logo smaller on your shirt?" Now it was Rick we were laughing at, the caricature of a sponsor getting bent out of shape over the size of his logo. Dan admitted he changed the proportions on his T-shirt as well because he thought his design looked better. Rick, of course, was very amused.

I always think back on this conversation as perfectly expressing Dan Wheldon. At this level, race car drivers must be extremely precise, and that describes Dan at every level. He expected perfection, and that included his clothing. If the team shirts weren't up to Dan's standards, he would make his own.

On Race Day, I sat in the suite with Rick. While nothing beats being in the broadcast booth, it was a welcome change to sit back and let my heart root for a favorite to win. I wanted Andretti-Green Racing to win because my son Brian was on the crew.

Growing up around racing, Brian knew he wanted to be a part of it somehow. Traveling with me as a high schooler, Brian saw an era when crews showed up a few days before the race and had much more downtime. Teams still spent lavishly on hospitality tents and entertainment. Brian couldn't believe the activity at the track after hours—every team had open doors and people visited around the paddock. He remembers watching Team Penske's crew play a game of roller hockey one evening at Michigan. It was false advertising for Brian. By the time he signed on, it was all business and tight spending.

Still in high school, Brian disassembled wrecked race cars for Derrick Walker's team. Robby Gordon gave Brian a lot of work that summer. The crew started calling him "Half-Page" because he was half my size, half as famous, and only around half the time. It stuck, and he's known in racing circles as Half-Page to this day. Being the little guy had benefits. At eighteen, he sat inside and steered the race car as it was towed to and from the pits.

Brian started working for Andretti-Green in his college days. He and Dan Wheldon lived in the same condo complex for a while, and Dan always offered him a ride to the airport. When Dan tried to order a "cup of hot tea" in his English accent at the local McDonald's, Brian usually had to translate for the confused staff.

Back in the suite in 2005, our hopes sank as Danica picked Dan's pocket on a restart out of Turn One on lap 190 to take the lead. Four laps later, Dan retook the lead. Rick leaned over and said, "Let's go down." We lost the radio signal as we rode down the elevator. We held our breath until the echoes from the public address system assured us Dan still had the lead.

In the pits, everybody was nervous. Several crew members refused to even look at the racetrack. They just sat with their fingers crossed looking down, listening to the public address system. After the white flag came out, the last lap seemed to go on forever. Sebastian Bourdais' crash behind the leaders sent up the yellow flag. They all realized Dan Weldon just won the 500. The team erupted in a frenzy of elation as Dan came around for the checkered flag.

I found myself at the center of a celebration I had reported on for so many years from the broadcast booth. As Dan's car rolled in and the crew followed to Victory Lane, I remained behind and watched.

This was the big moment for Dan, my son, and the rest of the team. They would go on to win the series.

As for me, I just felt what it was really like to be in a winning pit at the moment of victory at the Indianapolis 500. It's something I'll never forget and almost as good as being in the booth.

Almost.

In my career, I generally avoided stick-and-ball sports. I covered a few college football games and a Dolphins-Raiders game, but not very well. I had a rough time naming the right players. I have a degree of dyslexia, and somehow having players with the same number on each team threw me off. Maybe I just didn't want to do it. Maybe after seeing Don Shula walk buck naked out of the showers once was enough.

At the Dolphins game, I met Danny Thomas, the comedian. My Marlo is named after his daughter, Margaret "Marlo" Thomas, an actress and feminist icon who starred on the '60s sitcom *That Girl*. Danny kindly wrote something on the back of a program for my Marlo, a little girl at the time. I'm very proud of Marlo. She works in marketing in New York City.

A better fit for an old gearhead, the network put me on its coverage of National Hot Rod Association (NHRA) drag races with Marty Reid. In the off-season, the network replaced Todd Harris on the Indy 500 with Marty and moved me up to Marty's spot at NHRA. Again, the logic of the network escaped me. Why move the dragster expert to Indy cars and the Indy car expert to dragsters?

May of 2006 saw the return of Michael Andretti and Al Unser Jr. after temporary retirements. Sam Hornish Jr. took the pole. Tom

Carnegie called his farewell race on the public address system, hanging it up after sixty-one years. Never again would we hear, "And he's on it." In a lull in the action, Tom's go-to line was "Where's Mario?" It always elicited laughter and cheers from the crowd.

I was far away from Indy, in Topeka, Kansas, covering the NHRA Summer Nationals during the Indy 500.

On Race Day, Dan Wheldon dominated 148 laps and looked poised for a repeat win, but late pits shuffled the leaders. Michael Andretti found the front on lap 198 with Marco Andretti close behind. In the truck in Kansas, the crew installed a monitor on the floor so I could watch the 500. On that lap, I had to turn it off to record a segment. I thought for certain the Andretti curse had been broken. I was shocked to find out neither Andretti took the checkered flag.

In the last two laps, nineteen-year-old Marco Andretti snatched the lead from his father Michael, with pole-sitter Sam following in tow. With the white flag flying, Marco led the Indy 500 coming out of Turn Four, but Sam drafted up close. Sam took advantage of a small mistake by Marco and pulled alongside less than five hundred feet from the yard of bricks. The photo finish put Sam barely a car length ahead. Time and again, the Indy 500 delivers the most exciting and unexpected finishes.

Brian and I raced in the Wide Open Baja in a Porsche-powered two-seater with Yokohama tires. We camped out in the desert before our leg of the race. Our encampment included the mechanics and a crew filming the documentary *Dust to Glory*. Without radio contact, we sat and waited for the car. It got stuck in the silt with all the others and had to be dug out, putting it eighteen hours behind schedule.

Off-road racing is something different. Getting bogged down in areas with loose sand is maddening. The "goat trails" we took up the

rises were only as wide as the car. Brian has an engineer's tempera-
ment, and he frequently told me to slow down. At least in retrospect,
I think he considers it a great father-son adventure.

By the mid-2000s, the signature innovation and competition among
manufacturers would stall for several years. Every chassis would
soon be a Dallara. They all used Firestone tires. The rules prevented
almost any changes to the cars. Even the teams' own mechanics were
prohibited from tinkering with the leased engines. The manufacturer
assigned one of its engineers to each team to work on them. It called
into question which series runs the stock cars.

In the 1990s, the chassis moved to carbon fiber, first the wings
and then the frame. The composite bodies achieved a consistent
stress superior to metal. The engines became more and more electronic, including the throttle, and most controls moved to the steering wheel.

The information age arrived with sensors to detect every movement of a wheel, shock absorber, or wing. Accelerometers, GPS, and
infrared sensors allowed measurement of the slightest changes in a
driver's path or angle or height above the track. The exact contours
of the track could be known with near microscopic precision. Testing
cars moved from the track to simulations on the seven-post rig where
engineers could literally replay entire races. Manufacturers built wind
tunnels that fit full size cars running at full throttle on a treadmill-like
conveyor belt. All of this could be done without a driver.

For testing on the track, drivers were expected to become
machines as well. The rule for improving a car is one miniscule change
at a time. That requires consistent runs, not daring feats. With the
data, engineers began to know more about drivers than the drivers
might know about themselves. They could see the light brush of the
brakes to heat them before hard braking—styles and techniques that

are often subconscious. While instinct drivers with little technical knowledge could still compete, the best drivers studied the telemetry as closely as the engineers.

It's a long way from the seat-of-your pants, driver-turned-mechanic days, coming up with something completely new every year, like a sidepod or a turbine engine. On the other hand, the cars became much more reliable. Even in the '90s, engines only lasted about six hundred miles. On Carb Day, teams often limited their drivers to fifty miles to save the engine. Today, engines rack up 2,500 miles before replacement. Winning more often comes down to the skill of the driver, not the bad luck of a blown engine.

In May of 2007, the cars turned to biofuels, with ethanol instead of methanol—the first change in fuel since gasoline became obsolete with the mandatory pit stop rules enacted after Eddie Sachs's death. Pole Day had lots of action: Helio Castroneves and Tony Kanaan both withdrew and made second attempts for the top spot. Helio's gamble paid off and he captured the pole. It would be the last 500 for Michael Andretti (sixteen total) and Al Unser Jr. (nineteen total). Fans can only wonder what records, and curses, might have been broken if their careers at Indy hadn't been interrupted by the split.

On Race Day, rain arrived on lap 113 with T. K. in the lead. If the race didn't resume, he would get the win. I hung around his pit, watching him pace back and forth during the excruciating three-hour delay. The track dried, and the green flag flew again. A crash took out T. K.'s hopes. When the rain returned, the Scotsman Dario Franchitti had the good fortune of being out front and found his way to Victory Lane.

Out of broadcasting the race, I stayed involved in other ways. One of my favorite events I still attend is the Borg Warner dinner, where the new face on the trophy is unveiled. Bobby Unser and I have long been tasked with making the event fun for the reigning champ, and a bit of a roast. These intimate evenings with champs old and new are indescribably special.

When I started covering Nathan's Hot Dog Eating Contest, I got a lot of ribbing from my buddies on the Indiana State Police ERT. Sitting in a bar after a training session, they really poured it on. In response, I proposed a trip to New York City for the next contest. I would make them my VIP guests. Several of the guys heartily accepted, and we detailed plans for this serious stag trip. Naturally, as soon as these macho alpha-males got home, their wives and girlfriends put the kibosh on any guys-only trip to NYC. Only my good friend Patrick Etter was still in.

Patrick is a hulking figure right out of an action movie. Even in his late forties he could outrun nearly any new recruit on the obstacle course. And that's after surviving a horrific rear-end crash from a car traveling at 70 miles per hour while he was parked in his cruiser along the interstate. Broken back and all, he returned to duty less than a year after doctors told him he would be filing for permanent disability.

As I did at summer camp in the Guard, I play an "aggressor," one of the bad guys, during ERT training exercises. My handle is 5-P (5-1 is the leader, Mark French). They also call me the Sneaky Old Man or the Cheatingest SOB because I use my knowledge of their tactics to my advantage. But it's good training, as some criminals may have been in the military and learned a thing or two.

I might also have a reputation for playing a little bit mean. Though it's against the rules, I'm not above bouncing a soft round off someone's helmet. The trainees ought to know if they've left their head where it could get blown off. I can't get written up for it—I'm just a volunteer. Likewise, if an old man like myself can creep up from behind and shoot you in the rear at point blank, you deserve the welts that come along with it.

Special Agent Bruce Guider vividly recalls when we first met during an FBI SWAT training:

> During a night operation scenario into a large venue, Paul, who was hiding inside armed with a paintball weapon, "shot" me in the head. I still remember hearing his distinctive evil bad guy laugh.

I can't tell you the red tape he had to go through to allow the publication of that quote.

In New York City, I made sure Patrick got the full VIP experience, and he's joined me a few times backstage at Coney Island. I love watching thirty thousand people gather for the contest before heading to the beach. The ragged edge for an Indy driver is going deep into a turn, for Joey Chestnut, it's dropping seventy-three hot dogs in about ten minutes.

I arranged a few trips for the guys. We went to Las Vegas on a trip to Nellis AFB and to Daytona for a supercross event. My kindness was not always reciprocated. We often held sniper practice at a private range on a farm south of Indianapolis. We always left our car keys on top of a tire in case someone needed to move it. When I drove my Ferrari to the farm, I looked back and saw it was gone. Patrick had moved it—by way of a forty-minute tour of the countryside. As the afternoon progressed, at least two more Indiana State Troopers stole my Ferrari for joyrides.

I still join them for practice on occasion. Marlo even helped out as a pretend hostage when she was in college. I know these troopers adopted me as a bit of a mascot. I'm honored to spend time among them, and I hope they feel my gratitude for the dangerous work they do for all of us.

By May of 2008, CART and the IRL had merged, quietly ending the American open-wheel racing civil war. On Pole Day, Scott Dixon seized the top slot. A native of New Zealand, both of Scott's parents raced on dirt tracks. At twenty years old, Scott claimed the title of youngest driver to win a CART race—his fourth race in an Indy car. When he switched to the IRL two years later, he won the series.

On Race Day morning, Sally and I sat in a coffee shop, still undecided if I would attend. My love of the race won over any bitterness. I could relate to the words of Wilbur Shaw:

> I can't stay away from the speedways. I know it makes a certain torture, but I go to every race . . . and wander about like a lost soul looking into Paradise. . . .

> For this is the penalty I pay for racing—I've quit in body, but my mind still lives on the track.

Sally dropped me off just in time for the green flag. I used my press pass to get inside. I let that old familiar haze of absorbing the race overwhelm me once again.

Tony Kanaan broke the record with seven consecutive Indy 500s leading at least one lap, but he drifted too high and lost it in the marbles, ending his day. Late in the race, Vitor Meira made one of the most amazing double passes to come from third to the lead. Leading 115 laps, Scott Dixon shuffled back to the front and staked his claim on the Borg Warner Trophy on his sixth try.

A lot of the postrace coverage focused on Danica Patrick, who exited the race in an incident in the pits with Ryan Briscoe. Danica stormed toward Ryan's pit, clearly looking for a fight, until intercepted by security. Officials later fined both drivers for their conduct.

Among the women at Indianapolis, Danica was unique. When Janet Guthrie arrived in 1976, she was a thirty-eight-year-old aerospace engineer. Lyn St. James became the oldest rookie of the year at forty-five years old. Sarah Fisher was an honor student studying to become an engineer at Ohio State when she got her start in Indy cars. Only a teenager during her first Indy 500, Sarah had the downhome charm and humility of the girl next door. The fierce nature of Danica had no precedent.

Danica followed the path of many storied drivers: a kid from the Midwest who dropped out of high school to pursue racing. She arrived with passion, intensity, and star-power good looks, if not personality. Like a lot of drivers, she earned a reputation as a hothead who didn't resist throwing her crew under the bus when things went wrong. Danica is also known for a bone-crushing grip when she shakes hands.

An instant celebrity, Danica could claim any sponsor she wanted and drove great cars from the very beginning. I wandered through the ABC trailer her first year and 90 percent of the features taped to the wall were Danica. But she earned the rookie of the year honors by posting the fastest practice lap by any driver that year, and she went on to take three poles that season. She is the only woman who has won an Indy car race: Japan in 2008. More than any of the women before her, Danica was willing to go wheel-to-wheel to fight for it. I recall a ten-lap stretch between her and Tony Kanaan at Homestead that proved she was as tough and aggressive as any of the greats.

Danica went on to NASCAR, a safer sport with more races and better financial opportunity, but she returned for a farewell race at the 2018 Indy 500. To the very end, she showed what she thought of the boys and their silly superstitions: driving a green number 13. But luck wasn't with her, and she didn't go the distance.

When F1 dropped its race in Indianapolis, the Speedway picked up the MotoGP race for its road course. I covered the play-by-play on the IMS Radio Network with Jeff Ward, a great rider and Indy car driver. I'll always prefer race cars, but motorcycle racing takes the danger, daring, and speed to a whole new level.

I had no exposure to motorcycle racing before the early '80s when NBC sent me to cover a dirt track race at San Jose. The bug bit me immediately. World Championship racers like Kenny Roberts from Modesto, California, had brought a new style of riding. Previously, everyone sat upright. Kenny raced low on the bike, tucking behind the windscreen and shifting his body to offset the weight as he ripped through the turns.

I got my first taste of supercross at Anaheim Stadium in California. Gearheads love speed, but height and acrobatics can be just as exciting—what those riders did seemed impossible. Ricky Carmichael elevated supercross into an art form, and I later worked with him in the booth for the Summer X Games.

The most unusual motorcycle race I covered was in Assen at the Netherlands' Ice Speedway. The tires with hundreds of inch-long spikes looked right off the set of a Mad Max movie.

In May of 2009, Mike King graciously asked me to return to the radio booth as part of the one hundredth anniversary of the Speedway. I stuck around during the race to offer commentary. The track's skyline lost the old Speedway Motel. Tony George stepped down from the Speedway's leadership.

On Race Day, pole-sitter Helio Castroneves jumped the green flag, causing a restart. In a scary moment, Tony Kanaan wrecked hard but survived the life-threatening G-forces. Vito Meira broke his back in another vicious crash. Taking the lead on lap 142, Helio kept everyone in his rearview mirror. With Dan Wheldon and Danica Patrick close behind, Helio crossed the yard of bricks to become a new legend with three Indy 500 wins.

Indianapolis was the second big triumph for Helio that year. He had also been acquitted of tax evasion. The charges had derailed his career and forced him out of racing for an entire season. It was also something we had in common.

I had income from lots of sources: the network, our production company, speaking engagements, etc. Like professional athletes, I paid income taxes in each state I worked an event. Naturally, I paid an accountant to handle it all. One year, the IRS determined I failed to report some income. More accurately, my accountant blew it.

I walked into a meeting with the IRS with a check in hand to cover the taxes due plus interest and penalties. Instead of accepting payment, an IRS agent showed a gold badge and told me I was being criminally charged. His partner explained that they did this every year to make an example out of someone.

The IRS expected me to roll over and plead guilty and let them have a headline in the paper. Those agents soon learned that under no circumstances would I plead guilty when I had done nothing wrong, no matter the cost in legal bills. I fought them tooth and nail. They made several lenient offers, almost begging for a plea agreement. But I would only agree to a dismissal, so we went to trial.

Judge Sarah Evans Barker presided. She did not suffer fools and gave me faith in the legal system. My character witnesses were Bruce Jenner and Bobby Unser. To my relief, the jury acquitted me. I sued my accountant, but it was still an enormous financial drain: all because someone in the IRS thought it was more important to make an example of me than to look at the facts.

Helio and I chatted a lot during his ordeal, and I let him know what to expect. I tried to keep his spirits up. I was pleased with the outcome but outraged the IRS had learned nothing from my case.

In May of 2010, Helio Castroneves started from the pole again, back-to-back, and tied A. J. Foyt's four poles. The field had unprecedented representation by four women: Sarah Fisher, Danica Patrick, Ana Beatriz, and rookie of the year Simona de Silvestro.

I returned to the radio booth to provide commentary. I finally knew how it felt to be Donald Davidson, the long-time track historian. He'd been on the network, sitting behind the scenes, offering a bit of historical trivia here and there during every race since his first interview with Sid Collins in 1964.

On Race Day, the actor Jack Nicholson was the honorary starter. Speedway officials felt a bit nervous about the seventy-three-year-old actor climbing thirty-eight feet up the metal I-beam ladder that leads to the "pirate ship" flag stand. Jack nimbly made his way up and loved it so much he didn't come down until fifty laps later.

Dario Franchitti owned the race and led 155 laps. Tony Kanaan, who started thirty-third, made a great last effort, but low fuel caused him to pit late. A nasty wreck at the end of the race sent Mike Conway into the catch fence, breaking his back. Flying debris injured a couple of spectators. Dario's delayed pit strategy paid off, and he nursed his tank for his second checkered flag at Indy.

Reading Wilbur Shaw's autobiography, one of his stories always made me think of my Uncle Harry. In a hurry to get a race car ready,

Wilbur became careless while machining a part on a drill press. The metal piece slipped from his grip and he suffered a serious cut requiring a trip to the hospital. He felt he might have lost his hand had he not been wearing his clunky Scottish Rite ring.

The Scottish Rite is a branch of Freemasonry. As a young man, I assured my uncle I would join the Masons someday, and some years after his death, I received his Masonic ring. In 2005, I fulfilled that long overdue promise, and I could finally wear my uncle's ring with pride.

Masons are simply men of a common mindset regarding tradition, objective truth, and character. It is best described as a course of moral instruction illustrated by the art and tools of architecture. Its roots go back to the builders of the great cathedrals of Europe. Some of the greatest minds and leaders in Western history found value in it, from Voltaire and Rousseau to Washington and Franklin to Theodore Roosevelt and Winston Churchill.

While it is by definition a fraternity and limited to men, its inclusivity was far ahead of its time. For centuries, men of all races and religions have found brotherhood in Freemasonry. Conversely, authoritarian creeds like fascism and communism have feared the organization's democratic and Enlightenment ideals.

In my life, I have endeavored to seek out people who inspire: race car drivers, navy pilots, astronauts, FBI agents, paramedics, SWAT members, and combat veterans. Most of these people have a certain bedrock character that enables their success. That same type of character is valued by Freemasons. Though like any organization, not all members live up to its ideals.

The Speedway has been shaped by Masons from its beginning. Frank Wheeler, one of the four founders of the Speedway, and driver and owner Eddie Rickenbacker were both Masons. Indy 500 winner Sam Hornish Jr. is a member, as was public announcer Tom Carnegie, master mechanic Herb Porter, and long-time superintendent Clarence Cagle. All Masons like to find symbolism. Whether by design or not, the Field of 33 has significance, as does the checkered flag.

May of 2011 marked the one hundredth anniversary of the first Indianapolis 500. The parity among the cars was unprecedented. After several years with the same engine, the difference between the fastest and slowest car qualified was a gap of less than 4 miles per hour. In the early '80s, the gap was as much as 20 mph.

Alex Tagliani captured the pole. Simona de Silvestro, the "Iron Maiden," crashed during practice and suffered burns to her hands for the second time in less than a year. She put it behind her and qualified in Row 8. Later that season, a US Customs Agent denied the native of Switzerland entry because he thought she lied to him about her profession. He couldn't fathom a woman might actually be a real race car driver, and Simona missed the race at Sonoma.

On Race Day, I sat again in the radio broadcast booth as an analyst. My son Brian crewed Dan Wheldon's car, and he tells a great story from 2011. One of the hardest things for a late splash-and-go pit stop is adding just the right amount of fuel. The engineer calculates the amount of fuel, but the fueler puts it in the car. The fuel tank has a small sight gauge, similar to a coffee decanter, to indicate how much is in the tank. The math is precise, but the fueling process is not. The engineer is stuck on the other side of the pit wall. Add too much, and precious seconds are lost in the pit and extra weight slows down the car. Add too little, and the car runs out before the finish line. Teams practice with water before every race.

It all fell on Brian's shoulders as the engineer to get it right. It kept him up the night before. Bryan Herta Autosport mostly raced the Indy Lights series, the minor league of Indy car racing. The 500 was its first IRL race of the season. The young team didn't have some of the fancier equipment used to communicate with the fueler. As Brian walked through his garage the morning of the race, he noticed his bag of golf clubs. He reached over and grabbed the longest one he had. After an hour standstill in traffic, Brian heard on the radio that a stabbing resulted in the credentials gate becoming a crime scene. Brian turned around to find a place to park. He found a tattoo shop at 30th and Lafayette. Lugging his equipment and the golf club, he hoofed the two miles to the Speedway.

Getting into the Speedway and finding the correct parking lot is always an adventure, even for the teams and broadcasters. Traffic patterns are changed all the time and without any notice. Yellow shirts are trained to allow no exceptions. One year, Jack Arute drove Brian, Marlo, and me to the Speedway. Jack became frustrated with a yellow shirt and just drove around him. The yellow shirt hopped right onto the hood of the moving car. At some point Jack stopped. Marlo always liked Jack; he made her laugh.

Brian remembers a trip to the track when a car struck a motorcycle police officer. Our pit reporter, Dr. Jerry Punch, hopped out of the car to treat the officer. I yelled at him to get back in, saying, "That's not your job." But it was.

The 2011 race came down to fuel strategy and the maxim: "Be the first car to make the last stop." In the final stretch, Bertrand Baguette, Scott Dixon, and Danica Patrick all pitted early. Others, including Dan Wheldon, held off, thinking the early birds jumped the gun. Dan pitted with two gallons left in the tank, and the fueler jumped into action for a splash-and-go. Brian reached over the pit wall and held up his golf club. He thumped the fueler on his back when it was time to stop. Crude but effective, Dan roared back out.

The leaderboard changed as drivers ran out of fuel from pitting too early or blowing the quick fill. J. R. Hildebrand held the lead as the white flag dropped. With Dan in third, Brian felt satisfied with a good race, but his teammates soured at losing such a close one. Brian looked up to see Scott slowing—out of fuel—and Dan moving up to second. A glimmer of hope flashed through the pit.

Eyes glued to the monitors, the team couldn't believe it when J. R. went too high to pass Charlie Kimball, who'd run out of fuel coming out of Turn Four. They instantly knew J. R. had to lift. J. R. lost traction, hit the wall, and slid along toward the yard of bricks. Dan found his way through traffic and reached the checkered flag two seconds ahead of J. R. Dan's team put him in the right spot to win his second taste of Victory Lane.

Before the race, Mike King and I just happened to discuss the best way to prepare for the last two laps of the race. We agreed you must memorize the top five drivers to be ready for lead changes. In case of a crash right before the finish line, you can't focus solely on the leader. When J. R. hit the wall, Mike broke that rule. He gave a great narration of the crash, but he didn't watch for the actual winner. After a short pause, he turned to me and asked, "Who won it?" I said, "Wheldon. Dan Wheldon."

Dan never had the chance to return to Indy to defend his title, losing his life in that horrendous eleven-car wreck at Las Vegas. Everyone loved Dan. He had a boundless enthusiasm for life, and it was absolutely contagious. He also deeply cared about the people around him. When Brian and four crew members were injured in a serious accident in San Francisco on the way to the airport after a race, Dan turned around and picked up Brian and another crew member from the hospital.

Brian never completely recovered from Dan's death. He promised himself he would never become close friends with a driver again. If the unthinkable happens, the pain is just too much. A. J. Foyt learned that lesson when he saw the charred body of his mentor Pat O'Connor at his first Indy 500. Bobby Unser came to the same conclusion back in his sprint car days. When Swede Savage died, Sam Posey lost one of his closest friends. The death of a driver leaves deep wounds on so many others.

As the years have gone by, Brian has amassed several Indy 500 rings to choose from. He always wears the ring from Dan's second win. When J. R. Hildebrand joined the team, he wasn't pleased with Brian's choice in jewelry. But he knew the mark Dan left on Brian and all of us.

I choose to remember Dan for all he was in life, and not the tragedy of losing him so young.

CHAPTER 17

The Voice
Once Again

Oval tracks favor aggressive drivers that like
high-speed corners. We have balls and we use them.
—*Tony Kanaan*

I n May of 2012, innovation and competition returned to Indianapolis with engines from Honda, Chevrolet, and Lotus, all with relative parity. But Honda held back a second engine until Carburetion Day. With the new Honda engine, it became clear that Dario Franchitti and Scott Dixon would be much faster than pole-sitter Ryan Briscoe.

On a hot, ninety-degree Race Day, the lead changed thirty-four times. With five laps to go, Dario, Scott, and Takuma Sato fought it out. Dario led as the white flag fell. Sato made a daring attempt to pass in Turn One but lost it and found the wall. As the race ended under the caution, Dario captured his third Indy 500, with

Scott and Tony Kanaan right behind. All three lined up to cross the yard of bricks, side-by-side, as a memorial to Dan Wheldon. The Speedway handed out white sunglasses resembling Dan's signature shades. Dario dedicated his victory to the lost reigning champ, and the sea of fans wearing those shades roared for both of them. Dan would have loved it.

In a backbench role in the radio booth, I could watch the others react under pressure when something went wrong with the equipment. A good save in the broadcast booth is a thing of beauty. My best moment was at Tamiami Park in Miami. NBC often "bicycled" its sportscasts, meaning it would record the show and play it back on a short delay. It allowed a same-day broadcast that fit the time-slot and avoided ill-timed commercial breaks. Commercials during live broadcasts are magnets for big moments in a race, like a great pass or a wreck. To catch those moments, Don Ohlmeyer used a technique he called Memorex. He would cue up the tape thirty seconds before the big moment and run it right after the commercial break and we narrated it as though it was happening live. Sometimes that confused Bobby Unser. I remember a crash at Michigan during a commercial break. When the Memorex went live, Bobby forgot it was a replay and blurted out, "He crashed again!"

In bicycling, the show typically begins airing with the race still in progress, and that happened in Miami. We finished narrating except for the final few laps, which we would call live and simultaneously with the delayed broadcast.

Our temporary booth, a scaffold with tarps to ward off the rain, sat a few hundred yards from the broadcast trucks. Cables ran our audio to the truck and the director's circuit back to our headphones. The power for the TV monitors and lights in our booth came from a generator on the ground below us. Don Ohlmeyer counted us down from thirty seconds to go live. At fifteen seconds, our booth went dark: no lights and no monitors. The generator ran out of gas.

Light ebbed in from streetlamps and temporary lighting in the broadcast corral. Our headsets picked up the sounds of the race as it aired. Don said, "Just follow my cues. Leader starts the second to last lap." Bobby just stared at his darkened monitor, speechless—a first, but a good thing. I heard the drivers shifting and jumped in, "Danny Sullivan heads for Turn Three with three cars close behind." Don asked in my headset, "How'd you do that?" I ignored him, and he wisely let me do what I do best. Each turn, I drew on the sounds and my memory. I heard Don say, "Checkered." I dropped in, "And there is the checkered flag for Danny Sullivan the new PPG World Champion!" Don rolled in the footage of the victory circle interview and said, "That's a wrap."

Bobby looked at me trying to understand what just happened. We announced the end of the race completely blind and in the dark, and no one ever figured it out. It was a great save.

In May of 2013, Ed Carpenter, stepson of Tony George, took the pole. One of the lesser-known Race Day rituals for drivers is running for the bathroom right after "Back Home Again in Indiana." Having forgotten one year, Bobby Unser admits to a true pit stop at the Indy 500, relieving himself mid-race, in his fire suit, right in the car. On this Race Day, Tony Kanaan and a couple of other drivers at the end of the line for the bathroom worried it was taking too long. They ran over to use the women's room. Janet Guthrie would have laughed.

In a magnificent stint of uninterrupted action, the green flag flew for over 130 consecutive laps with no cautions. The lead changed a record sixty-eight times and came down to a battle between T. K. and Ryan Hunter-Reay. Trailing out of the caution with three laps to go, T. K.—known for aggressively winning restarts—jumped ahead of Ryan in Turn One for the lead. T. K. held it until a crash brought out the yellow flag, cementing the win. At long last, the fan favorite got the checkered flag on his twelfth try. The Speedway never heard roars so loud. When T. K. took the microphone, the outspoken driver didn't disappoint. Holding up the giant silver Borg Warner, he said, "Hey, I'm finally going to get my ugly face on that trophy."

T. K. is one of the best oval drivers—nearly all his wins have been all left turns. Like Bobby Unser, he is great at mind games. Whenever his car was fast, he said to his teammates, "It's too loose for you, but not for me." The Brazilians really speak their minds. Fellow countryman Nelson Piquet shared T. K.'s feelings on street courses. He scandalized F1 by saying that racing at Monaco was like "riding a bicycle around my living room."

As a gearhead, I've always had a soft spot for drag racing. In 1973, I covered the NHRA at Indianapolis Raceway Park for WNAP—my second time announcing a race live on the radio.

During the old Diamond P productions of NHRA on TNN, I covered a lot of drag racing. I could write a couple of chapters on those days with Brock Yates, Steve Evans, Don Garlits—who we just called "Big"—and our producer and director John Mullin. I covered Mike Dunn in his racing days, and our paths crossed a few times over the years. I was excited to work with him covering the NHRA on ESPN.

Drag racing is completely different from Indy cars. Top Fuel and Funny cars fire up 12,000 horsepower, while Indy cars are under 1,000. Indy car drivers are tied up all the time. PR people serve as gatekeepers between the media and the team. Drag racing still has the feel of racing in the '50s and '60s. You can walk up to a driver and talk. At the end of the day, grills come out for burgers, brats, and ribs. Many of the top teams and manufacturers are headquartered in the west suburbs of Indianapolis in Avon and Brownsburg; I call the area Nitro City.

When I started working NHRA for ESPN, the first six months were a nightmare for me. The style of broadcast was difficult to master. Everything about it felt different.

Isolated from the track, our "booth" was the back end of a windowless semitrailer. At Pomona, we felt every bit of Tony Pedregon's engine explosion. Things were knocked from our walls; we heard the tinkle of car parts hitting the roof and walls of our truck. Our "cave" had eight TV monitors and a staff of two announcers and a stat guy.

Drag racing begins at eleven in the morning and may go as late as ten in the evening. It's a big task to convert such a long day into a seamless two- or three-hour-long show. Because of the starts and stops, I might narrate one sentence and wait an hour to do the next. One night at a race at Brainerd, Minnesota, I sat exhausted from a long day and told my producer I might not be able to do these broadcasts properly.

Naturally, I felt inadequate next to Mike Dunn with his exceptional eye for detail and unparalleled memory. I never saw someone multitask like him, talking to his family, reading the time sheets, and ready on a dime to narrate another run. With Mike's help, I finally got it. Part of my job was to set Mike up so he could wax poetic. He'd take off, and every word was money.

Many competitors, like John Force, would come by our booth and hang out. John reminded me a lot of Bobby Unser—he understood showmanship. John had a hard time censoring himself, and our team spent a lot of time bleeping out his interviews. Finally, we told him we would quit interviewing him if he kept it up. Somehow, almost overnight, he got control of that mouth.

All good things must come to an end, and in my seventh season covering NHRA, my producer tipped me off that the brass wanted new talent. So ended my career in network sportscasting, like an aging veteran driver losing a spot to the next hotshot.

The folks at DreamWorks hired me for voiceover work on an animated movie. As I walked into the theater for the screening, I had low expectations. My other screen credits hadn't turned out well.

A decade earlier, I voiced an announcer in a film about Indy car racing. With actors like Sylvester Stallone and Burt Reynolds, I expected a blockbuster. Unfortunately, it was horrible. Sly mentioned *Driven* as one of the movies he wished he never made.

I caught a prerelease showing while in town for the Long Beach race. It was bad—cars-crashing-into-a-playground bad (an actual scene). After the poor feedback from the screening, they substantially recut the film. I was asked to come in with Larry Henry to re-narrate some sections. A bunch of us caught a showing the night before the race at Texas Motor Speedway. Parker Johnstone sat next to me as we sunk lower and lower in our seats during that still miserable movie. Thankfully, I wasn't included in the credits. A decade before that, I was cast with Jack Arute as announcers for an even worse and more obscure film, *Checkered Flag*.

I tempered my expectations when I visited DreamWorks's beautiful campus: koi ponds, recreational facilities, open creative spaces. The large studio had posters of the animated characters near the microphone. The animators watched from another room where they could pick up the actor's movements and mannerisms. Director David Soren worked one-on-one with me and offered great instruction.

Still, the plotline seemed a bit doubtful to me: a garden snail races against real cars at the Indianapolis 500. With actors like Ryan Reynolds, Samuel L. Jackson, Maya Rudolph, and even Mario Andretti making a cameo, I had some hope.

Like all DreamWorks movies, *Turbo* began in the clouds with the boy sitting on a crescent moon with a fishing line. The footage dove through the clouds to an aerial view of the Indianapolis Motor

Speedway, as my voice narrated. The animators transformed the Speedway into the magical place it has always been in my mind. Watching *Turbo* with my grandkids is always a special moment for me.

When Mike King moved on after fifteen years behind the mic, I jumped at the opportunity to once again become the Voice of the 500, exactly forty years after my first stint as a pit reporter on the IMS Radio Network. In a lot of ways, the radio broadcast is much more rewarding. In television, the producer chooses the camera angles and tells much of the story. On radio, the announcer is the creative lead.

May of 2014 began with the inaugural Grand Prix of Indianapolis on the road course. Juan Montoya and Jacques Villeneuve returned, the first for each since their victories in 2000 and 1995 (arguably that made for three "defending champions" in the field). Ed Carpenter seized the pole for a second time in a row. NASCAR champ Kurt Busch earned the rookie of the year honor—I covered him in NASCAR, NHRA, and Indy cars.

On Race Day, Jim Nabors sang his farewell "Back Home Again in Indiana," and Mari Hulman George invited Jim to join her in the command to "Start your engines." A new scoring pylon tracked the car's positions.

Surpassing the action from the year before, the race cars screamed around the track for 149 laps without a caution.

After Townsend Bell's wreck on lap 191, the officials brought out the red flag so the race would not end under caution. With only six laps to go, the green flag dropped with Ryan Hunter-Reay in the lead and Helio Castroneves close behind. Electrified fans cheered as Ryan and Helio passed and repassed each other four times. Ryan led by just a nose as the white flag dropped. In a mad dash out of Turn Four, Helio crossed just 0.06 seconds behind Ryan in one of the closest finishes in Speedway history. Ryan claimed his spot on the Borg Warner on his seventh bid.

Marco Andretti followed in third place. It marked the sixty-ninth try by someone with the last name of Andretti. Forty-five years after Mario's only win, the curse continued.

Returning as the Voice put me back on the circuit covering the whole series for the IMS Radio Network, thirty-six years after that season with Bob Jenkins. Back on tour, you can't help becoming nostalgic. All you want to do is tell stories, and pranks are always a favorite. The art of the prank is one of the oldest and most enduring traditions in racing culture. Some pranks can only be retold after the statute of limitations has expired.

Everyone feared Bobby Unser for his pranks. It might be a tarantula in a glove box or a fire extinguisher discharged under a hotel room door. A prank or a fistfight—those were the risks of a night out with Bobby in his heyday. If he felt a fight coming on at White Front, in a split second he'd whip out his leather belt and its big turquoise-encrusted buckle, his weapon of choice. A Bobby prank often involved real vandalism: M-80s destroying some part of a restaurant bathroom. Without warning, "the King of the Cherry Bomb" would give his companions a look that sent them running for the car, fleeing the scene of the crime seconds before the boom.

As Johnny Rutherford learned, any ride with Bobby could be an adventure. When he stopped at a red light with Bobby riding shotgun, J. R. looked over to see Bobby pull out an M-80. Before J. R. could protest, Bobby tossed the sparking incendiary onto a freshly poured concrete pad. The concrete worker, unfazed, sprayed it with his hose thinking that would extinguish it. He soon learned that water won't put out a cherry bomb. It blew before the stoplight changed, blasting a crater in the still wet concrete and splattering the worker from head to toe. J. R. burned rubber as he rushed off.

Legend has it that Bobby's systematic abuse of rental cars, after purchasing full insurance coverage, led to an industry-wide policy of banning motorsports athletes from renting cars. He once took me up Pike's Peak in a rental car. He constantly pretended to lose control, veering off and taking us over the three-foot piles of sand used for winter snow. It made us feel like we were rolling off the cliff. You can imagine the shape of the rental after that hill climb.

Late for a flight after a race at Talladega, I broke down and gave Bobby the keys. He promised to get us there in time. I immediately regretted it as he darted in and out of traffic, clearing big rigs by just inches. I closed my eyes and kept saying to myself, "He's a three-time Indy 500 winner and one of the best racers ever. I'll be fine." As we neared the airport, I still didn't think we would make the flight. Then Bobby sped down the lane for departures rather than rental return. He left the keys in the ignition and popped the trunk. As he saw me wondering how we would return the car he said, "Somebody'll take care of it." So we left it there and caught our flight.

A. J. Foyt always tormented Jack Arute over his fear of snakes. Live on the air, A. J. would toss a toy snake at him, or slowly slide a black rubber hose just along his peripheral vision, causing an instant reaction. It happened repeatedly every season, and Jack always recoiled with the same horror.

In the old days, the row of phones in Gasoline Alley caused untold mischief. Everybody could hear everybody else's business. When the public address speaker announced, "Call for such-and-such on Phone Three," anyone might get there first. It's also hard for a driver to explain, if he's standing beside his wife, how his "wife" is also holding for him on Phone Two.

I will admit participation in one prank: As a clothes horse, Dan Wheldon's massive closet looked like it belonged to a supermodel. He meticulously arranged every item and perfectly organized his enormous shoe collection. On a visit to his apartment on the north side of Indy, two of us distracted Dan while the third pretended to head to the bathroom. Instead, he turned Dan's perfect closet into a perfect wreck: mismatched shoes, clothes strewn everywhere, it looked like a bomb went off. Then we casually said goodbye and left him to find our petty vandalism. We couldn't get Dan to tell us how long it took him to set it all back.

Dan's fashion sense made him an easy target. On a trip to Japan, a teammate went through Dan's luggage and mailed back home one of each pair of shoes he brought along. It left Dan in the predicament of wearing mismatched shoes or buying new ones.

Some of the most diabolical pranks are the least expected. One fine day in May, sweet Sarah Fisher announced to her crew that Nickelodeon had expressed interest in sponsoring the team. She said the network wanted the team to make a promo video of a day in the life of the crew while wearing SpongeBob SquarePants attire. She brought in T-shirts and boxer shorts festooned with the iconic cartoon character. The husky mechanics and egghead engineers all complied and went about their work as Sarah filmed them.

Next, she wanted group footage on the track. Still in the SpongeBob apparel, Sarah marched them out of the garages, into the track, and through the pits—all in view of the other teams, officials, and media. She assembled them in front of the scoring pylon and had them shout in unison, "We're the #23 SpongeBob SquarePants Team." Finally, she held up a sign indicating they had been pranked on "Speedway Spoofs." Sarah perhaps broke a track record as she ran back to the garage with her crew in hot pursuit.

Robin Miller tells the story of one of the greatest pranks of all time. It involved Eddie Sachs and LeRoy Warriner, a driver who spent several Mays at the Speedway but never found a spot in the field. LeRoy later owned the Speedrome track. Like many great stories, it began at White Front. Late on a snowy winter night after having a few drinks, LeRoy asked Eddie to go with him to meet a girl.

LeRoy drove to a house in the neighborhood. They walked around to the back door. A man answered with a gun in his hand and asked LeRoy, "Are you the one who's been sleeping with my daughter?" (Perhaps in stronger terminology.) Before Leroy could answer, the man fired the gun and Leroy fell back in the snow. Eddie ran like hell all the way back to the bar, a couple of miles away. Once inside, frantic and out of breath, he saw Leroy and the man from the house, sitting together at a table and casually tilting back beers. It was a complete setup.

In May of 2015, Scott Dixon took the pole. James Hinchcliffe faced a life-threatening wreck on a practice lap when his leg was impaled. Quick work from the Speedway medical team probably saved his life as he very easily could have bled out.

Davey Hamilton joined me in the booth. Davey suffered severe injuries in a wreck at Texas Motor Speedway, and doctors even considered amputating his legs. After dozens of surgeries and over a year in a wheelchair, he eventually returned to racing. I will always be inspired by the determination and resilience of race car drivers.

On Race Day, a late caution for debris sent the lead cars to the pits for fuel. All bunched up and just fifteen laps to go, the green flag unleashed a mad scramble with Will Power in front. Four lead changes later, Juan Montoya made a stunning high pass around Will in Turn One with three laps to go. As they sprinted to the checkered flag, Juan held on to the lead by a tenth of a second. Fifteen years after his first win, and only his third Indy 500, Juan proved himself one of the greats.

When Juan first came to Indy cars, he went by Juan Montoya, and that's how his name was spelled on the Borg Warner Trophy the first time. On his return from F1, he went by Juan Pablo Montoya, and that's how his name appeared on the trophy the second time. To me, he's always been Juan.

At the Indianapolis Motor Speedway, Juan and Jacques Villeneuve have a special place in history: competing in the Indy 500, the Brickyard 400, and the US Grand Prix.

On the radio network at Pocono, I found myself facing the worst moment in motorsports broadcasting one last time. Late in the race, Sage Karam lost control in Turn One and crashed head-on into the wall, sending debris everywhere. The nose cone bounced up and struck Justin Wilson's helmet. The blow knocked him unconscious, and he veered into the wall. After an airlift to the hospital, Justin required life support. His family made the decision to turn off the machine and have his organs donated.

The cars now have aeroscreens that might have prevented Justin's death, and others' as well. Open-wheel racing has always meant open-air cockpits too. But perhaps it is time. Seatbelts weren't mandatory until 1951, though that dated to an era when the cars' heavy construction meant being thrown from a car might be safer than being strapped inside. Nostalgia isn't worth a driver's funeral.

May of 2016 marked the one hundredth running of the Indianapolis 500, which is not entirely accurate. The sixth Indy "500" in 1916 was "The International *300-Mile* Sweepstakes Race." Everyone just ignores that year, the only one not billed as a 500-mile race. In commemoration of the one hundredth race, a new "gold" brick, cast in bronze, glimmered in the yard of bricks. The yard's other gold brick honors A. J. Foyt as the first to win four 500s.

I couldn't sleep the night before the race. I've been haunted by the same recurring dream for over forty years: I'm stuck in traffic on Georgetown Road, everything is at a standstill, and I'm going to miss the race.

When I arrived at the Speedway, I breathed in the prerace festivities. I knew I would call the pace laps and the start of the race before handing the microphone to the next Voice of the 500, Mark Jaynes.

James Hinchcliffe took the pole. Alexander Rossi's fuel strategy gave him the lead late. For the last few laps, his crew told him to nurse his tank at 4.7 miles per gallon. That would be nearly impossible, but the rookie admitted to me he didn't know any better at the time. According to my son Brian's calculations, Alexander entered Turn One on the white flag with less than a mile's worth in the tank. Brian signaled to owner Bryan Herta who yelled over the radio, "Full Throttle! Full Throttle!" Alexander dropped the hammer—he needed enough speed so that when he hit empty on the backstretch, he could coast the rest of the way. As Alexander rolled on empty, teammate Carloz Munoz closed in with a 219-miles-per-hour lap. Four seconds ahead of Carlos, Alexander crossed the yard of bricks at an actual speed of only 135 mph to take the checkered flag.

Fans love it when an old veteran finally molds his face on the Borg Warner, but the lifeblood of the Speedway is renewed with a rookie's win.

Racing is a wonderful metaphor for life. It's a sport of risk and reward, physical danger and monetary success, a great many contenders and a chosen few who rise to the top. The rest of us on the sidelines are inspired by those whose hard work and daring pay off. But everyone hangs up their racing gloves sooner or later. As I removed my headphones, I knew I had followed my passion to a place I revered, doing what I loved. My 500 miles were run, and I had no regrets.

EPILOGUE

S ince my semiretirement in 2016, I still find myself in the radio broadcast booth each Race Day to offer what wit and wisdom I may as a "Voice Emeritus."

As I look to the future, I have much optimism. I felt overwhelmed by excitement and relief when I learned Roger Penske would become the next owner of the Speedway. The brilliant business sense and commitment to excellence that Roger has applied to his enterprises and racing teams will no doubt benefit Indy car racing immensely. Equally important, he understands the role of stewardship that the Hulman-George family has so generously established across eight decades.

Then a May came and went without a Race Day as the whole world paused. In August, the 2020 Indy 500 became a race without fans—something of an oxymoron. As I can attest from witnessing that eerie and surreal day, the greatness of the Greatest Spectacle in Racing comes from its fans.

It was also broadcasting without a booth, as I socially distanced in an empty room behind Ed Carpenter's pit. When I had something to report, I went outside to get the sound of the cars. I recorded my comments on my cell phone and emailed it to the booth. At an opportune time, they played it live on the broadcast. It was seamless, but far from ideal.

I have a photo taken from Turn One shortly before the race. The Field of 33 is lined up in perfect rows and columns. But the drivers and crews had been ordered to return to the pits. It's haunting: the race cars on the track moments before the Indy 500 and not a soul around.

In 2022 I was honored with induction into the IMS Hall of Fame. An incredible moment for me and my family. A great close to a life of passion.

With Roger Penske at the helm, and the fanless race of 2020 behind us, a new golden age of racing awaits. I can feel it: the call of Race Day at Indianapolis. And it's spectacular.

ACKNOWLEDGMENTS

A s I look back on my life, I realize how fortunate I am to have had the support of so many outstanding people over the decades. Without Sid Collins and Tony Hulman, I would have never been the Voice. Without the lessons learned from Lou Palmer and Jack Morrow, I would have never mastered the trade. Without Pat Patrick welcoming me onto the team, I would have never understood motorsports well enough to tell the story on Race Day.

Don Ohlmeyer ensured excellence and two Emmys, while my great directors and producers, Bob Goodrich, Steve Biem, John Mullin, Deb Luginbuhl, and Bruce Watson, brought out the best in me. Several hundred more names should be added for my outstanding crew members over the years.

No one can excel in the booth overlooking the track without the help of friends in the racing business, and I owe so much to Roger Penske, Dan Luginbuhl, Bill Donaldson, and Steve Schunk. Likewise, I am so blessed to have lifelong friendships with Johnny Rutherford, Nigel Mansell, Al Unser Jr., and Rick Mears—in spite of unloading that ultralight on me.

Sportscasting requires great chemistry, and I had that in spades with Bobby Unser, Sam Posey, Danny Sullivan, Tom Sneva, Scott Goodyear, Derek Daly, Parker Johnstone, and Mike Dunn. They all became family to me on and off the set.

Gail Sherman helped my career greatly and made me happy.

My son, Brian, makes me proud every day and envious that he made a very successful life in the sport as a racing performance engineer.

As for my extracurriculars over the years, I am so grateful for the incredible experiences I owe to Bear Pickavance, Phil Engelauf, Mark French, and Patrick Etter. Also, Bruce Guider, I'm sorry I shot you.

Of course, I'm most fortunate for the support of my wife Sally, who has stood beside me in all of my successes.

For the wonderful remarks in the foreword from Mario Andretti: I am deeply humbled. Likewise, I am indebted to Helio Castroneves, Bobby Unser, Roger Penske, Nigel Mansell, Derek Daly, and Mike Dunn for their generosity and kind words.

I am grateful for the help of my fellow journalists, Robin Miller, Gary Gerould, and Bob Jenkins—I found much solace in their memories being as faulty as my own.

From the racing side, thanks to Johnny Rutherford, Arie Luyendyk, Scott Goodyear, Bobby Unser, Al Unser Jr., Scott Dixon, and Alexander Rossi for still picking up the phone when I call.

A huge debt of gratitude goes out to Russ Thompson and Brian Page for fact-checking.

Likewise, I owe many thanks for the recollections and assistance of Phil Engelauf, Patrick Etter, Dan Luginbuhl, Tim Cindric, Jeremy Shaw, Dr. Terry Trammel, Dr. Stephen Olvey, Donald Davidson, Sally Page, Marlo Page, Bill Donaldson, Bob Goodrich, Merrill Cain, Art Garner, Bruce Guider, and Jade Gurss.

I deeply appreciate the support from Doug Boles, President of the Indianapolis Motor Speedway, and the assistance of Martie Grey and the staff at the IMS Museum and the IMS Radio Network.

The team at Blue River Press, including Dani McCormick and Tom Doherty, made this a reality.

And Lee Klancher and Tom Heffron at Octane Press for publishing the second printing and keeping this dream alive.

Finally, I cannot express the depth of gratitude for my coauthor, whose patience, diligence, and wit truly captured my story and the story of the Indy 500.

BIBLIOGRAPHY

Alesia, M. (2016). *100 Years, 100 Miles*. Pediment Publishing.

Arute, J., & Fryer, J. (2004). *Jack Arute's Tales from the Indy 500*. Sports Publishing.

Berger, P., & Bortstein, L. (1977). *The Boys of Indy*. New York City: Corwin Books.

Binford, T., & Kichler, F. B. (1993). *A Checkered Past: My 20 Years as Indy 500 Chief Steward*. Carmel, Indiana: Cornerstone Press.

Bloemker, A. (1961). *500 Miles to Go*. New York, New York: Coward-McCann.

Cochrun, T. (2011, Winter). *A Time of Hostages: A Reporter's Notebook. Traces*, pp. 14–21. Retrieved from *Dead Man's Line*.

Complex. (2012, February 22). *An Oral History of Black NASCAR Drivers*. Retrieved from Complex: https://www.complex.com/sports/2012/02/an-oral-history-of-black-nascar-drivers/

Daly, D. (2013). *Race to Win: The 7 Essential Skills of the Complete Champion* (Second ed.). Octane Press.

Davidson, D. (2012, May 24). *IMS Radio Network Celebrates 60th Anniversary*. Retrieved from Indianapolis Motor Speedway: https://www.indianapolismotorspeedway.com/events/indy500/news-multimedia/news/2012/05/24/ims-radio-network-celebrates-60th-anniversary?startrow=1

Davidson, D., & Schaffer, R. (2006). *Autocourse Official History of the Indianapolis 500*. Northant, England: Crash Media Group.

Dorson, R. (1980). *Stay Tuned for the Greatest Spectacle in Racing*. Speedway, Indiana: Carl Hungness Publishing.

Economaki, C., & Argabright, D. (2006). *Let 'Em All Go: The Story of Autoracing by the Man Who Was There*. Fishers, Indiana: Books by Dave Argabright.

Garner, A. (2014). *Black Noon: The Year They Stopped the Indy 500*. New York, New York: Thomas Dunne Books.

Garner, A., & Siegel, M. B. (2016). *Indy 500 Memories: An Oral History of the Greatest Spectacle in Racing.*

Gurney, D. (1979). *Formation of CART.* Retrieved from Dan Gurney's All American Racers: http://allamericanracers.com/formation-of-cart-dan-gurney/

Hallbery, A., & Olson, J. (2016). *Lionheart: Remembering Dan Wheldon.* St. Petersburg, Florida: Lionheart Books.

Heseltine, R. (2007, December). *A Life Less Ordinary.* MotorSport, pp. 82-84.

Hilton, C. (1995). *Nigel Mansell: The Lion at Bay.* Somerset, England: Patrick Stephens.

Kennedy, P. (2018). *Indy 500 Recaps: The Short Chute Edition*. Bloomington, Indiana: AuthorHouse.

Kennedy, R. F. (1968, April 4). *Robert F. Kennedy Remarks on the Assassination of Martin Luther King, Jr.* Retrieved from American Rhetoric: https://www.americanrhetoric.com/speeches/rfkonmlkdeath.html

Moses, S. (1979, April 30). *A Way to Upset CART.* Retrieved from Vault: https://vault.si.com/vault/1979/04/30/a-way-to-upset-cart-a-feud-between-organizations-that-control-indy-car-racing-has-now-boiled-over-and-the-indianapolis-500-might-have-only-one-past-winner-on-the-grid

Olney, R. R. (1966). *Daredevils of the Speedway.* New York, New York: Grosset & Dunlop.

Posey, S. (1976). *The Mudge Pond Express.* New York, New York: G. P. Putnam's Sons.

Reed, T. (1980). *Indy: Race and Ritual.* San Rafael, California: Presidio Press.

Reinhardt, J. C. (2019). *The Indianapolis 500: Inside the Greatest Spectacle in Racing.* Bloomington, Indiana: Red Lightning Books.

Rutherford, J., & Craft, D. (2000). *Lone Star J. R.: The Autobiography of Racing Legend Johnny Rutherford.* Chicago, Illinois: Triumph Books.

Scalzo, J., & Unser, B. (1979). *The Bobby Unser Story.* Garden City, New York: Doubleday.

Shaw, W. (1955). *Gentlemen, Start Your Engines.* New York, New York: Coward-McCann.

Sports Illustrated Staff. (1983, June 6). *Idol of the Indy Airwaves.* Retrieved from Vault: https://vault.si.com/vault/1983/06/06/idol-of-the-indy-airwaves

Waltz, K. (2010, March 23). *Schoolteacher Arlene Hiss Is First Female Indy Car Driver.* Speed Sport.

Wenck, E. (2016, May 27). *500 facts: broadcasting*. Retrieved from NUVO: https://nuvo.newsnirvana.com/entertainment/sports/facts-broadcasting/article_e28e5821-1416-52fa-87c7-d388f32fc28a.html

Whitaker, S. E. (2015). *The Indy Car Wars: The 30-Year Fight for Control of Open Wheel Racing*. Jefferson, North Carolina: McFarland.

SERIES AND EVENTS
PAUL PAGE COVERED

America's Cup — Auckland, NZ (2003)

Arcata to Ferndale Kinetic Sculpture Race — Arcata, CA

Calgary Winter Olympics — Voice Over Only

Can-Am Series — Various North American Locations

College Football — Salt Lake City, UT

Figure Skating — Various Worldwide

Flat Track Motorcycle — San Jose, CA

Formula 1 — Long Beach CA; Las Vegas, NV; Montreal, Canada

Full Contact Karate — Belgium, Canada, US

Global Rally Cross — Various American Series

Ice Speedway — Assen, Netherlands

IMSA Road Racing — Various US Locations

IndyCar (All Forms) — Worldwide

International Race of Champions — Various US Locations

Motocross — Farleigh Castle, England

MotoGP — Indianapolis, IN

NASCAR Truck Series — Various US Locations

Nathan's Hot Dog Eating Contest — Coney Island, NY

NBC SpeedWorld — Various Worldwide

NFL Football — Los Angeles, CA

NHRA Championship Drag Racing — Various US Locations

Olympic Speed Skating — Nagano, Japan

One Lap of America — Round the Borders of the US

Olympic Fencing (Olympic Trial)	Princeton University
Powerlifting	Gothenburg, Sweden
Rally Cars	Various US Locations
Rubik's Cube World Championship	Budapest, Hungary
Russian Olympics	Canceled by President Jimmy Carter
SCCA Amatuer Racing	Indianapolis, IN
SCCA Trans Am Series	Various US Locations
Snow Cross Series	Various North American Locations
Summer X Games	Various US Locations (fifteen years)
Sumo Wrestling	Tokyo, Japan (seven years)
SuperCross Series	Various US Locations (six years)
Swamp Buggys	Naples, FL
Unlimited Hydroplane Racing	Various US Locations
USAC Sprint Cars	Various US Locations
Widowmaker Hill Climb	Salt Lake City, UT
Winter X Games	Various US Locations (twelve years)
World Championship Bob Sled	Cervinia, Italy (six years)
World Championship Motorcycle	Europe (numerous cities)
World Championship Snowmobile	Eagle River, WI (ten years)
World Championship Water Ski	England
World Championship Weight Lifting	Odessa, Russia, Tatabanya
World Nike Masters Games	Portland, OR
World Outdoor Games	Florida, Nevada, Wisconsin
Yacht Regatta	San Francisco, CA

Paul Page is an award-winning journalist and member of the Indianapolis Motor Speedway Hall of Fame. His television coverage of the Indianapolis 500 twice received the Emmy for Outstanding Live Sports Special. He is also a member of the Indiana Sportscasters Hall of Fame and received many press awards during his time as a radio journalist.

J.R. Elrod is a writer in Indianapolis with a background in law and politics.

Made in the USA
Middletown, DE
17 June 2024

55901226R00189